W9-DDO-539

I Am Not Prince Hamlet

I Am Not
Prince Hamlet

Shakespeare   Criticism   Schools of English

D K C Todd

BARNES & NOBLE
BOOKS
10 East 53d St., New York 10022
(a division of Harper & Row Publishers, Inc.)

The author acknowledges assistance received from the Research Fund of Durham University.

The three lines, from which the title of this book is taken and which are printed on the jacket and on page v, come from 'The Love Song of J. Alfred Prufrock' by T. S. Eliot (*Collected Poems* 1909–62). They are reproduced by kind permission of Faber and Faber Ltd.

ISBN 06-4969312

First published 1974

Published in the U.S.A. 1974 by
HARPER & ROW PUBLISHERS, INC
BARNES & NOBLE IMPORT DIVISION

Printed in Great Britain by
Cox & Wyman Ltd,
London, Fakenham and Reading

No! I am not Prince Hamlet nor was meant to be;
Am an attendant lord, one that will do
To swell a progress, start a scene or two . . .

1

No, I am not Prince Hamlet, let me make that plain (nor King Lear for that matter). I shouldn't like to be known even behind my back as the man who thinks he's Hamlet, still less as the man who pretends to think he's not. 'No! I am not Prince Hamlet, nor was meant to be', said J. Alfred Prufrock. Do I wish to associate myself, then, with Eliot's anti-hero? Perhaps. Hardly: Prufrock murmured 'I grow old ... I grow old ... I shall wear the bottoms of my trousers rolled' — could he have been in the prime of life? If he wasn't, I am: if he was, my feelings are more positive, less negative anyway. There is a confidence, which is not quite qualified out of existence by all the uncertainties. Nowadays, I no longer worry about being muddled as much as I did when I thought I was clear-headed.

It is an odd paradox, this assurance with this uncertainty. I have a sort of conviction that I am going in a given direction. At any rate I know what interests me, what seems of value, what will conjure up energies (the presence of energy recommends itself as the absence of it does not). Supported by some inexplicable conceit I easily fall to thinking that anything right for me must be right for the world, and for the English Departments of universities in particular. But then I remind myself that there are different sorts of people: it is surely a serious mistake to assume that everyone is fundamentally like oneself — our shared humanity is one thing, uniformity is another; though perhaps the mistaken assumption enters largely into our attempt to sympathise with each other, and that cannot be wrong. I remind myself that there are different sorts of people, and once this thought takes hold I know I cannot possibly hope to understand what people are like who are not like me at all. They have their being. Their thoughts and actions run counter to mine. I may talk or argue, there is frequently an air of communication, yet when we go deeply into things I catch glimpses, at once terrifying

and utterly discouraging, of their alien vision. My sympathies are
defective. I have intimate friends but no intimate enemies; many
acquaintances. For this reason I could never write a play. Why do I
think about plays so much?

Despite everything I seem to move, to have been moving, in a
given direction. This is a mere belief, an impression. It appears quite
possible to be supported by an inner confidence of sorts (which
may well be immodest and which certainly owes little to reason)
without advancing one's claims to the point of irrational absurdity.
Yet I suppose the nettling words 'fate', 'destiny', must be grasped, or I
shall be stung by them (not that I really expect to be protected by an
adage, which I dare say is no better than a bunch of dock-leaves).
The trouble about fate and destiny is that they invoke the supernatural in one of its most troublesome forms: people are apt to
assume that all their necessary thoughts on the subject took place
years ago; their minds are made up, although the appearance of
fresh thought is often produced by discussion. Fate and destiny,
however, need not be apprehended in any metaphysically developed
way. They are sops to hunger, although they can become a banquet at
which philosophers fall to blows. Pabulum, or how to move in a
given direction. Some impression of fate and destiny, with the supernatural hardly apparent, may be familiar to many people – and, if
the impression is not familiar to everyone, what of that? Life's
journey: or to change the description again, life's pattern. On the
whole we do not regard the years which pass as altogether pattern-
less. Equally, they do not seem altogether patterned – a sense of confusion vies with the sense of order. In remembering our lives, trying
to conceptualise them, we seem to involve ourselves with a peculiar
duality of meaningful experience: as though we only know the
pattern because it is concomitantly not there. I find myself emphasising the pattern because no pattern can be less than it truly is: yet at
the same time the need for such emphasis bears witness to the
existence of confusion.

Pattern comes to look like destiny, not because of any fully
developed idea of the supernatural, but because I experience a certain
awe that it should be there at all. Somehow pattern takes on an independent authority: it has come into being by itself – if that is the
same thing as saying that the willed efforts of my life have not wholly
caused it to exist; so far as my efforts have contributed at all, they

have contributed indirectly, without of course any reference to 'destiny' as the objective. One knows about the monkey at the type-writer working on the script of Hamlet, and one is in the habit of saying that, when he finally succeeds, as sooner or later he will, chance was the only cause, anything more grand-sounding was never a factor. But in a way this great proof of chance, designed to rebut foolish fancies by force of reason, produces contrary results. If one accepts the rational conclusion, it is not without amazement. Frankly, one did not expect the monkey to succeed: and that he has done so seems far more remarkable than that Shakespeare should have done so, for Shakespeare was after all not a monkey (ah! perhaps he was, you see, they are looking for the bones). My point is that there are other types of belief: intellectual monkey-business is not fool-proof: so far as we are fools we continue to depend on these other types of belief in areas of experience foreign to the intellect. The accidental and chance quality of my life, beyond the will, seems to me more than accident in its pattern. On a scale how-ever trifling, it seems like personal destiny. What increases the (never overwhelming) awe, is the obscure conviction that the pattern is still being made. It will be fully understood, will be recognised for what it really is, only later. Perhaps destiny is better described after all as a sense of direction – the goal unknown – for pattern is not pattern unless already known.

A man's destiny can be petty, neither tragic nor heroic: his destiny then is to fall short of tragedy and heroics. In a way this is his tragedy and heroism – as the modern concern with anti-heroes shows. Doesn't 'the tragedy of the little man' consist in the fact that he is not a big man? – which may mean (paradoxically) that he is judged to be one; he had a sort of right to be big, like a midget born of full-sized parents. Do we, because we fear the decline of nature, insist on it as a fact? We play safe, saying how impossible is heroic tragedy in this day and age. Yet it is by no means certain that we deny tragedy in ourselves. The most modern, the most personal destiny, points to death as tragedy. What is true of Hamlet does not apply, and yet it does, to us. The destiny of the tragic hero ministers to our own.

Now, we think readily enough of tragic universality, indeed we accept that all literature has to do with ourselves. Yet the tragic hero's destiny is seen in his story. The closing events of his life lose

most or at any rate much of their meaning if the development
towards the destined end is not known. The pattern must be appreciated in full, or it is not really appreciated. Perhaps all this is self-
evident: one can say, surely, that the hero's destiny is the story of his
destiny. Why labour the point then? I have the feeling that most
criticism treats story very much as the poor relation of 'themes',
'symbols', and the like – even 'characters' have been given precedence
over their story. Not that story has been exactly disregarded: naturally it has been continually alluded to: but still, it seems subordinate, and (one may feel) merely there. I don't want to exaggerate.
Aristotle knew the importance of story: the importance of story
must at all times, and by all people, have been felt. However, our age
has thought fit to shift the emphasis, so that now the whole idea of
story often seems naïve; we have known the need to guard against
'story-telling', which is an uncritical activity.

We should ask – and not solely with regard to tragic stories –
Why does a certain train of events interest us, that is, cause us to like
dwelling on it? How, unless by conforming with something in ourselves, does a train of events come to be called a story? – a mental
patterning, or need for patterning of a certain sort, lets us recognise
some sequences as stories; all the rest remain sequences only, having
no story-interest. It is true that myths are often viewed as manifestations of the psyche: but I doubt whether even the most trivial stories
depend on a different principle. Here I become particularly aware of
my own confusion and uncertainty, although the road goes onwards
which I shall follow. Perhaps criticism has been not unwilling to
undertake the assimilation of story: but is it still criticism, so far as it
has dealt in myth, and in the interpretation of myth psychologically?
A partisan situation has arisen which no one can avoid: possibly no
one wants or should want to avoid it. I don't think I do. Yet it seems
to call for decisions, and I can't seem to arrive at appropriate ones.
For there exists, there is practised, a sort of critical apartheid. I
cannot pretend to be one of the blacks. As a matter of fact I prefer
to live with whites – I know where I belong. Nevertheless, the bar-
baric fantasies of negro psychologists, Freud and Jung especially,
seem to me among the great achievements of the age. I affirm, theirs
is a potent medicine, apartheid notwithstanding. And after all,
literature belongs to anyone; a pernicious, or at best contemptible
doctrine, some critics will say, for as critics we like to arrogate

literature to ourselves. My own feeling – and I imagine it is a fairly general feeling among us – is that the approach of psychologists towards literature is not altogether satisfactory. I am often prompted to use ideas that derive from psychologists: this approach is one which I value, but at the same time the bent of my mind is not finally 'psychological', and the only expertise to which I can lay the slightest claim is critical. In short I won't say I've gone bush: but having wheeled nimbly around like a flummoxed rhinoceros ('white' of course, that is 'wide' or big-mouthed) I resume the trail, keeping my horn well out of sight, ploughing a lonely furrow.

The tragic stories of literature, many of which (Hamlet among them) are associated with folk-versions, clarify the indistinctly perceived patterning of personal destiny. Yet they are also known to be more extreme, and hence not quite personal after all. We are not Hamlet, but Hamlet is us, Lear is us too, any other hero is each of us. The fact that all heroes are ourselves shows that they are all extrapolations from our less patterned, less heroic lives: that is why we are interested in them, and need them: yet in our realising of each hero, the alternatives are excluded, the latent possibilities. It is necessary to know what we might become with Hamlet (as with other figures) in order to know what some of the forces are, which contribute to our actually becoming something else.

My reactions to Shakespeare's Hamlet have changed over the years. First, in my youth, I thought it fairly interesting and yet (notwithstanding) fairly meaningless too. There followed a long period during which I simply got used to it, without changing my basic opinion: somehow, though, it did seem a bigger play. A time came when it was suddenly what it had always been, huge, densely coherent, bewildering rather than meaningless. It has become persistently compelling, my thoughts keep turning to Hamlet, of late especially. Its fascination, known I presume to generations of admirers (or it would not interest us so much?) has always the element of mystery. Mystery, any mystery, exists apart from exploration, although without mystery exploration is not possible. Hamlet commentary would, if it could, explore away the mystery which it depends on, perhaps which the play depends on. I wonder whether the desire is laudable, to explore, but I cannot resist it. Do I secretly hope that I shall fail? If so I am not likely to be disappointed. I do not know whether the mystery of Hamlet is altogether associated with the mystery of unconsciousness: but certainly I feel that the play's peculiar sway over my mind involves the origin and development of my own life. As far as the concept of unconsciousness is at issue – and I shall not object if it is treated merely *as* a concept, without reference to its truth or error – I find it to be immensely valuable; speaking, of course, from my own point of view; other people will already know what to think about the unconscious, and will estimate my remark accordingly. Rightly or wrongly one can try to explore *Hamlet*. I have to anyway, although the impulsion may have nothing to do with the play. Surely, it must have to do with the play.

2

Freud and Sophocles had at least the Oedipus story in common: and Ernest Jones, the disciple of Freud, thought he saw the Oedipus story again in Shakespeare's *Hamlet*, a drama composed before the invention of psychoanalysis and at a time when the alternative Humours theory was strongly entrenched. I doubt whether *Hamlet and Oedipus* (1949) is the uncritically silly book which its detractors have claimed it to be. The fact that it presumably has the approval of Freudians need not mean that it lacks critical interest; part of their approval might even arise from its being critical. Detractors would seem to imply that anyone approving the work in any way is not, and cannot be, a critic: I suppose they argue that Freudian psychology and criticism are totally separate and opposed. But many who call themselves critics, and who are not, therefore, intent on being psychoanalysts, reject this too sharp distinction. It is possible to be suspicious of Jones whilst acknowledging indebtedness.

A respectable matron in my home town eloped with her brother-in-law, abandoning her children. A thrill of excitement passed through the nearby streets. Tongues wagged. No doubt present-day trends in entertainment have led to our dismissing commercial incest with a world-weary shrug, but real-life incest among the neighbours is another thing, we cannot be indifferent to that. Wife with brother-in-law still means incest, and the lady's respectability greatly heightened the drama, somehow reminding us of probable improbabilities and immanent evil (or so the gossips averred). Yet Gertrude and Claudius, though making an incestuous union, are guilty mainly in Hamlet's eyes. He is, as school examination papers sometimes recall, obsessed by his mother's incest, even more than by his father's murder. It is possible to think that Hamlet's obsessional interest in a case of incest not his own, amounts to an indication of his own incestuous feelings. To some, this idea will be as attractive as god to atheists: and critics less open-minded will also feel the force of the possibility I refer to.

So many puzzling or meaningless features of the play begin to make sense if this idea is entertained – the nasty key fits into the lock. Hamlet's incest can be, and has been, inferred psychologically from his speech and action: but I do not think it rests only on interpretation of that kind. The play's lay-out and design seem to make their own kind of statement about Hamlet's attitude. The statement is not a language-statement, although naturally language is going on all the time, uttered by the characters whose words make up the play. Hamlet nowhere says he has incestuous feelings for his mother, nor is he ever accused of having them: a circumstance which has given more trouble than it need have done. Suppose – I am not attempting conjectural emendation – that Hamlet somewhere *did* declare a sexual desire for his mother. There would then be no difficulty, presumably, about agreeing that the play's whole design reflects, incorporates, this element of Hamlet's mind, just as it reflects other elements of his mind. Because he makes no such declaration the evidence from design is held to be suspect, to be forced interpretation, mere assertion or guess. Is the absence of declaration so decisive, however? It might be held to show either that he had no incest feelings for his mother, or that he had: the latter is not less likely than the former; surely, I may fail to recognise my desires for what they are, and not least when I am at my most self-righteous.

Sometimes I think that the state of Hamlet's awareness, so far as it concerns incest, has become confused with the equally problematical state of Shakespeare's. Even assuming that the design of the play, regarded as a kind of statement, can prompt a verbal rendering, translation, formulation – for example the formulation, 'Hamlet's incest' – this does not mean that Shakespeare felt such a prompting himself, he may never have verbalised what he conceptualised dramatically. That he could create a character in a dramatic situation, allowing the situation to reflect the character's complex and not fully aware reactions: that he (the playwright) should thereby demonstrate a penetrating and convincing understanding: these things seem to me possible without the accompaniment of verbal conception such as (in simple form) 'Hamlet's incest'. To the question of whether Shakespeare knew about Hamlet's incestuous inclinations, therefore, one can only reply that he knew it in the language of drama, but not (perhaps) in the language of English; I may mention here, since it is indirectly relevant, that in the common case of dramatic irony no one insists upon characters *saying in words* what the structure *says without words*. Of course, it remains possible that with the verbal parts of his understanding Shakespeare *did* know of Hamlet's incest: he may have chosen to portray a hero less verbally aware, in this respect, than himself. Dramatic structure, as I have admitted, is finally a structure of words: I want to emphasise that the context of a verbal statement can alter its meaning – not a very remarkable truth, one might have thought, but those people disregard it, whose only reason for insisting that Hamlet has no incestuous desires, is that he never tells us he has them. I dwell on this point because it is often supposed that nothing but a belief in Freudian theory could lead to a belief in Hamlet's incest; and it is hotly argued, with some appearance of probability, that Shakespeare lived before Freud's time. However, Shakespeare knew about incest. The incestuous union of Hamlet's mother and uncle is firmly indicated. I do not feel that the possibility of Hamlet's own incest, or rather of his incestuous attitude, should be dismissed or scouted merely on the grounds that Freud knew about incest too.

Hamlet's incestuous desire for Gertrude could conceivably show itself as an obsessional interest in, revulsion from, the incest that subsists between her and Claudius. Without question Hamlet is deeply perturbed: and, granted that the subject is a proper one for disgust, the audience must sometimes wonder whether his strictures on the pair are not excessive. Disgust of this intensity, hatred over and above what one would (simple-mindedly) expect, could arise from the fact that his mother's new husband stands towards him as a father. A son may love his mother incestuously – that is one of the meanings which the word incest has. A son who *does* love his mother incestuously will find himself frustrated by his father; indirectly by his mother too, through her commitment to his father. He will meet with frustration even should he fail to recognise his own love fully for what it is; in either case – love recognised or not – he will hate his father. There are people – ingenious or ingenuous, I am not sure which – who bring themselves to believe that *since Hamlet has no incestuous love* incestuous love does not enter into his hatred of Claudius. These good folk accept anything but Hamlet's incest – doubtless their feelings do them credit. All the same, the 'father' in

the play is the mother's 'brother', and it is therefore the case that
Hamlet's hatred occupies an incestuous context: and Hamlet's
hatred of the 'father' which occupies an incestuous context *is also*
(one could say) hatred of incest.

The plot follows genetics in giving Hamlet only one actual
father, and this need surprise no one. A man cannot have more than
one father, yet a playwright may legitimately distribute the facets of a
complex idea through more than one stage character; so Claudius,
who plot-wise is uncle and step-father, is not precluded from being
a psychological father to Hamlet. Indeed, if such distribution is to
take place at all there can be no *narrower* separation than that between
father, and uncle on the father's side. Claudius is a father to Hamlet:
but, of course, Old Hamlet likewise is a father, and is so in a psychological as well as a genetic sense. The two facets of a complex idea
have been split up and embodied in separate dramatis personae.
Shakespeare frequently has recourse to this technique. We have to
consider a particular case in which two types of father/son relationship are exhibited, whose real-life equivalent would be a single
relationship having two aspects.

May I comment on my use of the word 'psychological'? – or perhaps I should say comment *again*. In these opening remarks on the play
I am constantly having to ask myself whether, or how far, the
theories of psychologists are determining my approach. The fact that
I have been influenced by the theories – and indeed am glad to have
been influenced by them – must count for something, but what? I
am not aware of treating *Hamlet* as a secondary or derivative manifestation of twentieth-century psychology. I am wholly opposed to
the view that twentieth-century psychology is in some way definitive,
everything else being merely illustrative of its essential truth.
Nevertheless, I feel that a given psychological theory is a form of
truth, a truth-form, a form, and I accept that it will be related to other
forms: *Hamlet* is cognate. I cannot believe that my whole inward
experience of life has been dictated by theories which I have learned
about, and which seem to fit in with it: my inner life was not just
put there by the theories, although to a certain extent I have allowed
it to become involved with what the theories are. Forms are always
being sought, and when found they modify the previous state: the
forms of psychology were found. *Hamlet* was another form found,
and it too modifies my previous state. It is *Hamlet* which I am prim-

arily looking at. My psychologising, such as it is, is important to me as a viable mode of language: it does not imply a desire to match the play precisely to any other existent form; the phenomenon of cognate forms is a happy if expected accident, which may be turned to account when one comments on a particular form. Hamlet is, so to speak, of the inward life. It is a form characteristic of that medium – drama – which deploys actors to present a story (though not of course a *narrative* story, which is something different again). The story is symbolic, and thus there is nothing knowable behind it, for knowableness is what has become evident in it. Certain of our needs are satisfied, whose nature is grasped only through the nature of the satisfaction; needs which may enter into separate forms of satisfaction, without the various forms being properly substitutes for each other.

Distribution into separate personages, though a common means of dramatic expression, is not however always desirable. Gertrude is a single dramatis persona who reveals contrasted appearances: she functions as a duality, one side of her having married Old Hamlet, the other, Claudius. Just as the son (Hamlet himself) has two fathers, so he has in a sense two mothers, Gertrude by name. He is the fruit of the one marriage, or of its alternative, dependent upon his attitude of mind: and whichever parentage he owns, father and mother define themselves mutually as a pair. What it feels like to have a father (not a simple feeling, to Hamlet or to anyone else) is part and parcel of what it feels like to have a mother. Attention may be directed towards one parent, yet the assessment of each involves awareness of both. Insofar as it is true that Hamlet's principal preoccupation is with the mother, his father is of crucial importance. His feeling for her is modified by his feeling for him; though at the same time Hamlet's view of the father (not actually his main concern?) takes the form that it does precisely because the mother enters the assessment. The mother/son relationship seems an agreeable thing to Hamlet when the father/son relationship is also agreeable: the one implies, co-exists with, contributes to the meaning of, the other. At such times he will emphasise and approve the marriage of Gertrude and Old Hamlet. He will emphasise and resent the marriage of Gertrude and Claudius whenever the fact of his sonship appears painful, that is, when he is dissatisfied with the mother/son relationship, and dissatisfied with the father/son relationship simultaneously.

It must be realised that the stage personages are at once the cause of Hamlet's feelings about them, and also in a way the personification of what those feelings of his are like. This fine distinction does seem to make a difference in practice. For instance (to shift for a moment to a fairly late point in the play) when Gertrude in the closet scene is persuaded to reject her new wifehood and to re-adopt as far as possible her old wifehood, this should be understood in terms of Hamlet's experience of the mother/son relationship. Her change causes his affection to flow, recreates currently something of the earlier relationship: yet the good aspect which she wears is not only cause but effect. It describes what the relationship is, no description other than Gertrude's changed aspect being necessary. I doubt whether this process is peculiar to drama. It may be implied by the terms mother-figure, father-figure, when these appear in a more general psychological context: perhaps we regard actual mothers and fathers in the same fashion, rating our own response, indirectly, through their perceived qualities. The consideration is not less applicable to drama, however, for being general. It seems especially relevant, so far as the structure and movement of Hamlet's story are held to evince the nature of his sonship.

Hamlet is of the inward life: the hero is surrounded by his dramatised psyche, which is also ours. Yet against this inwardness I must set the apparent outwardness of Shakespeare's characters. Whilst I admire this quality I find it oddly disconcerting, for it seems to introduce an alien principle, one which is under no obligation to conform itself to the hero's internal figuration. The characters who surround Hamlet are not abstractions: they function in the stage world as though to themselves at least they were the centre of it. I recognise that, in the end, one may speak after a fashion of a 'real' story. Hamlet could have happened. At the same time, the rare special case must be supposed, in which life-circumstances are at once authentically objective and symbolically subjective. To put this another way, one knows that Hamlet is an artefact arranged to make the two elements coincide. But the principle actually adopted and pursued, the guiding if concealed principle, is nevertheless inwardness.

Gertrude's duality, her doubleness as a mother-figure, now good, now bad: this duality of hers embraces (almost literally) both halves of the play. Her position in the story, as well as her characterisation, sustains much tension. In elementary terms the play's design can be said to comprise a strong antithesis between alternative systems. The Claudius/Hamlet/Gertrude system is expressive of Hamlet's negative attitudes, and this system holds sway whenever the positive system does not hold sway: the positive system comprises Gertrude/Hamlet/Old Hamlet. It would hardly be too much to say that the elimination of either system is the appearance of the other, so opposite are they, so mutually dependent in their function of mutual exclusion. Yet in point of fact – though I defer discussion of this – the play is much more than an unstable arrangement of relatively simple alternatives; for elements of confusion, really principles of development, are latent. But the story's opening approximation has been my immediate concern rather than its subtle central disturbance.

3

It seems both possible and impossible to accept that incest has to do with oneself. There are of course no memories: one commonly says 'of course no memories' as though other people's incest were thereby rendered all the more likely – ignorance the great proof – but is the lack of evidence such convincing evidence in one's own private case? Does one believe in the 'Oedipus complex', really believe? Perhaps the most difficult ghosts to lay are those which only may be there. Whether I experienced an infantile incestuous desire, and, if I did, how my present state is thereby influenced: these questions are coolly rational, or are they visitations? Why does *Hamlet* fascinate? One cannot say with any certainty that it fascinates by touching upon inaccessible personal experience, although it might be doing just that.

I cannot remember when I became aware of sexual differentiation (the sophisticated expression is ludicrously attached to childish perceptions): but I have convinced myself that the discovery, when it was being made, was not other than important – I mean that it was a major discovery even at the time, despite its being the West Indies rather than mainland America. I think about the time when a child becomes aware not simply that its parents are two different people, but that somehow they are different *sorts* of people: that there are two different sorts of people in the world, men and women. And which sort does the child belong to? This problem, in whatever shape or form presented – presumably another shape, another form, than this I articulate – must appear to the child urgent and increasingly urgent. To the extent that I have here outlined the problem as something separate in itself, I have certainly misrepresented it. For a child's awareness of differentiation by sex is intricately and inseparably connected with his (or her) perception of the family situation as a whole, within which sex is identified as meaningful. Inevitably this total situation is seen (I feel prepared to assert) as a modified

version of the bond between mother and child, a bond which
originally did not take account of the third person in the family.
The modification is anything but slight, however. Between the
original bond and the modified totality there is an advance in complexity which prompts comparison with Jehovah's modification
into the Christian Trinity; and though I mean to limit the comparison to a matter of complexity, it does occur to me that there may
be and probably are other significant similarities despite the fact that
Jehovah is no goddess. For are not the cosmic assumptions of
religion connected with family? The ancient Egyptian trinity, which I
am told prefigured in some ways the Christian Trinity, was a complete family, consisting of divine father and mother with divine son.
The ordinary human child, mother-bound, discovers that the unre-
garded third member of the family is actually bound to the mother
too, has claims upon her. At some point or period of time the sharing
of the mother, perhaps the competing for her, is felt to involve a
distinction between father and mother which extends itself to the
child; that is to say, the child succeeds in making a viable classification into two sexes, and recognises personal affinity with one of the
classes. If father and child are found to be of the *same* class, a boy's
situation is apparent: if they are of a *different* class, then the situation is
a girl's. Although two sexes are recognised, the act of differentiation
is single: maleness is not-femaleness, and simultaneously femaleness
is not-maleness. The character of each sex lies in its difference from,
i.e. relation to, the other. Now, if maleness (for example) has to do
with womanhood, the relationship between two males cannot have
nothing to do with womanhood. The boy who finds that he is like
his father and unlike his mother forms a relationship with his father
in which the mother counts. Furthermore his perception of sexual
classification is intimately wrought with the mother's primacy, her
central position in his life: his feelings for the father are therefore
necessarily intense too. The whole situation is made inescapable by
the fact that father and mother have a relationship with each other
which has to be reckoned a part of their relationship with himself.
Perhaps one can hardly overestimate the complexity that is revealed
in a child's awareness: surely the emotional dynamics of his situation are as intricate as they are real. Freud's analysis, as it has passed
into common knowledge, suffers by being too well known and not
well known enough. The boy loves his mother, finds himself at a

disadvantage in competing with his father, identifies with his father so that, through him, he can reach the mother by another route. The case of the girl is less applicable to the present discussion. Her situation is not a precise reversal of the boy's, and I think this is ultimately because both boys and girls are attached primarily to the mother, but girls are of her sex and boys are not. True balance would exist only if boys were born of their fathers (I have heard young children, though only girls, make just this assumption).

All this seems suppositional yet also factual: and I believe it to be both, or I try to, unsuccessfully perhaps, for as between supposition and fact is there not a problem of mutual exclusion? In somewhat the same way — but the cases are very different — it is hardly possible to believe both that the authentic convictions of Christianity are mental projections, and that they are not, referring rather to an external god outside the self; though again I try to exercise these incompatible attitudes simultaneously. Belief cannot also be doubt (this is particularly true of doubt believed in). Still, on some footing or other the Oedipus situation lives in my mind. I tend to think of it as an experience common to all males, despite lack of evidence from memory. Therefore, amid non-sequiturs of every sort, it may be said that Hamlet appears to have much to do with life as I know it.

A House of Cards has this advantage over a cathedral: when it falls down it much more nearly doesn't, for when it was up it hardly was.

Furthermore, if I may press the word into service, there are moral considerations which somewhat separate me from the play — perhaps I only partly share its assumptions. Simply, the play evokes a moral universe: or a universe morally broken: but in either case the Oedipus situation would have to be assessed by Christian standards of an independent and indeed entirely self-sufficient kind; that is, Hamlet's moral universe bears upon his incest dilemma. By contrast I really don't know whether I can summon the term 'moral universe' to my aid, and in any case (this may explain why) I can't but feel that my experience of the dilemma caused my moral awareness (such as it is) at least in some degree. Or was my morality called into being for the first time by the dilemma, to which I responded accordingly? The play, not inconceivably, may reflect just this situation: Shakespeare may have explored the moral universe through family relationships, which are not separable from the greater whole although they do not cause it.

It occurs to me that those earlier comments about suppositional/factual belief in the Oedipus situation, about belief in religious projection and in god beyond the self, must have some sort of bearing on the question of my moral outlook. I dare say I am confused, and the confusion is so to speak all of a piece. On the other hand the confusion does not seem to amount to disorientation – it is viable and far from amorphous. A lack of systematic principle is only a painful and urgent condition when the people around one (of firm principle) are having their own say and their own way. One is then under pressure from alien wills. The characters in a Shakespeare play serve to figure forth the mind of the hero, though this technique is not inconsistent with their separate identity. The characters in life who surround a given person have separate identity, sure enough, but do not contribute to any symbolising of the 'hero'. Life is not art. And yet it must be true that the person, the 'hero', sees everything around him including people in accordance with perceptual processes which are his own. That is to say, his experience of the world about him *does* figure forth what he is, his perceptions are his being – all he can know of his being. The stimuli that activate his perceptions are things outside himself (I don't doubt it) but the perceptions, once activated, are always himself. That these stimuli can take the form of people, perceivers likewise, merely means that the 'heroic' focus can be endlessly shifted, person by person. In a sense each person is the playwright of his own play, himself the 'hero'. But as he is a deficient hero, so he is surely a worse playwright. For, whilst the total play (more truth than pun) of his perceptions, stimulated from without, sets forth fully all that he is, it does this inefficiently, indiscriminately, without benefit of the symbolic structuring which both evinces and evokes an otherwise scattered order. He is a poor playwright in the business of living out his life because he cannot select or control in any adequate way the stimuli by which he is affected.

Still, he has some control, however little, in that he retains power of choice and action. If I have implied – and I think I have – that a man is composed out of, accumulated through, his perceptions, then perhaps it appears to be of little importance what his perceptions are (this, that, or the other) for they can only and always add up to the sum of himself. I can't help wondering whether this is really true, although the only alternative is to believe that identity will change – and not necessarily superficially – with the change of his environment. Perhaps identity can so change: people may choose to live abroad because they know (nor are they in error) that there they become different people, who they prefer to be. So far as the individual can exert any control over his environment, therefore, he may be altering himself along with it, and this kind of change may be for the better; he need not flee abroad to accomplish it, either. Better for whom, according to whom?

The people who stimulate, activate, a man's perceptions will give rise to moral experience, which is included under the general head of perception. They and their behaviour, to use ordinary parlance, will seem good or bad. Now, although their moral effect is in, and of, me, still they caused it, by being the sort of stimulus they are; a stimulus which, of course, might produce a very different result when applied to another perceiver than myself. Given my moral experience, I must deal with it. I ought to do what I can (perhaps it won't be much) to limit the power of the stimulus that emerges in me as a perception of evil, and to further the power of the stimulus whose perceived result is good. The great problem – I mean apart from bringing persuasion to bear on other people – is to distinguish between evil and good, so as to decide how to act. What seems evil may be evil, or may not. Conversely, interrelatedly, good may be good, or may not. The moral dilemma is often deeply obscure: one does one's best to relate it to that ordered vision of another drama (those ordered visions of other dramas) which real-life drama is for ever seeking to improve itself into.

My morality for what it is worth, relativistic and subjective or whatever else, ought to be exercised according to occasion, and not least in the teaching of English at university, since that is the official context of my life. My confusion must be as a knife going through butter. How to bring that about? Aye there's the rub must give us pause, there's the calamity to make a man grunt and sweat (First Quarto).

4

In one sense the conflict between the royal brothers Old Hamlet and Claudius is a clash of moral opposites, yet in another sense it is not. Good and evil are eternally opposed, and this has often seemed the most simple and basic of truths. However, so far from being straight-forward, the struggle has revealed a perplexing paradox, made all the worse by the need (nevertheless) to act. It is as though good, vindi-cating itself against evil, hence being true to itself, is not being true to itself after all. Resisting the destructive encroachment of evil, and itself encroaching upon evil, good apparently becomes in the process destructive and evil. In short, good is unable to do battle, because that implies an aim to destroy which is the mark of evil: the attempt to destroy destructiveness – even that which belongs to evil – seems doomed to fail: indeed, seems guaranteed to advance the cause not of good but of evil. The alternative is not to fight, in which case does not evil triumph anyway? A good man combats with a bad man, and presently (whoever wins) there is one bad man, he a murderer. What might be called the militant 'solution' to the problem of evil has always been exposed to this dilemma. That a morally sophisticated solution exists, the sacrificial, perhaps makes more cul-pable the continued practice of militancy. Yet is militancy, which has so much the look of righteous human reaction, altogether irreligious? Not inconceivably the world might be an even worse place without it. Militancy may be necessary morally, despite its being morally sus-pect, or even actually immoral. Unfortunately we are likely to be confused by further complications. For, in order to be militant, a man must be good before he decides to fight, and must enter the battle on behalf of right. He may mistake both himself and the cause. His enemy may have been better than himself, or no worse.

Claudius murders Old Hamlet: evil murders good. This over-simplified view need not be entirely despised. Shakespeare charac-teristically avails himself of our most automatic responses, and does

so because he wants to explore them. The conflict between the royal
brothers we reckon to be a moral conflict. If we jump to a moral conclusion which is too crude, if we are betrayed into a moral approximation which is too easy, we have at least made morals our concern.
Furthermore, whatever may be the subtlety of the brothers' situation
we are presumably right in seeing Old Hamlet as essentially good,
and Claudius as essentially evil. In other words the first and over-
simplified view is perhaps not wholly false. Uncertainties may arise
and complexities increase, but our developing awareness seems consistent – does it not? – with our original guess. What happens is that
moral judgement becomes more fully, more painfully, exercised.
Hamlet's own opening reactions are sometimes simple, sometimes
subtle.

The oversimplified view is first exposed as inadequate by the
doubt cast on the status of the Ghost, whose appearance might
denote deceit – a possibility of which Elizabethans were well aware.
Hamlet's subtlety (where he is subtle) is directed at this aspect of
things. He conjures with a metaphysical problem, but hardly
seems to judge of the Ghost's actual behaviour, or his father's. He
accepts the revenger's role at the Ghost's behest, without directly
questioning revenge ethics. I know that this consideration impinges
on the related topic of revenge as literary convention, but still I hardly
feel easy about saying, 'Of course he doesn't question revenge ethics'.
For the Ghost's general status is questioned, repeatedly, and I don't
think the points at issue are merely dramatic suspense and Hamlet's
metaphysical bent. The Ghost is not Old Hamlet the mortal man,
but obviously the two beings are partially identified. It seems to
me that anything which could have a bearing on the relationship
between Old Hamlet and Claudius ought to be noted. If the conflict
of the royal brothers is other than a simple matter the Ghost may
enter into the case, and the ethics of revenge may enter into the case
too.

Interestingly, the appearance of the Ghost is linked at first with
the ancient struggle between Old Hamlet and Old Fortinbras of
Norway. In a long and contorted speech (I, i, 79–107[1]) Horatio
establishes the necessary political background. We are later to learn

---

[1] I have used throughout the 'New Shakespeare' *Hamlet* (Cambridge
University Press), ed. John Dover Wilson (rev. ed. 1954).

that Claudius encompassed the death of his own brother by dishonourable means and for most dishonourable reasons: Old Hamlet in
the early battle seems to have behaved with honour. Perhaps, even so,
he did not need to respond to the challenge that was offered: Old
Fortinbras, 'pricked on by a most emulate pride', had after all only
dared him to combat. The King of Denmark did respond, however,
being proud enough to accept the challenge. He was blessed (if
blessed he was) with success.

When Shakespeare writes ambiguous sentences – especially, I
would say, when his syntax is ambiguous – one is aware that he is
often responding to, and furthering, genuinely ambiguous dramatic
situations. The 'emulate pride' of Fortinbras could be Old Hamlet's
too, a possibility which should at least be considered.

>   . . . our last king,
> Whose image even but now appeared to us,
> Was as you know by Fortinbras of Norway,
> Thereto pricked on by a most emulate pride,
> Dared to the combat . . .   (I, i, 80–4)

It may be agreed that the line 'thereto pricked on by a most emulate
pride' seems to hang curiously in the sentence. As coming after
'Fortinbras of Norway' it is evidently designed to explain the action
of that King. But what action? Well, he dared Old Hamlet to combat,
surely. No, he did not. Rather Old Hamlet *was dared* by Fortinbras:
Old Hamlet ('our last king') is the subject of a passive verb, Fortinbras is not the subject of an active verb. Although 'pricked' appears
to have an adjectival relationship with the closely preceding 'Fortinbras of Norway', it has also an adverbial connection with 'was . . .
dared'; and hence ultimately a connection with the subject of the
sentence, 'our last king'; the verbal function inherent in 'thereto'
supports this reading. The sentence is prevented from becoming
meaningless by the near-equivalence, as regards the human outcome,
which subsists between daring and being dared. The giving of the dare
tends to result in, is expected to result in, the taking up of the dare.
'To dare' is active in grammatical form and points to further human
action; 'to be dared' is passive in its grammatical form yet it likewise
points to further human action, in fact to the *same* action. Old Hamlet
is dared: but this can mean, and here does mean, that he responds in
anything but a passive and acted-upon fashion. Thus the words

'thereto pricked on by a most emulate pride' (and indeed 'emulate' gives further substance to the ambiguity) are applicable without absurdity to Old Hamlet, as well as to Old Fortinbras; although it seems to me plain that the speaker intends to apply them only to the latter.

There are further considerations, associated with Old Hamlet's pride and likewise tending to bring him under moral suspicion – however slight. For when I say that his moral status comes under suspicion I am not (at least I think I am not) affirming him to be really an evil man. I am of the same opinion as anyone who chooses to go on calling him good. Yet I believe that one's confidence in him has to be maintained against disquieting elements: nor is this surprising if one considers that even the best of men cannot be perfect. Certainly Old Hamlet is heroic: he and Old Fortinbras, however, before the combat, enter into an arrangement which so far as it concerns their sons is perhaps dubious. Shakespeare relies a good deal in this play upon the English response to hereditary title: he does so whilst at the same time allowing, or seeming to allow, or not denying, alternative systems. Our commonly held notion of hereditary title is compounded of the following notions: (a) the title passes to the eldest son (b) any present holder of the title is guarding it for his heirs, having no right to give it away, for it is theirs as much as his. One feels and is intended to feel that Hamlet ought to have become King after his father's death, notwithstanding two counter-principles (themselves somewhat at variance with one another) which the play presents; viz succession of the next brother, and election. Less strongly, one feels that perhaps Young Fortinbras ought to have ascended the throne of Norway, although the legality of his uncle's succession (brother of the dead King, and by name another Fortinbras) is never adversely judged. The bargain struck between Old Hamlet and Old Fortinbras, despite its being 'well ratified by law and heraldry', has the effect of denying to the loser's son certain rights. It is one thing that your father should have part of his (your) lands stripped from him by force, and another that he should cede away your inheritance to the enemy. You stand to gain if he is victorious, for then the gamble pays off, but this does not mean that the risk can properly be taken. The unlucky son, as things turned out, was Fortinbras: the reduced Norwegian inheritance passed to Old Fortinbras the dead King's brother. Hamlet might have been the unlucky son: Hamlet, who, years later, never inherited his father's increased lands, being kept from possession by the dead King's brother, Claudius. A powerful vagueness invests the play's treatment of inheritance. The Ghost of Old Hamlet can appoint his son avenger, and Hamlet can accept the role. Yet with Claudius evil enough to call forth vengeance, is not Old Hamlet in some degree evil for the same reason? – arousing as he does a desire not unlike revenge in Young Fortinbras;

> . . . which is no other,
> As it doth well appear unto our state,
> But to recover of us by strong hand
> And terms compulsatory, those foresaid lands
> So by his father lost . . .   (I, i, 100–4)

The Ghost of Old Hamlet, and Hamlet himself, may be wrong to seek revenge. However, Young Fortinbras is allowed a triumph at the end of the play – and his is surely a triumph of goodness. One notes also that he has Hamlet's 'dying voice'. The basic idea which I am pursuing is simple enough in itself and perhaps sound as far as it goes. I fall back on it. Old Hamlet's moral status is open to some degree of doubt: and so is the validity of the revenge which his Ghost would exact.

Old Hamlet seems a paragon to Hamlet, who strangely is able to preserve intact this view of his father; strangely, because from the moment of first seeing the Ghost an awareness of metaphysical predicament impresses itself on the mind of the Prince –

> Angels and ministers of grace defend us!
> Be thou a spirit of health, or goblin damned,
> Bring with thee airs from heaven, or blasts from hell,
> Be thy intents wicked, or charitable,
> Thou com'st in such a questionable shape,
> That I will speak to thee. I'll call thee Hamlet,
> King, father, royal Dane. O, answer me!   (I, iv, 39–45)

From that moment onwards Hamlet knows that he is dealing either with supernatural good or supernatural evil, and he cares which. Also, he does not care which. His not caring is tantamount to a willingness to pursue evil. His caring shows him determined to pursue good if he can. Yet Hamlet is open to these moral complexities only in regard to the Ghost: Old Hamlet himself, the memory of him, remains simply good. The son is willing enough in one way to identify the man that was with the spirit that is, even whilst keeping them apart in another way (he keeps them apart by speculating not at all about the one, and about the other a great deal). The Ghost himself, notwithstanding his unwavering and self-righteous demand for revenge, does not claim to have been perfect in the mortal world, rather the reverse. This is greatly at variance with Hamlet's conscious ideas about his father: one might say in fact that the Ghost's attitude makes apparent in terms of story and staging the aspect of Hamlet's awareness which conflicts with Hamlet's beliefs; I don't mean that the Ghost exists merely as a figment of Hamlet's imagination. Certainly Old Hamlet's moral condition is evident enough to the spirit-being who now suffers the consequences. To treat the confessions of the Ghost as though they were proof of a good man's modesty seems to me less than satisfactory. There is no indication that the 'sulph'rous and tormenting flames' (I, v, 3) are an unjust infliction: 'I could a tale unfold', says the pained spirit, 'whose lightest word/Would harrow up thy soul, freeze thy young blood'. Old Hamlet's sins were 'foul crimes' according to the Ghost. Either the sins were by human standards really foul, or human standards are false in accounting them less than foul. In neither case can we quite accept Hamlet's uncritical estimate of his father's goodness.

Old Hamlet's *innate* imperfection? – his original sin, his fallen human state. Several points arise. In the first place, Old Hamlet hardly gains an excuse: if he is guilty of original sin he is guilty of it, and there is no case for pretending that somehow this kind of sin doesn't belong to him, doesn't count, is unimportant. In the second place, the guilt of original sin is not necessarily Old Hamlet's only guilt – he may in his life-time have committed crimes over and above those of a new-born baby. But should one assume that original sin has to be reckoned with at all? Is there, perhaps, an allusion to the Fall in the story of the murder? After the first call to revenge the Ghost addresses Hamlet in the following manner:

> . . . now Hamlet hear,
> 'Tis given out, that sleeping in my orchard,
> A serpent stung me, so the whole ear of Denmark
> Is by a forgéd process of my death

> Rankly abused: but know, thou noble youth,
> The serpent that did sting thy father's life
> Now wears his crown.   (I, v, 34–40)

Evidence of Shakespeare's knowledge of, feeling for, instinct about, the Fall, can be detected I think in most of his plays: but I have to qualify my statement in that way because it is quite wrong to think that Shakespeare confined himself to allusion. Allusion means reference to material elsewhere existing, existing in definite form: the definite form yields the significance: that is to say the allusion itself is derivative and secondary, and remains so no matter how complete-in-itself the new rendering may be (which is often, however, just a hint). Now, allusion is a perfectly legitimate technique, and of course Shakespeare chooses on occasion to use it. But sometimes he is only assumed to be working in this way, and then interpretations are offered which are strained: or else, perhaps because the interpretations do seem strained, it is sometimes denied that he is working in anything like this way, with the conclusion that his meaning must be quite other. But I have somewhat the same notion here that influenced me when I tried to comment on Shakespeare and Freud. Shakespeare knew nothing of Freud's theory of the Oedipus complex, whereas he knew a lot about Christianity: just as he could render in his own way material which Freud was to render in another way, so he (Shakespeare) could make a rendering of material which Christianity had formulated already. If Christianity is valid it is so because it conforms itself to, and gives form to, underlying psychic patterns: from these, new forms can be imaginatively evolved. In view of the fact that a huge mass of conscious material, Christianity, was (unlike the Oedipus theory) actually present in the mind of Shakespeare, there is likely to be an overlapping of the form Christianity takes, and the forms his imagination creates. The overlapping could then be mistaken for allusion, especially as the authentic and direct technique of allusion is employed not infrequently. The case at present under discussion, that of the serpent which stings Old Hamlet, I feel is an imaginative parallel rather than a thorough-going allusion to the Fall: Shakespeare's image and the religious myth spring from common roots, though a degree of overlapping is obvious. The evil serpent referred to by the Ghost stings a man, not a woman. Yet in the Ghost's next speech a woman is introduced:

> Ay, that incestuous, that adulterate beast,
> With witchcraft of his wit, with traitorous gifts,
> O wicked wit and gifts, that have the power
> So to seduce; won to his shameful lust
> The will of my most seeming-virtuous queen.
>
> (I, v, 42–6)

It seems to me legitimate to recall the Fall of Man, and even to be *advised* by it – if one may express the myth's interpretational influence in that way: nevertheless it is not altogether the source, not the focus, of the tale the Ghost tells. The serpent's sting, i.e. the poison which Claudius pours into the ear of the sleeping King, is comparable with humanity's original fall, but it also seems to figure forth Old Hamlet's later and so to speak *post-original* immorality: for not only is evil instilled into innocence, but that same evil, the killing of a brother King, belongs already to the victor of the emulate combat, ugly in his dying and cut off even in the blossom of his sin –

> . . . a most instant tetter barked about
> Most lazar-like with vile and loathsome crust
> All my smooth body.   (I, v, 71–3)

The goodness of Old Hamlet is subject to doubt, and the revenge which his spirit calls for is thus equally doubtful. The ethics of revenge are not overtly called into question. It is noticeable, however, that the insistence on revenge lessens as the play advances. The spectre potent in the first act is attenuated at the end of the third to a form which only Hamlet can discern; and if Gertrude's attitude prevents her from seeing it, the apparition must still be called enfeebled even as Hamlet sees it. From this point onwards Hamlet refers less frequently to his father and to revenge. He utters neither of these key *words* when he finally kills Claudius – 'father' must be inferred from 'murderous', and (less directly) 'revenge' from 'Drink off this potion'; the absence of the word 'revenge' at the end of a Revenge play is of course a considerable omission. But Hamlet's procrastination, his whole approach, is notoriously hard to explain. It may have at least something to do with a need to assimilate the seeming simplicity of revenge into an altogether more complex moral framework. The assimilating process could well occur without discussion of revenge as such.

I have already tried to explain how Old Hamlet and Claudius jointly render Hamlet's notion of fatherhood, and I suggested also that they could be regarded as personifying the relationship they caused: they are aspects of fatherhood seen from a son's point of view, and they show by their characterisation the nature of the double relationship which the son feels. It is possible to refer to Hamlet's feeling of partnership and rivalry respectively; other paired terms of a like nature may prove themselves necessary, such as loyalty and rebelliousness, or love and hate. Old Hamlet figures forth Hamlet's feeling about partnership with his father (yet the partnership is between a junior and a senior) whilst Claudius figures forth the feeling of rivalry (again, perhaps, though less clearly, between a junior and a senior). Whatever Old Hamlet and Claudius do in the story, we may understand as rendering the conflict of these elements in Hamlet's mind. His feeling of partnership is in conflict with his feeling of rivalry: in dramatic terms, two characters are placed in conflict, and the third, who is really both of them, must take sides and settle the outcome.

Conflict exists because the tendency of the one feeling is towards the exclusion of the other − partnership and rivalry are opposites, and neither of them can come fully into its own unless the other falls into abeyance. Now, the nature of the rivalry relationship is such that it wants not to be a relationship at all. It wants relationship eliminated, it wants no father in the way. In stage terms this calls for the killing of Claudius: rivalry will thus consummate itself in victory. The triumph of rivalry and the death of Claudius would necessarily imply the end of partnership (Old Hamlet); for what does rivalry mean, if not the rejection of feelings of partnership?

The pursuit of rivalry requires the death of the father, Claudius. Partnership, of course, requires the father to live, though the father then is Old Hamlet, not Claudius. Indeed, partnership can have nothing to do with Claudius, must reject him utterly: in stage terms the success of partnership calls for the killing of Claudius. Only the killing of Claudius can show partnership predominant, and only the killing of Claudius can show rivalry predominant. It is the case, therefore, that each of these two opposite attitudes, to reach fulfilment, must culminate in one and the same event, namely, Claudius's death: there is a choice and no choice. This analysis is certainly over-simple, and I shall shortly explain why: but there are, I think,

valid implications to explore first. Perhaps Hamlet's delay in killing
Claudius reflects his underlying uncertainty about the meaning of this
action. He seems satisfied that Claudius's death is wholly desirable,
yet his conviction stems from two different sources, only one of
which is to be accepted, the other rejected. Until he can commit
himself he cannot strike, when he strikes he is a partner for ever or
he is a successful rival who has struck his enemy dead. Once again
it is as well to say that Hamlet does not discuss these things in plain
terms, nor is it necessary that he should. His reaction when he
mistakenly kills Polonius may not be unconnected with the dilemma
as I have described it:

Queen	O me, what hast thou done?
Hamlet	Nay, I know not,
	Is it the king? (III, iv, 25–6)

But neither here nor elsewhere do the words prove the existence of
the structure and its statement; they merely invite interpretation in
accordance with the structure perceived. To the extent that he is (so
to speak) in the structure and reacting to it, Hamlet is aware of it:
and all the more painfully so because he tries to base his behaviour
on much simpler assumptions, whose tendency is to deny the
existence of any integral conflict or personal dilemma. He is determined to treat revenge as though it were good, even though he
knows it may not be, and this determination is grounded in the un-
questioned assumption that Old Hamlet must have been entirely
good. A sort of moral wilfulness, which he wilfully sets up as moral,
limits his response to a very complex situation (which thereby is
rendered more complex still) but the wilfulness lacks power to
enforce its assumptions in the face of Hamlet's deeper awareness:
it is to his whole experience that he necessarily finds himself
responding, his conscious interpretation being much less than the
whole.

Because Claudius is bad it follows that Hamlet's feeling of rivalry
is bad: the evil locates itself in the father-figure who embodies the
relationship, and thus Hamlet, by self-deception of a kind, frees his
emotion of hatred from the guilt which, nevertheless, is his. Hamlet
feels himself to be good in another way too, more or less an opposite
way: for does he not treat his feeling of partnership as good, represented in the persons of Old Hamlet and the Ghost? There is less

self-deception in Hamlet here, no doubt these figures are primarily good – nevertheless we know that their goodness is hardly what it appears, and Hamlet is evil in being blind to their evil. How is the taint of evil to be understood in terms of the incest situation? I am far from sure.

In the play incest-evil seems gradually to intensify, and as it were to draw nearer by stages. The approach towards recognition of it, never quite completed, seems almost to *create* evil, transforming what was formerly innocent into what it never was when unknown. Perhaps the process has to do with maturation: the infantile relationship with the mother, which prevails before the father is noticed, perhaps cannot properly be called incest at all, since it entirely lacks the evil connotations which subsequently arise: where incest is truly innocent it is not truly incest. The myth of the Fall yields its comparisons; that story which has always been accorded such importance, which appears so centrally 'about' the human condition. When the father is noticed the first change in the original mother-relationship occurs: partnership with the good father, Old Hamlet alive, could seem to Hamlet wholly good, although, by implying a changed awareness of the mother, perhaps the partnership engendered some hint of evil – indirect, remote, sexual. Did Old Hamlet (that aspect of Hamlet) successfully fight the evil off, at any rate for a time, when he slew Old Fortinbras? Old Hamlet's subsequent death was somehow connected with this, was a kind of counterpart to it: and at that later stage the full evil of Claudius became apparent, whose incestuous contact with Gertrude evinces the state of Hamlet's moral perception – incest is now fully incest, rejected though it is as not his own. Yet in Hamlet something like a rebellion is mounting, which is obscurely a part of the still looming and developing incest-evil: whether the rebellion is against good or against bad, how far it is aimed at Old Hamlet, how far at Claudius – these are deep uncertainties: Young Fortinbras musters his more or less rebellious army. The one-ness of the father-figure, Old Hamlet's good totality (a goodness always inherently doubtful) has by now yielded to division. A strengthening of evil has overwhelmed it, innocence is a thing of the past. Perhaps in a way the good has been intensified too, but it has been changed and narrowed into the Ghost. The Ghost's goodness – if that is what it is – shares the total arena with Claudius's successful evil. The Ghost's goodness must insist strongly (one could put it like this) on the right route to the mother, since the wrong route is closer to being recognised. In addition, the rightness of the partnership represented by the Ghost (so far as it can still be called right) is allowed to include, besides love of good, hatred of evil; for its primacy has been destroyed and its very existence is threatened by evil. Love that hates evil is kindred with evil hatred: in a curious way the Ghost is as murderous as Claudius. Hamlet's attempt to legitimise incest by taking vengeance on incestuous Claudius is perhaps suspect, and a move away from the relatively pure goodness of the past: nevertheless, surely it is preferable to the incestuous desire itself, which is become so nearly present? The whole complex situation is further complicated because, in however qualified a fashion, rivalry could after all have something to recommend it above partnership; at any rate, the son may have to challenge the father eventually, and challenge him for a woman.

The play's opening structure presents alternative systems apparently exactly opposed, which, however, are subtly out of balance. If the system represented by Old Hamlet/Hamlet/Gertrude is to be preferred before the other system of Gertrude/Hamlet/Claudius, the fact remains that in approving the former we in some degree approve the latter: equally, it is true that rejection of the bad system goes some way to implying (whether we like it or not) rejection of the system that seems good.

5

There is always a possibility, perhaps it is a probability, that one's professional judgement even at its best is no more than concealed self-justification, seemingly absolute, but the outcome of and apology for identity. In *Hamlet* the apparent outwardness of things is made to reflect the hero's inward condition: and his inward condition, apprehended as the play's form, is compounded of psychological and moral elements which seem not only inseparable, but virtually indistinguishable – I mean that the psychological and moral elements seem all elements of a single type, described by either term with equal fitness. Hamlet's dilemma is of terrible complexity and difficulty, yet one may say it is in some sense idealised. The dilemma itself is ideal, and it is ideally worked out. In real life the perceived outer world does not display the nature of the perceiver in any very perfect or ordered fashion, and there is no certainty that inward psychological and moral elements are unified ideally, or unified at all: nevertheless it is incumbent on each one of us to change the outer world in the right way, that is, in accordance with the right sort of inwardness. The impossible task has to be undertaken as though it could be done: for of course it must be that it can be done. To impinge upon outwardness is a legitimate attempt; it is a necessity imposed upon inwardness, perhaps by inwardness itself. The psyche seems much concerned with things outside it. Why should God need to become incarnate? – furthermore the contemplation of Christ as no more than an idea is somewhat unsatisfactory; for although, in being a figment, he possesses the force of an active and prepotent symbol, in that form he lacks the strange authority of, and over, matter. To change the world beyond the psyche we must change matter certainly: people, however, we must change too, who are psychic entities in their own right besides being material creatures. It occurs to me that art, so psychic, involves itself with an outward medium in order to *become*, and that, having become, its

effect impinges on outwardness further: the playwright's medium –
language spoken by actual people moving on a material stage – partakes to a marked degree of the world: control of the medium is a
controlling of some part of outward reality (more than is the case
with most arts?), and this control occurs whatever the more far-
reaching impact of the play may happen to be.

The attempt to control the outside, including people as well as
things, is entirely proper, although it is finally (as with free will
generally) subject to moral evaluation; thus if the result is evil the
attempt had better not have been made, but it had to be allowed and
encouraged because of possible good. Everything will depend on the
nature of the inward state which is being substantiated. And the
nature of the inward state is not easy to assess, for evil deceives: perhaps evil's most characteristic quality is to look like, but not to be,
good. We may be in a deceived condition when we assume that some
dear stance, dear aim, is good, which makes us glow with righteous-
ness. Our professional judgements and actions may be deceived. It
seems to me (unfortunately I may be deceived, but what can I do,
what can anybody do but his best?) that principles basically simple
and few in number are especially likely to be associated with a state
of deception: I emphasise *basically* simple and few, for intelligent
elaboration of them, though it may become impressive, is undertaken only in the service of the original deception. Simplicity is likely
to be deceived, and is likely to be an evil simplification, because
might we not have expected that a few simple principles will occupy
little place in the phenomenon of existence, whether that be divinely
or naturally appointed? Principles of that sort do not necessarily
lead to evil, but complexity associated with inward awareness perhaps has more chance of leading to good, the evil of deception being
akin to blindness.

Inward attention by no means guarantees freedom from deception: yet when one considers the risks of a simplistic outlook one
feels compelled to opt for complexity, being cast into a life which is
inevitably moral and hence perilous. Sometimes simple principles
seem almost to detach themselves from inward reference. The pas-
sionateness with which they are held shows them to be *actually*
inward, yet in a curious way it is as though the passion belongs to
the outward state of things, the inward reference is hardly acknowledged, significance is not so to speak inwardly accountable. It is a

limited approach, and naïve, and powerful. Now, one of the most
influential forces in modern society is the idea of efficiency. This
idea is certainly not new – perhaps it is as old as the idea of progress,
which is as old as the hills. But progress has shown its variants,
having been conceived of differently from age to age, and efficiency
likewise is no longer quite what it was. It is still treated as though
it were a means to progress but it has really become an end in itself:
efficiency is progress. I exaggerate, but not much. Efficiency (part and
parcel of modern progress) is an article of faith, highly charged
emotionally, and widely believed to be applicable to everything. I
exaggerate and generalise – but how much? Is not inward complexity
usurped by this outwardness, which is simple-minded even when
elaborated into apparently subtle forms? There are actually strong
tendencies at work to check the advances of efficiency – as the people
who strive for efficiency are aware – but so far does it prevail that
whatever checks it can be called inefficient and thus condemned:
even people most responsible for opposing efficiency are prone to
feel a guilt that acknowledges it. They – the opposers – assume they
have no case to make. Because they are in many respects slothful,
ignorant, and muddled (and know it) they unhappily conclude that
only their faults conduce to their inefficient state. It may be that
efficient people lack these faults of the inefficient (an unlikely
enough supposition) but they also lack the merits. And even things
bad in themselves, which check efficiency, to that extent at least are
good.

Resistance to efficiency comes from many sources all over the
country. The staff of English departments in the universities are
among the people well placed to further such resistance if they
choose, though of course their influence on the national life is small.
Presumably the interest which we have in literature implies an
awareness of complex human issues entering through art. It may be
that in our fashion we do manage to stand in the way of efficiency:
certainly there has been no real succumbing in the three departments
I happen to have served in; nor is this statement meant as other than
a fore-handed compliment to past and present colleagues. Yet I have
the feeling that efficiency is 'in the air' which even literary academics
breathe, and perhaps its concentration is higher in some universities
than in others. The degree to which my remarks are resented, or
dismissed as absurd, or actually suspected of being ironical (with

efficiency as the true ideal) will give the measure of efficiency's hold in a given case. Naturally I am not advocating anarchy, real confusion. A department needs organisation, and some methods of organisation must be better than others. The line between efficiency and effectiveness (if I can so express things) is extremely hard to draw: significantly, it would not occur to efficiency to try to draw it.

The zealous spirit of efficiency, with its emotional fervour masquerading as objectivity, has no place in literary awareness or literary teaching. It detracts from our real function, fostering instead that kind of outward assessment (the joke is to make a joke of it) which gives credit to reading, methodology, publication, as such: these things may be all right, or they may be merely the outcome of those efficient-looking habits, enthusiasm and hard work, but again the point is that efficiency does not enquire whether in a particular case they are any good or not. The existence of an informing spirit of efficiency counts quite simply as a guarantee that all is well (the man is a go-ahead man, the institution a go-ahead institution). The truth is, as we all know in a way, that reading, methodology, publication, guarantee in themselves little if anything. Yet some respect is nevertheless accorded them, mainly, I think, because it is assumed that other people will insist on such respect, doing so moreover (unlike ourselves) from conviction; we shall be thought well of for thinking well of efficiency. But outward assessment, precisely because it is outward, judges wrongly. When once a particular outward manifestation is called a good sign, nothing but the sign need be reckoned with, and whoever reproduces it deserves to be rewarded. This would be acceptable enough (indeed perhaps it is inevitable) if the outward sign were subject to some kind of persistent inward reference. But here the difficulties are great, too great to be coped with by efficiency, nor does efficiency want to cope with them. Other things admitted for consideration than outward signs, the basis of efficiency is destroyed at a blow. Efficiency will have nothing to do with inward reference: this avoidance proves efficiency to be really efficient.

In a way efficient operators do admit inwardness into their plans, as their approach to university teaching shows. They often express their care for educational standards, giving the impression that these are no less important to them than standards of efficiency. They express their care as often as people do who care much more, so that a misleading appearance is created of basic agreement between the two sides, with merely marginal differences of opinion. The battle is joined, all the same. Those who favour efficiency argue with a humility which buys the right to a greater aggressiveness, that, though educational standards are naturally dear to them, they cannot and do not pretend to deal with these directly. Such matters, paramount in their way, must be left to experts. Efficiency has to do with the attainment of some particular objective: this might be supposed in the case of English to be literary skill. However, since experts insist that literary skill is many-faceted and indeterminate, efficiency is well content to settle for another objective, which is really the same thing (for is it not the sign by which literary skill is known?): the English degree. The attainment of degrees is something which efficiency can aim at without direct reference to inwardness. Let inwardness be dealt with by proxies who are necessary grist to an efficient university. Standards must be maintained, yes (whatever that means, but yes): firm facts are different, and are the real concern. The maximum number of degrees are to be produced for the cheapest price (the cost of degrees is terrible). I am aware that I have spread the implications of efficiency considerably: but English departments partake of a total academic context, and efficiency is one of the evils in our midst, whether it is actual or potential. English departments have their own true interests. There is no point in fitting ourselves to meet alien demands in a spirit of give and take, since it is only possible by that kind of compromise to give what we value and take what we don't.

In seeking to multiply the sign of the degree, efficiency apparently seeks to multiply the achieving of academic standards. However, degrees are not only a sign of standards: efficiency recognises in the same sign other types of reference, whilst always hoping or pretending that the one sign has essentially a single meaning. But is it likely that (for example) a financial reference, which efficiency accepts as pertinent to the production of degrees, will never conflict with the reference to standards? Naturally the government wants degrees to be as cheap as possible, and so the efficient production of degrees must take into account not only academic standards but also value for money. In theory efficiency can go about its business and be loyal to both aspects of the degree, even though these are quite unlike each other. In practice efficiency may find itself faced with the reconciling of incompatibles. Standards are only too likely to suffer, partly because they are at one remove from the outwardness with which

efficiency is chiefly concerned, and partly because, as it happens, the
more expensive methods of degree production are the only ones yet
known to be academically sound.

   Finance is prominent in another way too. It is believed that the
more degrees there are in the country the more riches will eventually
accrue to everyone, since our trading position as a nation will be
improved. With this consideration in view, efficiency is bound to
consider the production of certain types of degree – this constituting
yet another demand made upon it. Increased output of Arts degrees
would be costly indeed, but not so costly as an increase in the output
of scientific degrees: on the other hand the latter are deemed more
profitable. Save for the fact that spiritual wealth (not, unfortunately,
quite the same thing as material wealth) has also to be taken into
account, expenditure on the Arts subjects could be sacrificed in favour
of science. Science is certainly felt to imply spiritual wealth (and
trade implies it too) but the implication is more obvious in the case
of the arts, which have only this to recommend them. Is spiritual
wealth less important than material wealth, or might it conceivably
be more important? What is the bearing of the one upon the other?
Efficiency cannot suppose that efficiency is meaningless, impossible,
with questions of this kind unanswered and perhaps unanswerable.
Efficient universities must be possible.

   Widespread education at minimum price, leading to widespread
material and spiritual wealth, these ideas enter deeply and passionately into our democratic faith. Moral attitudes infuse this faith, so
that a person who seems to call the democratic assumptions into
question must expect to be called élitist, if not fascist swine; he must
expect his argument to be rejected automatically, as insidious evil is
rejected. Such persons do unfortunately exist; I am one of them,
democratic but dissatisfied with democracy, although as a matter of
fact still largely under the sway of its assumptions. I find myself
assuming that education does have a lot to do with income – education and money for everybody: and yet I don't know that I have any
great confidence in the blessings conferred by wealth. Extreme
poverty is undesirable on any terms, but is much wealth desirable?
Surely everyone must feel at times that possessions neatly arranged
and all in working order are in some curious way more worth getting
than having. Perhaps education is not directly proportioned to
material wealth – indeed we know perfectly well that it isn't – and

perhaps in any case we don't finally want material wealth. If, then, rather than material wealth we want spiritual wealth, can we believe that the latter is more convincingly related to education than the former: education and spiritual wealth for everybody? When educated people experience a sense of spiritual wealth they may well wonder whether their education is the necessary and whole cause. And in moments of spiritual bankruptcy the same thought may occur in reverse: is too little education to blame, or too much – is education to blame at all? Presumably it would be absurd, and subtly undemocratic, to hold that uneducated people are debarred from spiritual wealth. Since the consequences proposed from education, namely material and spiritual wealth, do not follow from it – do not follow only from education, nor are they necessarily caused at all by education – there seems little enough point in designating education a universal need, inseparable from democratic fairness. Equality of opportunity is proper: but if opportunity to be educated is held to be the unique good, a ridiculous limitation has been introduced which distorts and nullifies the proper principle. Why not replace this limitation by another? Everyone must have the chance to run a four-minute mile – each individual, no matter what class he belongs to, is coached with this performance in view from the age of five to twenty-one. A few manage it. For the rest, well, democracy has done its best.

I suppose the comparison is less than justified. Personally I value the education I have received, and am inclined to believe, when I briefly feel rich, materially or spiritually, that education has something to do with it: and whenever I am either way poor, I do not seem to believe that education might as well be abolished. Still, it is obvious to me that if education is used to measure success, if the highly educated condition is the one and only condition that can be thought of without condescension, something then has gone wrong with the theory of democracy. And I think the present-day emphasis on efficient expansion in the field of higher education shows this mistaken approach. The accusation that anyone who wants to reduce expansion is élitist can only be made from the false standpoint I have described: were it the case that education did measure success, were education the only acceptable condition, then the attempt to limit the number of people enjoying the advantages of it would indeed be insidious and pawky. But the advantages of education only become absolute if they are erroneously believed in. Otherwise (and more truly) education is not necessarily a matter of advantages, just as the absence of education is not necessarily a matter of disadvantages. We are most of us second-rate, and second-rateness can be achieved with a lot of education or a little. Nor is first-rateness, in the few instances where it occurs, confined to highly educated people.

I am sufficiently of my time to feel traces of uneasiness about the position I have adopted. But I remind myself that the allegedly grand and inevitable tendencies of our new civilisation, which to past ages would certainly have seemed unnatural, may seem less than grand, perhaps less than inevitable, when two hundred more years have gone by, or five hundred, or a thousand. I am of the time in dismissing notions of progress with difficulty: yet typical also of our time is a broad opposing movement, subordinate but not weak; I draw from that and contribute to it what strength I have.

The inward neglect, moral blindness, distorted outwardness of efficiency whether academic or administrative, the simple certitudes of progressive democracy in its approach to education at present, are all far removed from *Hamlet*. They have nothing to do with *Hamlet*, but *Hamlet* has something to do with them: they stand condemned by criteria such as those evoked in the play, where an altogether different vision of life is explored. Perhaps it is hardly necessary to say that *Hamlet* offers no advice on modern university planning, despite the hero's tenuous connection with Wittenberg; but I had better say it just the same, in case I am accused of holding to that view. Of course there is no direct connection, yet there must be a connection. A person who responds to the play is not another person when he does his work; should not be, cannot be. Does he not retain a responsibility of some sort towards his own perceptions as they are brought into form by the play?

6

The form of a play – of a work of literature generally for that matter – is revealed to the perceiver gradually, as seconds turn into minutes, and minutes into hours; I am merely remarking that the medium of words involves passage of time. Literature does not have the simultaneity of (say) sculpture. And yet the simultaneity of sculpture is evidently qualified by the fact that sculpture cannot be perceived from all angles at once, it is not perceived instantly: time is perhaps hardly less necessary than it is when words are to be appreciated, although they (words) are associated with time in a more formal way. But just as sculpture, simultaneous in form, nevertheless involves time, so literature, which in its form is temporal, does not lack a kind of simultaneity; obviously literature is more than the particular word whose turn for pronunciation comes, special though the word must then be. What might be termed literature's corporeal being is impermanent, renews and dies, renews and dies, in an order established: nevertheless, such moments do not entirely cease as they pass away, rather they persist through memory, which persistence is no less essential to literature than the corporeal transience. Few if any of the moments that have come and gone are exactly recalled to mind, and yet in some flexible, immensely complex way they make themselves felt. If this were not so, a work of literature could have little or no impact, all sense of development, of organisation, would be lost; we should be like Struldbrugs, the beginning of even single sentences being lost before the end was reached. But in fact, at the end of a whole work, when there are no more moments left, we retain awareness of its opening and its entire subsequent development. Time of course continues to pass: though the work is stilled into co-presence of its elements, within that stasis we move as we please. Perhaps our memory of the temporal sequence does not (should not, cannot) transcend time altogether, yet there is a very near approach to simultaneity as regards perception of form.

I have no further interest in sculpture than to bring out the vital and legitimate function of memory in literature. As a proposition, indeed, this might not have raised many eyebrows, but some of the critical implications might have done. It seems to me that the unfolding of story in Hamlet can be in some degree detached from the immediate temporal flux. The difficulty about handling a story critically is to avoid retelling it on more or less its own terms – the need to keep intact a temporal sequence is apt to be a self-sufficient and exclusive proceeding. The story's development can be registered in rather different but still relevant terms only if regarded as simultaneously present in the memory, there to be freely contemplated backwards and forwards around the moving centre of its 'present' – for the latter continues recognisable and acknowledged, the essential agent of the total fixity. I doubt whether the instinctive appreciation of literature works otherwise than this theory implies: strict temporal sequence binds literature itself, rather than the appreciation of it: criticism may be allowed to conform with appreciation. But perhaps criticism has need of a further process, which is distinguishable from appreciation rather than inimical to it. A kind of generalising tendency, akin to the original functioning of memory although more intellectual and finally simpler, gathers material into major phases, whose interior organisation and broader interrelatedness can then be analysed.

In Hamlet there are three major phases to the story, corresponding with beginning, middle, and end, or as we may rather put it ha ha boy (I, v, 150) sayst thou so, art thou there drachma (allowing for present-day inflation)? The middles of some stories are composed of several phases, but I do not think this is the case with Hamlet. Essentially, the middle phase of Hamlet is a modified re-working of the opening. From the relationship between the beginning and the middle arises dramatic meaning, which is apprehended without need of critical formulation. Apprehension does not need criticism. Criticism on the other hand, when it is attempted, has to derive itself from apprehended facts, must so to speak reconstruct the facts into its own image, yet do no outrage upon the facts as they were formerly. We modern practitioners of criticism thrive on confidence, our own and other people's: are not facts currency? Is it not written on each of our invaluable pound notes, 'I promise to pay the bearer on demand the sum of'? I promise to demonstrate a structural comparison, at the same time structural contrast, between the beginning of the play and its middle.

There may be connections between Hamlet and Young Fortinbras: but of course Hamlet is much more obviously connected with another son, Laertes. Where Fortinbras, who is bent at first on recovering the lands lost by his father, seems somewhat in a revenger's position, Laertes dedicates himself to the cause of a slain father specifically (here I look ahead briefly to the play's final phase) and like Hamlet specifically adopts an avenging role. Moreover, the vengeance of Hamlet is associated with a woman, and this holds true of Laertes' vengeance too; although the woman in his case is a sister not a mother. The activities of Young Fortinbras, vengeful or otherwise, are not associated with any woman.

The play's opening exhibits a massive structural split, as I have already tried to argue. On one side of the split are father, son, mother, and on the other are the same figures in a changed aspect – still the mother, still the son, still the father. Something of the first phase actually survives into, and becomes part of, the middle phase, but there comes into being also a new pattern, an evolution. All elements together, old and new, seem to result from the instability of the opening situation. So complex are the changes in this middle phase that one wonders whether, after all, complexity is not merely confusion. Instead of an organisation hard to understand, do we confront a lack of it inimical to understanding? The presence of two similar revenge situations hints strongly at organised arrangement.

If one thinks of Ophelia as a secondary female centre, is she surrounded by men in the same way that Gertrude is, who ambivalently connects with both halves of the play? Ophelia is the subject of a conflict between two young men: they are not her sons, but the conflict has to do with love: and Gertrude is concerned in love-conflict too. One of the young men close to Ophelia is Hamlet himself, and to that extent the comparison between the two women is all the closer. Indeed, it is possible to say that, like Ophelia, the Queen is the subject of a conflict between two young men (quite apart from her involvement with two men of her own age): it is possible to say this, if we allow Hamlet's two separate aspects to count as two separate people – for on one side of Gertrude is the son devoted to partnership and on the other is the son devoted to rivalry. After all, there are reasonable enough grounds for arguing in this way, because Hamlet's feelings about what it is like to have a father are objectified dramatically into two separate persons, Old Hamlet and Claudius, through whom respectively Hamlet's aspects are realised. So Gertrude has on one side of her a Hamlet, and on the other side of her another Hamlet. Ophelia has a Hamlet on one side of her too, whilst on the other side of her she has Laertes. Hamlet and Laertes are in conflict over Ophelia, and the two versions of Hamlet are in conflict over Gertrude. There appears to be a sense in which Ophelia's Laertes is equivalent structurally to one of Gertrude's Hamlets.

This view of the play does not take directly into account the older male figures. In the opening phase there were two of these, Gertrude's husbands, but Ophelia has only one father. Since both Hamlet and Gertrude are dual figures (each is a person showing contrasted aspects) we ought at least to enquire the status of Polonius – is he dual? With his son Laertes he has very close ties. But he is at odds with Hamlet: for Polonius it is who contributes largely to the break-up of his daughter's love-affair with the Prince; and by the Prince, afterwards, Polonius is murdered – accidentally, but it is worth recalling that had the marriage taken place (and Gertrude later says at the grave of Ophelia 'I hoped thou shouldst have been my Hamlet's wife', V, i, 238) Hamlet would have been Polonius's son-in-law. The old man is indeed, it seems to me, a dual character, one of whose aspects shows in the relationship with Laertes, and whose other aspect shows in the relationship between himself and Hamlet. Ophelia is therefore located as follows: Polonius/Laertes/Ophelia, Ophelia/Hamlet/Polonius. This arrangement seems not unlike that earlier one, which still persists: Old Hamlet/Hamlet/Gertrude, Gertrude/Hamlet/Claudius.

The son in the first phase of the play was dual, and the father was separated into two figures, but the situation is reversed in the middle phase, where the father (Polonius) is dual, and the son is separated into Laertes and Hamlet respectively; the woman in both cases (Gertrude, Ophelia) remaining dual. Laertes is a son in partnership with his father Polonius (first aspect), and thus he serves to reflect or represent Hamlet's partnership with Old Hamlet. This aspect of Hamlet continues to exist insofar as he is himself intent on revenge. But how intent on revenge is he? The fact that he opposes

Laertes is a structural way of emphasising Hamlet's rivalry. He is the rival of Polonius (second aspect) and of Claudius still. But now he seems associated with rivalry because in his own named person he is positioned as a rival: the alter-Hamlet, the son in partnership, goes under the name of Laertes.

My earlier optimism has faded and I can no longer persuade myself that my argument will convince everybody. Some people will reject it out of hand and in its entirety. Others may feel that it is misleading because it is oversimplified. But I have had to establish the basic structural affinities between first and second phases: I have tried to establish the basic meaning which the structure (a sort of language) implies. But now there are other things to add, modifying factors. Especially I must consider the moral components of the play's two sides in this its middle phase: and consider too, in so doing, the changed meaning of incest which attends a shift from the older to the younger generation.

For there is a shift of generations. Where the brother/sister relationship in the first phase exists on the parental level, it is on the hero's own level in the second phase; in the first phase Claudius and Gertrude, who are treated as siblings, in the second Laertes and Ophelia, actual siblings. Hamlet the son experiences the mother by way of his connection with the brother/sister relationship of his parents (the Hamlet of rivalry, that is): possibly in a comparable fashion Polonius the father experiences the daughter by way of his connection with the brother/sister relationship of his children. However, Hamlet's incestuous experience of Gertrude takes the form of a revulsion at the open and evil sexuality of the parental siblings, whereas Polonius's experience of Ophelia is different – he insists on a family solidarity and exclusiveness which is supposedly good, and which can seem so because the sibling sexuality of his children, and his own sexuality, are matters covert. An argument urging that covertness is not distinguishable from absence, and hence that the solidarity of Polonius's family might just as well have nothing sexual in it as something – such an argument I think would leave me unconvinced. My objections to it are based on other than psychological grounds: I believe it takes no account of a larger dramatic context. Apart from Laertes and Ophelia, the only other brother and sister in the play are Claudius and Gertrude, incestuously married. Why should siblings in the older generation, positioned decisively on one side of the play, appear in the younger generation on the other side of the play? Why should the Polonius family, with its young siblings, be structurally aligned with the family of Old Hamlet, which is hostile to incest and does not contain siblings? Why should this reversal occur at a time when Hamlet's position, too, has been structurally reversed — when for the love of Ophelia (no sister) he prefers rivalry with the father-figure Polonius, and when he stands opposed to his own alter-ego Laertes, who is the son in partnership with the father? These questions pull one along like an undertow of hints, and each seems to bring the Polonius family under a suspicion deriving from the dramatic context: there is a curious sense in which incest appears as a possibility, an opportunity almost. The members of that family forfeit the benefit of the doubt. Sexuality is between them, and it is none the less theirs for being imposed and revealed by outside forces. Polonius, Laertes, and Ophelia are inseparable from the rest of the play; of course their relationship does not amount to physical incest.

The incestuous feelings of Hamlet are towards his mother, but perhaps incest of that sort — i.e. across generations — is not the most potent. His way of registering his love is to dwell obsessively on sibling sexuality between his parents. It is true that in this way he can avoid recognising the love for what it is, since he himself is not the mother's brother. But it is also the case that this obsession of his pays tribute to the superiority of sibling incest over his own. His own is just as intense, but incest across the generations lacks power, and Hamlet must give way before the strength of Claudius. Only siblings are on a footing of equality, incestuous consummation is only between siblings: if the son were brother to his mother (a proposition which even the subjunctive mood is hardly able to contain) he would have the access and the potency implied by his love yet denied. A father's incestuous love for his daughter is likewise across the generations, inferior therefore to sibling incest. Polonius must yield precedence to his son as regards incest with Ophelia: Laertes and his sisters are of one generation, the brother being in a position to claim the sister's love as an equal. Within the play, circumstances of great importance work against the incest-pattern, strain it severely: for example Ophelia loves Hamlet unincestuously, even though the love is as it were held off by Laertes, and by Polonius whom she obeys. But this is not to deny, indeed it is to affirm, that some aspects of the play's form are directed to establishing and exploiting the incest-pattern.

The audience cannot finally withhold its assent from the love which is between Hamlet and Ophelia (or which was formerly between them) even though Polonius makes out a plausible case for interference. Hamlet's claim on Ophelia is felt to be more just than that of her father, more just than that of the potent brother. We recognise that Hamlet is essentially right to challenge the son-in-partnership, Ophelia's brother, in the grave scene: crying out as he does to his alter-ego Laertes –

> I loved Ophelia, forty thousand brothers
> Could not with all their quantity of love
> Make up my sum.   (V, i, 263–5)

Hamlet opposes partnership. Therefore he acts in a spirit of rivalry: or he acts at any rate from the Claudian side of the play. Yet once the shift of generations has occurred, how good is partnership? Alternatively, how good is rivalry? Neither attitude is the same as it was. Some significant crossing-over of values has been effected between the two sides of the play: to what extent have partnership and rivalry actually changed places?

Polonius enters into a compact against Hamlet, and so does Laertes subsequently: a compact with Claudius, who killed Old Hamlet and insidiously changed him in death, evil Claudius, who perhaps had much to do with the Ghost's suspect moral position. Partnership was originally opposed to incest but now includes it. Rivalry, which included it, now opposes it. The incestuous aim of the son was to meet his mother's sexuality on equal terms. In a sense Laertes has succeeded, sibling-status is his. The mother has become his sister, she is accessible to him because he now has the necessary power – the son is no longer in a position subordinate to his father. Yet he still shares the woman with his father: or rather, his father shares her with him, since it is the father who is become subordinate; or rather again, Laertes continues to behave as if it were still proper to reach the woman through his father, even though his actual position (that of sibling) could enable him to dispense with the whole strategy of partnership in favour of direct rivalry, and no sharing of the woman with anyone. Not that an incestuous connection with his sister is proper at all, of course, though Laertes is structurally placed to express the assumption that it is; Laertes who is Hamlet's alter-ego. The mother was made less real than a mother by the necessity of the son's aspiring to be her brother, so that she became a quasi-sister: and now the real sister is less real than a sister, by reason of the brother's need to be her son, which makes her thus a quasi-mother. In the first case the woman was pushed towards wifehood, in the second she is prevented from assuming it. She can, however, be a wife, real in being neither real mother nor real sister, neither quasi-sister nor quasi-mother: this realness of wifehood will be achieved if, and only if, the confusions of incest are abandoned. Ophelia can then be Hamlet's wife, and he will be the kind of husband that Old Hamlet was to Gertrude. The blood-tie must be broken for this to come about. Unfortunately Hamlet's awareness, which is located in the play's structural arrangement no less than in his statements of principle, is divided against itself, with the result that he cannot bring himself either to break the blood-tie, or keep it intact. He feels a need to do both, and even tries to do both. What is happening to him is this: His original attitudes have evolved and also persisted, an earlier conflict is in conflict with a later derivative conflict. The tensions are huge and unresolved.

7

Because Hamlet knows that partnership was once right for him, he supposes that it still is. Familiarity and obviousness guarantee it. The old morality props up the old morality. Good ought to be now what it always used to be. Commitment to revenge must follow, seems to follow, how can it not follow? Hamlet knows the simple truth: but he also knows that it is open to doubt. What is the moral status of this doubt? He convinces himself that it is evil. On the other hand he accounts it good, at least in part and indirectly, for he moves beyond his original position when responding to Ophelia. His passion for truth is such that his false beliefs need to be continually renewed or they will collapse, i.e. the need to sustain them shows them to be weak. Here I argue perversely, for Hamlet is perverse. His mind is powerful, active, trained at the university (he has often been regarded as Shakespeare's most learned hero): these qualities serve only to increase his agitation, for they are baulked of success on their own terms. The frustration − and yet not total frustration − is a kind of diffused awareness which awaits the change of truer formulation. Hamlet passionately and unavailingly pretends to simple truth: however, he is not among the people who can confine themselves to simple principles passionately applied. Such people − and I suppose I am thinking again of those who are dedicated to efficient progress − succeed in blinding themselves, whereas Hamlet tries to do so and castigates himself perversely for failing. The desire for self-delusion, that part of Hamlet, is by way of being a reaction against insight, and it is a reaction which has to occur because, first, the insight is apparent only as confusion is apparent: second, because the insight if it were stronger and clearer might prove to be something worse.

How much learning did Hamlet have, or for that matter Shakespeare? − Hamlet could not have more learning than Shakespeare but he might of course have less. Is there any relationship between

Hamlet's, or anyone's learning, and that person's psychic insight? I
wonder whether Hamlet's state of awareness, such as it is, is furthered
or retarded by his learning: or is his learning after all merely irrelevant? Would Shakespeare (can one ask this) have been a worse playwright with less learning or a better one with more? What of
audiences: can we say that the appreciation of plays is proportional
to the learning of audiences?

I seem to be making rhetorical gestures here, as though to
learning's disadvantage. I intended to be fair, and in fact I do not
find that the questions, carefully considered, work altogether against
learning: yet my prejudice has shown. Efficiency and progress are
obvious enemies of literature, and as ideals they must be entirely
rejected; a certain amount of organisation and a readiness to consider changes are not inconsistent with this rejection, since they can
occupy a context in which quite other ideals are paramount. Is learning, though less obviously, an enemy too? If this should in any
degree be the case, the ill-effects can only be multiplied by efficiency,
so far as efficiency succeeds in spreading learning. There is thus a connection between learning and efficiency in practice. Unlike efficiency,
however, which is simplistic, learning can display both flexibility
and subtlety. Not by any diminution of complexity does it threaten
literature: indeed learning is really a mixed influence, being at its
best partly good. Yet even that good becomes dangerous when
regarded as the only influence for good.

Learning has perhaps never been a uniform ideal, for it has meant
different things to different people; a state of affairs which not un-
naturally has led to persistent charges and counter-charges from
classical times onwards. Occasionally, large-scale controversies have
developed. The main outbreak in England took place late in the
seventeenth century and in the earlier half of the eighteenth. A great
many participants were engaged on both sides, but Swift and Pope
who entered on one side are of course best remembered.

It is easy to overlook the fact that attacks on scholars such as
Bentley and Theobald – attacks frequent in the Augustan period – make
use of allegations which are not only mixed but self-contradictory.[1]

---

[1] Bentley and Theobald as individuals influenced the form of the attacks
against them, but only to a limited extent. A general situation can be made
out which owes nothing to their human uniqueness, and in my view this is a

Scholars were held to be mindless plodders – this allegation one might expect. They accumulated knowledge in a misguided effort to compensate for feeble endowment, emphasising and developing a single strength, memory. But scholars were also believed to be men of dangerous and perverse mental vigour – this is more surprising. They manipulated scholarly material without reference to anything but the actual possibilities of manipulation: a heady extremism found favour, knowledge was subordinated to a false end. The strength of the plodding scholars, unlike the same strength when that occurred in a proper context, was worthless, just as the richer endowment of the manipulating scholar was worthless because the context was equally wrong. Either there was an over-factuality, or there was a sort of over-understanding; although in the former case there inevitably existed some understanding (which satire had to minimise) and in the latter there were certainly some facts. The critique of scholarship in both its aspects was perhaps grounded in a critique of scholars as men. Their learning was not admirable unless they were admirable. The truth of what they said proved nothing in itself; although if they spoke falsehood, so much the worse for them.

The underlying attitude of the attackers might I think be expanded as follows: The aim of life is to ascertain and develop the best of the human potential: exercise of the various faculties must be harmonised, since too much development in one place will cripple development in another, full potential being not then realised: the mind, achieving itself, must so conceive of itself as to take behaviour into account – that is to say contemplation must not seek to avoid action, nor does failure of action denote anything less than a failure of contemplation. This is a general attitude of considerable antiquity, but it is one in which learning, as a function of the intellect, may well prove crucial.

Shakespeare himself dramatises very much this kind of situation, through the implications of rhetoric, in Love's Labour's Lost. The King of Navarre and his companions, having vowed to study, break the vow

determining factor of more importance. For attacks on other scholars of the period are conducted along similar lines, despite further differences of personality. Again, earlier attacks on scholars often have much the same outline; this is true of those which appear in the seventeenth-century Character Books, where the aim is to produce recognisably typical portraits.

when they fall in love. This is finally seen as proper behaviour. They likewise become aware of their responsibilities towards the sufferings of others. And they realise, too, that a change in their habitual use of language is part and parcel of their changed outlook. The characters of the sub-plot, besides those of the main plot, exhibit the abuses of learning in various ways (and again language usage is important): Don Armado, learnedly fantastical; Moth, witty and perhaps too witty; Sir Nathaniel and Holofernes, pedagogic. Costard and Dull, the one a man of ability the other not, illustrate that particular abuse of learning which is simply the absence of it. For the play is not finally, in one way, against learning. Ignorance is opposed, knowledge is insisted upon as skill. Nature must neither be disregarded, nor perverted: by 'art' (in the old sense) it must be cultivated and refined.[2]

Love's Labour's Lost may seem to display an odd emphasis – it may seem to constitute, for our purposes, a rather marginal case; perhaps this is so. Yet I would wish to draw attention to the whole question of context, the range, the diversity, the unpredictability of context. There are in the play at least two scholars; the main focus of the attack is on rhetoric; I have declared my concern with attitudes to learning. It is difficult to relate together these elements. Are we confronted by major and minor categories, and if so, which is which? Are we dealing rather with degrees of centrality; in that case, where is the centre? Or are all the elements merely variants? Are they, even, virtually the same? These confusing problems are not confined to discussion of the Shakespearean play, but arise in regard to the later Ancients v. Moderns Controversy;[3] indeed they make themselves

---

[2] Numerous contemporary figures are alluded to in the play, but they are mostly, I think, wrought into composite and overlapping forms. I don't think the contemporary figures have a consistent one-for-one relationship with dramatis personae.

[3] Ancients v. Moderns. Under this name goes the earlier phase of a controversy (including the Phalaris controversy) which in my opinion, at least, extends into a later phase when the actual terms 'Ancient' and 'Modern' were less current. Swift engaged himself most obviously in the first phase, contributing The Battle of the Books and A Tale of a Tub: but Gulliver's Travels belongs to the second phase, where it is more central than is often supposed. Pope, virtually a generation younger than Swift, participated only in the second phase: The Dunciad, much revised and long-evolving, was his

felt elsewhere too. For there was historical uncertainty of a half-concealed sort, which ultimately had to do with the status of Antiquity in Renaissance Europe. The study of the Greek and Latin languages was important, so was the appreciation of classical civilisation, although these two overlapping pursuits could also seem separable. On the other hand whilst the ancient past had the importance of an ideal in shaping modern life it was not the only ideal to be followed: and this being the case it was not wholly applicable, might be seen as inadequate or even on occasion wrong. Opinions about such matters were never constant, and have since undergone further changes. At the very least it is true that the meaning of scholarship has altered in our twentieth-century world, and true that intellectual activity is more diversified and fragmented than it used to be.

The Ancients v. Moderns controversy is a richly muddled affair, exhibiting in its own way many of the uncertainties which I have described; of course one has to add that some few of the individual works are rich and not muddled. Allusions to, and displays of, scholarship, are frequent in the controversy: scholarship takes its place with other branches of learning, though perhaps it is accorded a fluctuating and inconclusive kind of priority – there is still at this date a lingering notion that scholarship is all-embracing. Scholarship, in the narrower sense at any rate, takes its place with other branches of learning: but also, learning at large including scholarship takes its place with intellectual activities which do not seem to be primarily learned: beyond these again are found aspects of life which are not even intellectual, but which are related to intellect, related to learning, related to scholarship. How does such richness as this bear on my present argument? As regards the Ancient side of the controversy, the influence of the life-criterion is everywhere pervasive – just as it was in the case of Love's Labour's Lost, with results already discussed.

Of the various learned activities which were attacked (for chiefly learning has to be considered) two in particular are relevant – philosophy and science. The attacks on philosophy are comparable with those levelled at manipulative scholarship: those levelled at plodding scholarship are on the other hand comparable with the

---

major contribution. In some ways the activities of the Scriblerus Club, of which both Swift and Pope were members, served to bridge the two phases.

attacks on science. Scholarship, we recall, drew forth two divergent types of allegation. Philosophy and science are admittedly not entirely distinct from scholarship, but they do not seem to be scholarship. It is, I think, true that the type of scholarship which (for example) humbled Milton's strains,[4] had a counterpart in the perversities of false philosophy. General connections, comparisons, were achieved by Swift in *A Tale of a Tub*, where wildly manipulative classical scholarship (parodied in 'A Digression Concerning Critics', and elsewhere) is finally at one with the philosophical excesses of Aeolism; for that matter, the abuses of Biblical exegesis (Section II) partake of the same madness. A philosopher – perhaps even more than his confrère in scholarship – might allow himself to be carried away by the delights of a speculative system, relying on it utterly: he disregarded the harmonious development of man, misapprehended the nature and function of his mental gifts. Of course Aeolism is only a satirical invention, but it has a general application to all absurd philosophising (also to 'common sense' – a terrifying twist, this, uniquely Swiftian). An early attack on actual philosophy was made by John of Salisbury, a twelfth-century English humanist writing in Latin. He loathed disputational logicians (his other aversion was for courtiers) :

> Consider the leading teachers of philosophy of our own day, those who are most loudly acclaimed, surrounded by a noisy throng of disciples. Mark them carefully; you will find them dwelling on one rule, or on two or three words, or else they have selected (as though it were an important matter) a small number of questions suitable for dispute, on which to exercise their talent and waste their life. They do not however succeed in solving them but hand down to posterity for solution by their disciples their problems, with all the ambiguity with which they have invested them.[5]

John's standpoint in this and in his many comparable attacks may be found represented in the following passage:

---

[4] Dr Bentley's 1732 edition of *Paradise Lost* was attacked by Pope and others for its conjectural emendations run riot.

[5] John of Salisbury, *Frivolities of Courtiers and Footprints of Philosophers. Being a translation of . . . selections . . . of the Policraticus*, ed. and trans. J. Pike, 1938, p. 244.

I have purposely incorporated into this treatise some observations concerning morals, since I am convinced that all things read or written are useless except so far as they have a good influence on one's manner of life. Any pretext of philosophy that does not bear fruit in the cultivation of virtue and the guidance of one's conduct is futile and false.[6]

We have witnessed in our own time attacks upon philosophy (upon the philosophy of A. J. Ayer, for instance) which are essentially similar.

The other and plodding side of scholarship (as opposed to the manipulative) I have suggested has affiliations with science.[7] Unlike philosophy, however, science can hardly be said to exist until a fairly late date: its learned origins are diffused through learned contexts which are more or less alien to its subsequent true character: so that early attacks on science are not to be expected. But certainly by the time of the Ancients v. Moderns controversy science had established itself. There are attacks on it in all Swift's major satires, perhaps the best-known examples being in Gulliver's third voyage; Arbuthnot attacked it in Memoirs of Martinus Scriblerus (if he was the author of that work, the publication of which was delayed until 1741); Pope put science within the empire of Dulness. In what way are science and plodding scholarship connected? Of course they are far from being identical – but then, philosophy and manipulative scholarship are not identical either, they merely share a common tendency. Science and scholarship (of the plodding sort) are alike in the immense respect which they accord to facts, external facts. The plodding scholar feels that facts are enough, are everything: they speak as it were for themselves, he has nothing to do but know them. He is alleged to be feeble-minded in everything but memory, so this sort

---

[6] John of Salisbury, The Metalogicon of John of Salisbury, trans. with an introduction and notes by D. McGarry, 1955; 'Prologue', p. 6.

[7] Pope expresses very generally the divergence within learning at large when he describes the Goddess Dulness:

Laborious, heavy, busy, bold, and blind,
She rules, in native anarchy, the mind.

(The Poems of Alexander Pope, ed. John Butt, 1963; The Dunciad in Four Books, Bk I, lines 15–16.) The long footnote to line 15, written or at least approved by Pope but satirically signed BENTL., is well worth consulting.

of thing is all he can do anyway. The scientist – who may not be feeble-minded – shows something of the same willingness to conform with things beyond himself: nature's own facts, own laws, must declare themselves using him as mouthpiece. That there is much of the speculative philosopher in the scientist is apt to be obscured by the force of his conviction that this is not so. His mental activity is aimed at a kind of passivity, in that he must invent nothing. A few years ago C. P. Snow delivered a controversial Rede Lecture which he called 'The Two Cultures and the Scientific Revolution'. He observed:

> The non-scientists have a rooted impression that the scientists are shallowly optimistic, unaware of man's condition.[8]

In the attitude thus described I seem to recognise the persistent ideal of learning as individual development. Elsewhere, this time giving his own opinion, he says of scientists, 'their imaginative understanding is less than it could be. They are self-impoverished.'[9] He also describes – his sympathies and criticisms are divided between both sides – the impression which scientists have of non-scientists (or 'literary intellectuals' as he calls them here):

> ... the scientists believe that the literary intellectuals are totally lacking in foresight, peculiarly unconcerned with their brother men, in a deep sense anti-intellectual, anxious to restrict both art and thought to the existential moment.[10]

From this representation I infer that scientists lay claim to the life-criterion no less than non-scientists, to the extent that they have human ends in view. However, the application of science to life is curiously impersonal, or is personal only at several removes. Scientists have never judged the truth of science by its effect upon the scientist: nor have they believed that the generalised purpose which they assign to science is quite the same thing as science itself. It is true that science is no longer confined to the world of matter; but, although the life-criterion has infiltrated certain scientific areas, science for the most part remains hostile to that criterion, in my

---

[8] I quote from *The Two Cultures: and a Second Look*, 1964 (being the Rede Lecture of 1959 together with Snow's later comment), p. 5.

[9] Ibid., p. 14.

[10] Ibid., p. 5.

view. I am not sure that the cultural gap which Snow speaks of *can* be closed:

> Closing the gap between our cultures is a necessity in the most abstract intellectual sense, as well as in the most practical.[11]

His basic division I would not want to dispute:

> I believe the intellectual life of the whole of western society is increasingly being split into two polar groups.[12]

Learning, then, has often seemed a highly controversial topic within the learned world: and one of my reasons for introducing this short discussion has been to remind myself and others that to comment on learning adversely, to attack an aspect of it which often counts as learning's true and only self, is not necessarily to place oneself in a uniquely absurd position. Yet in university English departments today, if my own experience is any guide, learning of a certain sort is venerated so strongly that anyone who seems lacking in it, or in respect for it, feels himself condemned. To hold out against prevailing theories is difficult, and the one I refer to expresses an unshakable conviction that something called learning is, as it always was, the raison d'être of universities. Not all members of staff in English departments really have such veneration, though no one is uninfluenced by it. In private it may often be set aside: but no lecturer in English could publicly declare, 'I do not much like learning, I am not very learned, I am none the worse for that', and expect to be officially believed on all three counts.

That some scholars of both the main types can still be found today as they were found in the past, will perhaps be agreed. If their outlook on life sets no special value on human development, then on their own terms they are not pedants (for this has been the derogatory term commonly used to describe them): rather, they will think themselves scholars who have succeeded. But a more interesting situation arises when, though accused of pedantry by others, they actually hold the same ideals as their accusers, i.e. they consider themselves to be men for whom human development *does* matter; and they may even believe that, within themselves, this same ideal is

---

[11] Ibid., p. 50.
[12] Ibid., p. 3.

fully embodied. The situation is more interesting because it suggests that there are differences of opinion about the degree of scholarly emphasis necessary to the cultivation of the whole.

Individuals contribute to the society they live in, and they also derive from it much of their identity. The scholar studies this mutual interchange as it occurred in the past: however he is caught up himself, and so to speak personally, in the corresponding interchange which is the present. He responds to the life which is within and around him, he seeks to know the forms of past life (those inevitably cognate forms, if one may thus broadly describe them). He understands the past, at least a few facets of it: yet understanding is a thing of the present, for it is a relating of the past to and by the man who lives – the dead don't understand anything. If he understands the past, perhaps he will thereby increase the understanding of himself; on the other hand it would seem impossible that his understanding of the past can exceed by very much the understanding of himself. The great range of past forms offers itself as a kind of teaching, so that the scholar who is a good pupil finds opportunities for personal development in the proper pursuit of his work – for inward development inseparable finally from behaviour – which he might otherwise have missed. Whether this in itself makes for continuous and unlimited human advance, I doubt: too many other factors seem to be involved. But travelling in the past may be like travelling in foreign countries – the traveller benefits by being exposed to alternatives, equivalents.

If scholarship were the only way in which human development could be brought about there would be every justification for giving it the ascendancy. But of course it is not. Indeed (I have been trying to suggest this) it seems certain that scholarship can only proceed, and yield up its benefits, if a primary inward life which is essentially contemporary flourishes in the first place. And this primary life can be extensively developed without much help from scholarship, though it cannot develop at all without help from contemporary society. The fact is that social continuity, and with it cultural continuity, ensures that the past influences the present, and it would presumably do this even if the present knew nothing of the past. Since scholarship exists and has never not existed, it must be reckoned an associated influence. Older scholarship, knowing something of what lay behind it in the past, contributed to its own surrounding present; which present evolved itself into the next age; fresh scholarship, partly dependent on the old, partly no doubt original, arose in turn and was newly influential; its influence like that of the scholarship before it was not the only, not perhaps the most important factor determining present or future. Knowledge of the past, then, helps cause us: but other causes are at work, which if they were ever known may long since have been forgotten – these (probably more than scholarship) are expressed in social and cultural continuity: and the nature of man, reborn into each generation, is an ever-present further causing. There is little justification for believing, because scholarship has always been with us, that the past is making itself felt today only for that reason. Scholarship is not decisive to the achieving of individual human development in a contemporary civilisation – nor can any civilisation be other than contemporary.

Perhaps I have falsified my position by generalising it; I am recalled to my native province, where a modest funeral is being prepared for me. How scholarly should the study of English literature be? Does literary response depend much, or at all, on the scholarship which has entered and influenced the perceiving mind, does response depend upon learnedness of any sort? The cultural contact that is made with an author is obviously an important factor in appreciation. Since cultural contact is not always made through learning, learning is not always necessary. The more remote the culture is in time, the greater the probability that scholarship will be needed for contact to be made. But scholars are apt to exaggerate the importance of cultural differences between author and reader, and indeed they exaggerate the actual extent of the differences, too. The similarities between our culture and that of Shakespeare's day, for example, vastly exceed the differences: we are still basically in the same culture, yes, I affirm it. To make the same or else another point, cultural continuity lets us feel Shakespeare's culture directly in our own. Naturally, literary mistakes can and do occur through ignorance, but how numerous and how damaging are they? The culture of Chaucer's day? Scholarship is needed, not least in language: yet one has to remember that Chaucer's listeners were not Medievalists. In some impossibly paradoxical sense the aim of scholarship is to promote an experience which will compare with the relatively unlearned experience of our reading later poets.

Scholarship is a means of effecting cultural contact, and it falls

short of universal necessity because the same end can often be
differently achieved. Cultural contact itself, however, is far from
being the only relevant factor in appreciation. If we do not make any
ignorant mistakes when we read Shakespeare, if perfect cultural contact has been achieved, has perfect appreciation occurred? A work of
literature is rather related to its culture than synonymous with it;
thus each of Shakespeare's plays is a different work, although the
cultural context of all of them is the same, barring changes that took
place during his life-span. The created work (that which in a special
sense is a *becoming* of language, a psychic manifestation of a most
complex sort) inevitably engages with the cultural context for the
proper achieving of its potential, but in some vital sense or other it
gives meaning from within, even more than it draws meaning from
without. Later readers have at their disposal a humanity of their own,
deployed through forms characteristically modern, just as humanity
was deployed into past forms. This humanity makes direct literary
insight possible for us: insight which whilst it involves, is not wholly
dependent on, the work's cultural context − whether that context is
accessible by way of today's forms, or brought into the mind by an
act of scholarly learning. Scholarship, then, is of some help:
limited help is help, certainly, unless it is too much relied on. One
has a duty, not to reject scholarship, but to reject the exclusiveness
of its claims: and though scholarship itself need not be rejected, it
may without apology be little regarded. The position is difficult to
maintain in practice, because scholars treat a partial acceptance of
their case as evidence that the opposition has crumbled − at any
rate they feel themselves confirmed and vindicated. This misappre-
hension ought to be countered.

8

Whereas Hamlet has been generally regarded as Shakespeare's most learned hero, there has been no agreement about his madness – beyond the fact that it is agreed to be an important issue. Is he mad, how mad is he? It seems obvious that, if he is mad at all, he is not mad quite in the way that Lear, for example, is mad when he thinks he is putting his daughters on trial at the end of the storm sequence, or when, crowned with wild flowers, he comes upon Edgar and Gloucester near Dover; nor for that matter is Hamlet mad in the way that Ophelia is mad in Act IV, scene v. Surely, his wits are not deranged? True, he sometimes behaves strangely, as towards Polonius in Act II, scene ii but in the famous speech to Horatio and the others, swearing them to secrecy, he seemed to hint at the possibility of a mad disguise –

> As I perchance hereafter shall think meet
> To put an antic disposition on. (I, v, 171–2)

True also that he sometimes behaves strangely even when the 'antic' plan is not being applied: presumably it was not being applied when he first visited Ophelia after her rejection of him, although there is only the evidence of her report to go on:

Ophelia   My lord, as I was sewing in my closet,
           Lord Hamlet with his doublet all unbraced,
           No hat upon his head, his stockings fouled,
           Ungart'red, and down-gyvéd to his ankle,
           Pale as his shirt, his knees knocking each other,
           And with a look so piteous in purport
           As if he had been looséd out of hell
           To speak of horrors – he comes before me.
Polonius Mad for thy love?
Ophelia   My lord, I do not know,
           But truly I do fear it. (II, i, 74–83)

Again, sometimes Hamlet's behaviour seems to be pitched ambig-
uously between calculated and uncalculated eccentricity, as in the
main 'love' scene with Ophelia, which Claudius and Polonius have
stationed themselves to observe. Yet notwithstanding that actors
usually play Hamlet in this scene with dishevelled dress, and often
make him somewhat distraught, he invariably appears to be on the
right side of sanity, at least to the audience. Ophelia declares afterwards,

> O, what a noble mind is here o'erthrown!   (III, i, 153)

but Claudius's assessment, in regard to the question of madness at
any rate, comes closer to our own:

> Love! his affections do not that way tend,
> Nor what he spake, though it lacked form a little,
> Was not like madness.   (III, i, 165–7)

Whether or not as a result of the 'antic' plan, many of the characters
in the play regard Hamlet as mad (including Claudius himself at
times, e.g. V, i, 266). How mad, it is not easy to say: are they at any
rate sure, like the audience, that he is far from raving? The question is
difficult, because these characters (who think the Prince mad) hold
to their belief mainly on the basis of Hamlet's unantic behaviour: or
perhaps this would be the conclusion to draw from the relative
infrequency of behaviour which is decisively and surreptitiously
antic: however, a conclusion of that sort is critically suspect, involving as it does only realistic criteria.

   At one point, in the closet scene, Hamlet insists passionately
on his sanity. Gertrude has called his vision of the Ghost 'ecstasy',
not having seen anything herself. Hamlet answers her:

>   . . . Ecstasy!
> My pulse as yours doth temperately keep time,
> And makes as healthful music – it is not madness
> That I have uttered, bring me to the test
> And I the matter will re-word, which madness
> Would gambol from. Mother, for love of grace,
> Lay not that flattering unction to your soul,
> That not your trespass but my madness speaks.
>   (III, iv, 139–46)

If Ophelia just before her death had been brought to the test of re-wording the matter, her madness would certainly have gambolled from it. Hamlet's cohesion is by contrast always present, and this is so even when he is antic – for then his behaviour is marked by a poised awareness, which is altogether different from Ophelia's (or Lear's) crazed mixture of confusion and insight. But although his mind, unlike theirs, remains cohesive, it is clearly subject to an immense strain. He does not lose himself in ecstasy, and yet, curiously, he chooses to make the 'healthful music' of Gertrude's pulse the standard of comparison for his own. Has she not committed trespass, does she not mistake her trespass for his madness? Can he insist on the fact of her trespass and deny the fact of his madness, if his pulse beats in the same way as hers? In claiming to be as well as his mother, how much does he really claim? Less than he thinks.

The Elizabethan milieu has been held to account adequately enough for Hamlet's madness. If we understand the Humours theory, and the Revenge tradition, we shall find our difficulties resolved. Hamlet's symptoms are associated with melancholy, which operated in a more diverse and intricate fashion than any of the other humours. Shakespeare was certainly well versed in the theory of Humours, and many of his plays incorporate it, among them Hamlet; very detailed connections with medical writings of the day have been traced. It is probably true to say that Hamlet's madness would be referred not simply to sanity as mental cohesion – though that would be a relevant issue – but more generally to any extreme manifestation of melancholy: a victim of melancholy was mad even if his wits remained intact. It is argued that nowadays, in wondering whether Hamlet is mad, we are likely to apply a wrong criterion – wrong because too limited. Using the Elizabethan criterion of melancholy we can understand the nature and meaning of the madness, and this is necessary to the proper assessment of Hamlet's character and the play as a whole. The Revenge tradition (we are further told) has to be considered alongside the theory of Humours; the form of the genre being partly determined by the form of the theory. Proponents of the genre approach, however, may insist on giving with one hand what they take away with the other: Hamlet's madness is referred to the stage rather than life, despite the pervasive importance of humorous melancholy. If Shakespeare could count on the more or less automatic response of audiences to expected stimuli, he needed to do no more than offer a few signals, without troubling much about the way things tied together. The audience expected madness (real or feigned) in a Revenge play, along with many other ingredients: Shakespeare supplies what can be recognised and hence readily accepted – whether his hero's madness is superficial or fundamental is a question which hardly arises.

One must take care not to be overwhelmed by Shakespeare's milieu – an unlikely eventuality, one might suppose, but hundreds are taken from us in this way each year. Research is needed, but not all that much. We ask no one to pay more than he or she can really afford. Please help us as little as you can, sending your contribution, on a postcard, to me at the following address. Thank you. You have been listening again to a foolish person; one who believes what everyone else believes, that it is not enough to establish analogues (Humours theory, Revenge tradition); who believes besides, to his discredit, that it is often unnecessary to establish them at all . . . For Shakespeare is a literary creator. Like the inventor of a new machine, he uses existing forms and methods, but these must be fitted to the new purpose: what they are going to be and going to do, not what they were and did, matter to him; though doubtless they serve unchanged, sometimes, in part. Analogues are pursued for the sake of a great play, but its greatness is not dealt with, only its supposed reliance on things more primary. The Humours theory does not fully account for the Elizabethan grasp upon human nature: furthermore, it tends to lead discussion away from the medium of drama, or to treat this as though it were incidental. The Revenge tradition indeed leads to discussion of the dramatic medium, but the exercise of comparing a play with others of the same kind is a curiously restrictive and selective process, despite its apparent scope. Similarities do not define what any one play is: its properties might just as well be, and often are, dissimilarities.

Why should Hamlet not be presented as entirely and unequivocally sane throughout the play? In other words what is the function of his so-called madness, why does Shakespeare bring his hero so elaborately into contact with the idea of madness? I have suggested that explanations based on the Humours theory and the Revenge genre leave something to be desired, and I feel this strongly: but whilst I see the need for more convincing answers I must admit that finding them is another thing. However, I am persuaded that the madness issue has to do with representation of the hero's moral position. Traditionally, sin is death. Into this formula, by a natural extension of thought, sickness is introduced, which is inimical to life.

The moral context of sickness is expressed by Gertrude:

> To my sick soul, as sin's true nature is,
> Each toy seems prologue to some great amiss.
>
> (IV, v, 17–18)

She is concerned lest her own guilty thoughts should stand as though revealed through Ophelia's madness. In a curious way sin and madness are being contrasted yet also compared. Certainly, if sin is sickness of the soul, madness is also soul-sickness, and it is difficult to avoid the conclusion that madness is, therefore, sin. Shakespeare in some of his plays seems to associate madness and sin insistently, though in anything but a straightforward manner. In King Lear, for example, Tom o' Bedlam is continually attacked by the foul fiend. When Lear asks the madman (III, iv, 84) 'What hast thou been?' the reply is a whole catalogue of sins: he was 'one that slept in the contriving of lust, and wak'd to do it ... false of heart, light of ear, bloody of hand; hog in sloth, fox in stealth, wolf in greediness, dog in madness, lion in prey'.[1] It is his own past evil that poor Tom in madness flees from. He is not only pitiable but in some peculiar way virtuous. It must be meaningful – or else it is oddly meaningless – that Edgar chooses this particular disguise, who is perhaps the most unsullied man in the play. As Tom, he helps his blind father on the journey to the cliff: guides him to suicide, the crime of despair. Yet saves him too, by a cruel deception which is kind. After the leap has taken place, Edgar assumes a sane role (though still guarding his true identity for a time): he furnishes Gloucester with the following account of Tom –

> As I stood here below methought his eyes
> Were two full moons; he had a thousand noses,
> Horns whelk'd and wav'd like the enridged sea:
> It was some fiend.   (IV, vi, 69–72)

---

[1] I have used throughout the 'Arden' King Lear, ed. Kenneth Muir (rev. ed. 1963).

Tom's madness (Edgar's madness) must evidently be understood in a moral context. So likewise must the madness of Lear himself. The hero's status is morally problematic; whether or not he is 'more sinned against than sinning' he has certainly sinned.

Hamlet's own moral position, I have tried to show, is extremely involved. One would wish to say, of course, that he is essentially good, and with a great deal of qualification this may be finally true. But although he struggles to do right, he is powerfully drawn to do wrong, and his dilemma is made worse by the fact that right and wrong are so likely to be taken for one another: what seems in some ways absolutely right seems absolutely wrong in others. I have explained how the structure of the play develops this moral complexity. It may be that Hamlet's morality sickens in the uncertain contact between good and evil; that the sickness can be mistaken for good health; that this illusion of health is sinful, being a further sickness, by comparison with which the first sickness is better, healthier. True moral health, however, would be incompatible with the existence of these problems. If the problems exist, madness can express the fact. Hamlet's madness is in doubt, the evidence being contradictory, therefore the existence of the problems is in doubt. His moral outlook may be sound, may not. He is *possibly* mad. In practice, though perhaps not in logic, this helps us to realise that he is imperfectly good, partly in the right and partly in the wrong. Imperfect good is no doubt a contradiction in terms: nevertheless we sympathise, we cannot think him evil, for he is well-intentioned. He carries our hopes.

When Hamlet first wooed Ophelia his approach was perhaps proper to adulthood: or perhaps it repeated the infantile approach to the mother, recalling the time before the father had to be reckoned with. The distinction may be unnecessary or impossible. But when Ophelia rejects Hamlet at the command of her father, Hamlet does seem to react in terms rather of the infantile than the adult situation. He sees the rejection as proof of a sexuality in her which is both excessively chaste and excessively corrupt: this was how he viewed his mother when, having recognised the importance of fatherhood and its dual nature, he put good partnership before evil rivalry. Hamlet's subsequent killing of Polonius represents an advance of sorts, yet it is problematically confused with the killing of Claudius. The interaction of forces at this point is finely controlled, and shows once again how structure can make for meaning – the play's larger movement is gathered into a climactic episode. Through the arras the sword is driven home. Does Hamlet aim to destroy Claudius? If so, does he strike as a partner or as a rival? It seems to me that the spirit of the attack is entirely uncertain, ambiguous: Hamlet is not even confident that the person in concealment is Claudius. Nevertheless he guesses at the King, brings no one but the King into question, and therefore the stabbing had at least some reference to the childhood system. Partnership, one of the elements supported in the uncertainty, legitimises the mother-relationship, whilst rivalry, also supported, attempts incest with her. The latter tendency is of course evil. Since the real victim, however, is not Claudius but Polonius, the rival's blow for incest is actually the rival's blow against incest. Laertes only is in partnership with Polonius: Hamlet is in rivalry, and unequivocally he acts out the legitimacy of his love for Ophelia when he kills her father. To the extent that the real nature of the action takes precedence over his confused intentions in acting, Hamlet may be said to have matured, but childhood attitudes predominate so far as his intentions count. The two factors are hard to assess for relative importance. Hamlet continues with his old obsession, undeterred by the discovery that Polonius is his victim: vehemently he lectures his mother about her two marriages: the Ghost re-appears. In this morally tortuous situation the possibility of his madness again comes to the fore (III, iv, 105 et seq). Later, the madness of Ophelia occurs. Perhaps her madness is his madness confirmed. Mad, she laments young love, but does so in the context of grieving for her father. Perhaps her madness (his madness) is destroyed in being confirmed – destroys itself; Ophelia dies. Hamlet is thus sane after all? Is his madness denied, is every possibility of it at last dismissed? When Ophelia is dead, Hamlet fights the right battle against Laertes in her grave, but the fact that the battle is being fought shows that it is not won; as regards Hamlet's love for that particular girl, the battle is for ever lost. Claudius and Gertrude (both of them sinful, however) can still call the Prince mad, V, i, 266 and 278. Although his position is not fully matured it is undergoing appropriate change, and I believe the possibility of his madness is essentially less than it was.

Hamlet's main scene with Ophelia occurs in III, i, a little *before* the middle of the play. His main scene with Gertrude (III, iv) occurs

shortly *after* the middle. In each of these scenes Hamlet is talked of as
mad. Before the scene between Hamlet and Ophelia occur the reports
of Hamlet's love-madness, when he was repulsed (II, i and II, ii):
after the closet scene with Gertrude comes the madness of Ophelia
(IV, v) a kind of love-madness in some ways, which is closely associated with Hamlet. Near the beginning of the play (earlier than any
of the parts mentioned, we learn of Hamlet's wooing (I, iii), and perhaps at that time he was not mad, although his passion was immoral
in the judgement of Polonius at least: near the end (V, i, i.e. later
than any of the parts mentioned) there is the fight in the grave, when
the hero is called mad, but is perhaps not. In regard to madness,
therefore, a degree of symmetry is discernible, an equal distribution
of dramatic weight greater towards the centre; although other sug-
gestions of madness abound, the ones listed are I believe among the
most important.

At the centre itself is the play-within-a-play (III, ii), when for the
only time Hamlet, Ophelia, Gertrude, and Claudius are all together
with speaking parts: not an episode where madness is given any
prominence. Yet the opposition of forces within it, the partial
reversal of these forces against themselves and one another, their
sheer intricate incompatibility, these are no less unharmonious, un-
reasonable, than madness itself, and no less morally divisive. It is a
pity the scene is so often cut down in performance. Something which
strikes me as important is that Lucianus, the character in the Mousetrap play who does the murder, is *nephew* to the murdered man
(Hamlet gives this information to Ophelia in line 243). I cannot
think it merely accidental that Lucianus is not a *brother*, since this is
demanded by the comparison Hamlet wants to enforce. Old Hamlet
was murdered by his brother Claudius, who poured poison into the
ear of the sleeper. But in the tragedy performed by the Players, poison
is poured into the ears of the sleeping Gonzago by his nephew. It is
almost as though Claudius were being murdered by his nephew
Hamlet, except that Claudius never was murdered: he will eventually
be killed, though, poisoned by Hamlet. The Mousetrap, designed to
catch the conscience of the King, apparently succeeding, seems
obscurely to hint at guilt in Hamlet too. That his moral position has
none of the simple rightness which he hopes it has, the whole structure and movement of the play shows. But Hamlet, perhaps, is mad.

9

One's temerity is recognised and admitted at last. The attempt to grasp *Hamlet*, to grasp it critically, brings on despair. This is a play of which one might say that its critical icebergs are visibly bigger only as they are invisibly more bigger: show me that Atlas of a critic who is Neptune enough to raise his lumpen world clear of the water: has he got the right fardel? One's system of thought, which seemed to be that of the play, becomes strained, will not develop enough to accommodate new material, is not flexible enough to do so. Who has ever coped with *Hamlet*, who ever will? Perhaps no art can be 'coped with' – for that suggests a sort of conquest, almost an elimination of the art. The critic has *won*, or thinks he has; nobody else thinks so, other critics least of all.

Critical despair has another side. Failure is pleasant enough when success is not wanted – when the sun shines on the garden outside the upholstered study, and life, instead of critical labour, can be pursued. The pendulum swings; or rather, upside-down, it sways metronomically to the other side; your metronome is a spirited contrivance which rebels if the pace gets too funereal and there it lies doggo, apparently in mourning, but why not basking in the last laugh? Perhaps the method I saw or thought I saw of alternating sections of my book was false to gravity. Summer proved too much for it – sabbatical summer: we in the universities enjoy the inestimable privilege of occasional terms of leave. Can one speak of spacious weather? The window is open, and I have a couple of laburnum trees in the garden heavy and easy with their own wealth. Tragedy died some other death, this is a different victory. Of course Hamlet himself comes close to the spirit of comedy at times. He has immense resources of humour – I use the word in its modern sense with a light heart. And yet the proximity of his humour, when he exercises it, to comedy, only serves somehow to separate it from comedy more terribly. His merriment (nowhere is it more evident than in the

play-scene) is genuine, a buoyant lift of the spirits distinguishes it
from wretchedness and anger, though both of these may enter the
mood: the merriment nevertheless is like a reversal of tragedy,
not like comedy.

It is sometimes said that tragedy and comedy are the two sides
of a coin, for tragedy and comedy are conceived of as opposites. Yet
if the image works, it works in a more elaborate way than might be
supposed; and perhaps it does not fully work anyway. Are we meant
to understand that, when tragedy is present, comedy is in some sense
present too? – for when the head is showing, underneath it is still the
very necessary tail (Hamlet would turn an old joke to account here
with interest): and vice versa (his perverse wit would go to town –
poor Ophelia). The actual presence of both the genres in tragedy singly,
as likewise in comedy singly, is suggested by the coin analogy,
and the possibility has something to recommend it. Yet how is
tragedy's tail displayed without a fresh toss, which comes down on
the other side and establishes true, proper comedy? Boggle numis-
matists. If tragedy and comedy are opposites, they are better thought
of as man and woman. Thus the feminineness which is in men is not
womanliness: rather, it is a characteristic of maleness. By the same
token a woman's maleness is part of her real womanhood. Whatever
may be the nature of masculinity's becoming, it does not come from
the thing which is maleness in women: neither is her femininity a
becoming of what must be called femaleness in him. The difficulty
of these ideas undoubtedly inspired a travelled troubadour, who
observed:

> A nancy boy of Khartoum
> Took a lesbian up to his room,
> He said, 'Look, wait, let's get this straight –
> Who does what, and with which, and to whom?'

There is plenty to worry about, yet sexual differentiation is
actually possible, and so are tragedy and comedy. The central figure
of a tragedy may have to be a man, the central figure of a comedy
may have to be a woman: on the whole, though, I think I was making
of sex a mere conceit, to replace that of the coin; I was carried away.
Am I mad in Hamlet's trail, as a hatter or a March hare, grotesquer in
flaming June? Hamlet's merry fit is the unborn comedy which must
haunt a tragedy: it is not live comedy: it is not dead comedy's ghost.

Ghosts, we know, confuse the judgement. Perhaps Hamlet's merriment is the photographic negative of a tragic print. Inky cloak is
wedding-white, gay as the weird dark face shadowed with lights.
Highly amusing yet positively no joke. And comedy: comedy cannot be
developed from Hamlet's tragic print used as though that were a
negative; a negative needs to be transparent, of course, but I suppose
the tragic print of Hamlet could actually be transparent if it were
what is called a 'colour transparency'. We must go in for colour
photography, although Hamlet is virtually a monochrome subject,
whey-faced in black weeds; a pig-headed attempt enough, because
of the expense, and why bother when the result is like a nigger-
minstrel playing Othello?

Colour is of interest, though, colour-theory, and again perhaps
not quite in the way of metaphor. I can't remember the factual
details, but it's the principle which is interesting, because of the play
of opposites. Suppose yellow is the colour you seem to see after staring
at blue for a long time, and then shutting your eyes. The mad yellow
of this optical illusion did not exist as you sanely looked at the blue –
did not exist for you as yellow, although something perhaps existed
which crazily became yellow when you turned blind. In the darkness
is the spot which has to be called yellow, for there's no other word
you can use: but how different from that faint retinal glare is the
capital yellow of these laburnums in the morning.

My book has seemed a matter of alternations, but alternations
what of? I have had a sense of polarised extremes, yet also of false
oppositions; antitheses, interpenetrations; of equipoise and un-
balance; knowledge and partial knowledge, confusion and ignorance.
This has been my state of mind: my book has seemed to alternate
between, or had I not better say among, these perceptions: has it any
form at all? The language of form is not easily approached, its
meaning in a given case is hard to interpret with certainty. There can,
however, be no approach to meaning if form does not exist. I seem
to have to deal in half-truths. Thus Hamlet – which I am sure is formed
– has alternated with other things, other aspects of my life. In some
fashion Shakespeare's tragedy illuminates my private life, and in a
sense (conversely) my private life's raw material is necessary to the
play. My private life (aside from its being partially connected with
Hamlet) is connected also with my public life. For me, public life
means academic life in a department of English, teaching Hamlet

(among other texts): and *Hamlet* is a play which illuminates my public life no less than my private life. The tragedy, the private life, public life, the tragedy: all partially connected, without precision. Without precision, therefore partially separated. The separation seems to imply that quite different systems of half-connection might be possible. The human predicament which traces itself into tragedy can find its end in comedy by tracing another route.

Under this blue sky, these laburnums. I should say, under this sky's *untragic* blue ... for didn't I have blue as tragic? Either I erred then or now, one way or the other I'm human (my critics will certainly know how to forgive). The laburnums with their fall of yellow – they at least belong to comedy. Or perhaps they are too un-English, being rooted in Latin. Not far from the horticultural soil, over the hill beyond the back-gardens, is Flass Vale, a sad strip of urban country, which is native and pastoral on a summer weekday. I draw towards my Arden; the grass is prime, myriad, wild with white flowers. Hamlet, Prince of Denmark, leaves the corrupt court and carves on trees the name of the Princess he serves, ROSALIND. Children playing in Flass Vale appear suddenly disappear (and if they eat laburnum seeds, children will be poisoned – is there any truth in that?). It is a place for lovers. Sin and death came with the Fall, but also procreation. Pastoral comedy is love; although it is satire, too, directed at the rottenness of civilised excess. I remember the Man of Destiny, with his ludicrous posturing; intellectually confused and deceived; a selfish hypocrite mouthing morals; sexually neurotic as any Hamlet; discontented; afraid to die. Fallen man's comedy rites are different: midsummer marriage – high end and new beginning. Even so, pastoral comedy is absurd, no less culpable than over-sophistication, as Touchstone knew with his treacherous courtier's wit. And in tragedy, too, satire is at home: it is then often close to madness. Hamlet is a satirist, so is Lear's Fool (a tragic Touchstone). But I am not Prince Hamlet. Am I, at times, a fool? Let tragedy claim its own again.

10

Lear's Fool is not mad, he is true to his office. Although Fooling is not actually disorder itself (is not madness) it appears nevertheless to be a symptom of disorder. Is that a real distinction? Indecorum in a Fool is licensed, is decorum indirectly. He is no respecter of persons – he must seem to make light even of his master, of his master especially. Moreover his contact with ordered society is by way of verbal fantasy and wit, which look like unreason although they are not. Madness and Fooling are easily associated, and yet the appearance of similarity expresses an antithesis between them. Reason loses itself in madness, the folly of a Fool then reflects this disintegration, is released by it, is part of the process: however, the process develops its own reversal, disintegration is overcome by Fooling aimed against madness for the purpose of restoring reason. It is true, a Fool does not invariably imply the presence of madness. Where reason already prevails he reminds it of itself, by being for its sake what it is not: but reason's corruption, this only, calls forth his full potential. The Fool in King Lear is brought specifically into contact with madness – to such an extent that the play's central climax finds him in a hovel whose occupants include the mad King his master, and Tom o' Bedlam the mad beggar. Soon afterwards (III, vi) he makes his final exit: he is subsequently referred to, but his importance has declined. Perhaps he can be regarded partly as a dramatic technique leading towards the more extreme device of madness.

That King Lear himself goes altogether mad, no one can doubt, and everyone can see in this madness a primary, dominant fact of the play. He goes mad, but he is not mad at first. Is this true? Rather, must not Lear be accounted mad within some meaning of the term long before his wits are affected? His eventual ravings seem the outcome and counterpart of his former state of mind, when he did violence to the true order of things. One might say that he is 'mad' in seeking to free himself from the responsibilities of Kingship (it cannot be

meaningless that he is briefly re-instated just before he dies). In an
action which is closely related to the giving up of sovereign responsibilities, he gives up — or else has never recognised — his responsibilities as a father. He feels no duty towards his heirs: he imagines that
their right is his generosity. He further believes that this generosity,
detached from all idea of duty on his part, should be exercised in
proportion to duty on their part, duty shown towards himself:
thus he is hardly generous (let alone dutiful) for his impulse to give
is qualified and controlled by the demands which he makes on others.
But the truth is, a father is a father whether or not his daughters are
daughterly. In repudiating the role of father Lear absurdly, madly,
invokes the ordered universe to his support:

> For, by the sacred radiance of the sun,
> The mysteries of Hecate and the night,
> By all the operations of the orbs
> From whom we do exist and cease to be,
> I here disclaim all my paternal care,
> Propinquity and property of blood,
> And as a stranger to my heart and me
> Hold thee from this for ever.   (I, i, 109–16)

No sanction can be drawn from the universe to cast off Cordelia,
rather Lear is threatening its existence. He abuses it again when he
calls on Nature to punish the bad daughter Goneril. He cannot possibly — yet he does — address to the forces of fertility this prayer:

> Hear, Nature hear! dear Goddess, hear!
> Suspend thy purpose, if thou didst intend
> To make this creature fruitful!
> Into her womb convey sterility!
> Dry up in her the organs of increase,
> And from her derogate body never spring
> A babe to honour her! If she must teem,
> Create her child of spleen, that it may live
> And be a thwart disnatur'd torment to her!
>   (I, iv, 284–92)

Kent from the first sees Lear's errors and risks everything to protest:

> . . . be Kent unmannerly,
> When Lear is mad . . .

> . . . To plainness honour's bound
> When majesty falls to folly. Reserve thy state;
> And, in thy best consideration, check
> This hideous rashness.   (I, i, 145–51)

And a little later it is Kent who uses an image of disease to describe
the King's condition: here the underlying thought is reminiscent of
Gertrude's association of sin with soul-sickness. Illness may make a
man turn on the doctor who could cure him. Kent before his banish-
ment thus addresses Lear:

> Kill thy physician, and thy fee bestow
> Upon the foul disease. Revoke thy gift;
> Or, whilst I can vent clamour from my throat,
> I'll tell thee thou dost evil.   (I, i, 163–6)

One could say, then, that Lear in his repudiation of lawful
reason is metaphorically mad, and is so long before the scenes of real
madness on the heath and near Dover. But equally well one could put
things the other way round, and say that those scenes are a kind of
dramatically realised metaphor designed to illustrate the King's perversity. Perhaps there is no need to suggest uncertainty as between
imagery and actuality: surely one can accept a connection between
different manifestations of unreasonableness without reference to
levels of realism: within the context of the play Lear's perversity and
his madness are presented as plot-components, and both these components are fully valid. Yet a mutual interpenetration of vital categories does seem to distinguish the play. This impression, perhaps
dispensed with when one tried to think only of Lear, re-asserts itself
strongly when one takes into account Gloucester. Lear's unreasonableness and Gloucester's, the evocation of madness and blindness, all
come together in a powerful effect of symbolism: symbolism is at
once reality and metaphor, yet in being both it somehow takes on a
different meaning from that possessed singly by either, a larger
meaning.

As early as the first scene Lear's situation is described through
imagery which approximates to the real subsequent situation of
Gloucester. It is Gloucester whom we shall come to associate with
blindness, yet when Lear commands 'Out of my sight!' Kent can
reply –

> See better, Lear; and let me still remain
> The true blank of thine eye   (I, i, 158–9)

Lear himself, his wisdom called into question when Goneril cen-
sures him for the behaviour of his retinue, cries out:

> Does any here know me? This is not Lear:
> Does Lear walk thus? speak thus? Where are his eyes?
> Either his notion weakens, his discernings
> Are lethargied – Ha!   (I, iv, 234–7)

And later in the same scene, weeping and cursing, he says:

> . . . Old fond eyes,
> Beweep this cause agin, I'll pluck ye out,
> And cast you, with the waters that you loose,
> To temper clay.   (I, iv, 310–13)

Towards the end of Act III Lear in some sense or other escapes blinding by one of his children through the intervention of Gloucester.
Gloucester's own blinding occurs on the stage within moments of
the following exchange:

Cornwall	Where hast thou sent the King?
Gloucester	To Dover.
Regan	Wherefore to Dover? Wast thou not charg'd at peril –
Cornwall	Wherefore to Dover? Let him answer that.
Gloucester	I am tied to th' stake, and I must stand the course.
Regan	Wherefore to Dover?
Gloucester	Because I would not see thy cruel nails Pluck out his poor old eyes. (III, vii, 50–6)

The immediate cause of Gloucester's blinding is that he helps Lear to
get away: but there is a sense in which he is blinded as Lear's proxy.
Lear therefore seems to avoid *actual* blinding, and the fact that he
avoids it gives us continuing permission to treat the blindness motif
as metaphorical in his case. We never have to think of his eyes as his
jellies. Nevertheless, the metaphor is brought into extraordinarily
close contact with actuality by the blinding of Gloucester in his
stead.

And the general drawing together of metaphor and actuality in
this play is taken even further by a sort of complementary process

carried out in respect of Gloucester. It seems simple to say that Lear
keeps his eyesight and loses his wits, that Gloucester keeps his wits
and loses his eyesight. There appears to be, in a sense there is, contrast. Yet is not Gloucester mad like Lear? — is he not, at any rate,
mad like the *early* Lear, before the dramatic image of actual madness
took control, or (using the alternative formulation) at the time when
Lear's original perversity was a metaphorical madness? Gloucester,
too, goes against the ordered universe. His desire to treat the bastard
Edmund as the equal of legitimate Edgar may seem on the surface to
denote fair-mindedness, may seem to claim our respect. 'I have a son,
Sir, by order of law', he tells Kent at the beginning, 'some year elder
than this, who is yet no dearer in my account: though this knave
came something saucily to the world before he was sent for, yet was
his mother fair; there was good sport at his making, and the whore-
son must be acknowledged' (I, i, 19–24). But fairness to Edmund is
unfairness to Edgar: to put this more fundamentally, Gloucester
shows himself willing to put the sanctity of marriage on an equal
footing with what Edmund calls 'the lusty stealth of nature' (I, ii, 11).
Gloucester not only disregards responsibility to moral law, doing
evil thereby, but he hardly understands that evil has been perpetrated — he has no grasp of the nature of evil, fails to deal with it.
Having made this mistake it is less than surprising that he takes it
further and readily assumes the bastard son to be *more moral* than the
legitimate son. Being deceived, he rejects Edgar in favour of
Edmund. In other words he is spiritually blind: 'I stumbled when I
saw', he admits (IV, i, 19) after the real blinding has taken place. A
little later mad Tom becomes the guide who will lead him towards
Dover, towards the cliff of despair, and towards the mad King:
''Tis the times' plague, when madmen lead the blind' (IV, i, 46).
The madness of Lear, which we can call actual, although in relation
to his earlier state it is also equivocally metaphorical, is thus the
dramatically realised image of Gloucester's madness too: the blindness of Gloucester, likewise an equivocal metaphor in relation to
Gloucester himself, is the dramatic image also of Lear's blindness.

Gloucester is deceived, and in the play there is much deception:
it may be thought of as an aspect of the blindness theme, or for that
matter of the madness theme. Edmund deceives Gloucester — not
difficult, as Gloucester is so willing to believe that 'legitimate Edgar'
is a monster of ingratitude. Goneril and Regan deceive Lear at the

outset by their gross flattery and expressions of love – again their task is an easy one; for self-deception is stimulated by deceiving tongues, deception being possible only by a willing blindness on the part of the deceived. However, this kind of double dependency may be lacking, and still deception may occur. It will then be wholly self-deception, for there will be no intent to deceive by the other person. Lear's unreasonableness is such (his blindness, his madness) that Cordelia's ungarnished statement of daughterly feelings seems to him wicked. Here is a good person trying to behave properly, and succeeding (though indeed with an unfortunate emphasis which is forced upon her by the need to separate her own responses from those of her dissembling sisters): the aim is the reverse of deception, yet Lear's autonomous self-deception requires no outside and mutual evil to operate it. One could put this in another way, and say simply that to an evil person who believes himself to be in the right, good looks evil. Kent as well as Cordelia looks evil to Lear, and to Gloucester Edgar looks evil.

Edgar, who becomes Tom o' Bedlam, the other madman on the heath with Lear, is driven to put on his disguise (a kind of deception?) perhaps because, essentially, reason looks mad from the standpoint of unreason – that is, again, because goodness looks evil to evil.

Edgar   The bloody proclamation to escape
          That follow'd me so near . . .

                              . . . taught me to shift
          Into a madman's rags, t'assume a semblance
          That very dogs disdain'd.   (V, iii, 183–8)

Edgar does not deceive Lear with evil intent, and his motives for continuing the deception of his own father are anything but evil:

          Why I do trifle thus with his despair
          Is done to cure it.   (IV, vi, 33–4)

He is therefore quite unlike Edmund. Is Edgar like Cordelia? He is good, but changes his appearance: she remains the same, although in Lear's eyes she may be said to have become someone else, someone evil. He is disguised, but so in a sense is she. Edmund occupies a position at the other end of the moral scale, along with the evil deceivers Goneril and Regan: must one not say that these characters, who assume an appearance of good, are in disguise too; at any rate, that there is an active analogy with the disguise principle? The case of Kent is very curious. He assumes a disguise when Lear, self-deceived, banishes him. But although Kent is technically a disguised person, not himself, he is to all intents and purposes the same character that he always was (unlike Edgar who is not the same character as Tom). Where Lear was formerly deceived in thinking that Kent was evil, he sees him as good once a mere figment of disguise is interposed; the stage convention of disguise is often arbitrarily employed, but I doubt whether this quite accounts for Kent's presentation.

Madness, blindness, deception, disguise, are all associated together, and all signify disturbance of the moral order. How are we to understand the nature of this disturbance? Our instinct may well be that madness, blindness, deception, and disguise are simply and automatically evil things, but presumably we cannot jump to this hasty conclusion. Lear is mad, and certainly evil in many ways, yet surely he is not wholly evil: and when he loses his wits he seems paradoxically to advance in sanity and goodness; he becomes less blind, one could say. And Gloucester, his eyes put out, understands at that very moment his former spiritual blindness, former madness:

O my follies! Then Edgar was abus'd.　　　　(III, vii, 90)

Lear and Gloucester, deceived in regard to their evil children, are also deceived in regard to their good children: it seems as though deception can have to do with goodness on occasion, although the morality of Cordelia and Edgar hardly makes moral the deception which results from it. And if Edgar, like the disguised Kent, is apparently wholly good, why has Edgar's disguise (Tom o' Bedlam) trafficked with the foul fiend? These points I recapitulate: taken together they seem to indicate a state of moral disturbance. Moral disturbance is obviously unsatisfactory, better there should be harmony. But again I wonder how we are to understand the nature of the disturbance – since it seems to involve good elements along with bad.

King Lear gives us a strong sense of confused oppositions. Perhaps all art contains and thrives on oppositions: sometimes these are easy to distinguish: sometimes not, for they may merge and change places, produce the most complex, if obscure, conviction of meaning. Uncertainty of a kind there may be in difficult cases, yet this does not amount to confusion, as *Lear* seems confused, even bewildering. Not that the play is *unpositive*. I am trying to express its baffling elusiveness, the feeling (which I at least experience) that its oppositions are not only ambiguous but without fixed orientation: nevertheless, the feeling also that it moves from its beginning through to its end with the utmost assurance. I cannot think of any work which produces quite this impression. In *Hamlet* moral opposites seem constantly to interpenetrate. It is as though they are for ever in the act of redefining themselves and reversing. But the hero's agonised attempt to sustain initial assumptions, against his own evolving experience and deeper awareness, gives the play a point of reference – his illusion of confidence, known in some sense by even himself for an illusion, and certainly felt by the audience to be unsatisfactory, allows the taking of bearings. Whereas, in *King Lear*, we cannot get our bearings, or cannot be sure we have got them.

One of the many areas of confusion in *Lear* concerns the gods. There may be something like thirty references to the supernatural, and these reveal little in the way of consistency. We could take just two examples. After his eyes are out Gloucester realises that he has wronged Edgar, who has been true to him: and notwithstanding his condition, cries out

> Kind Gods, forgive me that, and prosper him!
>
> (III, vii, 91)

In the scene immediately following, and speaking again in the context of his relations with Edgar, he utters the well-known lines

> As flies to wanton boys, are we to th' Gods;
> They kill us for their sport.   (IV, i, 36–7)

These formulations, whether thought of singly or in combination, may leave us hesitating. How can the gods be called kind after they have permitted Gloucester's bloody blinding? If the sufferer is not so much expressing a belief in present kindness, as praying for kindness in the future (perhaps a possible interpretation) why does he think it worth while to pray, why should such gods ever behave otherwise than they have done in the past? If (as in the second quotation) the gods seem unkind, why does Gloucester use the image of wanton boys, children? – who, when they kill flies, are not cruel in the fullest sense, being less than innocent no doubt, but also less than guilty. In any case wanton irresponsibility hardly consists with the possibility of forgiving the wicked and prospering good (first quotation). Of all the statements that are made concerning the gods in the course of the play, some no doubt should be accounted more significant than others, depending on the character who speaks and the situation in which he speaks. But even so there is an unusual and somehow emphatic degree of variation: the gods are just and unjust, benevolent, capricious, malignant, indifferent, any of these things, some or all.

That the status of the gods should seem thus to fluctuate is perhaps not surprising in view of the moral intricacies already discussed, of madness, blindness, deception, disguise: for moral disturbance among men must be related by men to the universe, and in their disturbed condition they interpret everything as they can and will. Man is fallen, often has difficulty in distinguishing right from wrong, yet tries to evaluate the supernatural along with the world he knows. The interpretational possibilities, even the basic categories of interpretation, are numerous. The better members of our race will see things properly, that is, in a more or less Christian fashion. God is omnipotent: he is good, but otherwise inscrutable. He judges humanity. Evil he punishes or forgives as he thinks fit. Goodness he rewards, finally; however, this is not to say that he rewards or even protects it on earth. These elements, separately or together, are given frequent expression in the play (notwithstanding its supposed paganism) and perhaps several of them are present in the exchange between Edgar and repentant Gloucester at the end of Act IV, scene vi:

Gloucester You ever-gentle Gods, take my breath from me:
            Let not my worser spirit tempt me again
            To die before you please!
Edgar   Well pray you, father.
Gloucester Now, good sir, what are you?
Edgar   A most poor man, made tame to Fortune's blows;
            Who, by the art of known and feeling sorrows,
            Am pregnant to good pity. Give me your hand,
            I'll lead you to some biding.

Gloucester   Hearty thanks:
   The bounty and benison of Heaven
   To boot, to boot!   (218–27)

But besides these elements of proper interpretation there are distorted versions, expressive of varying degrees of moral error. The
worst of fallen men adopt extremely involved positions, as does
Edmund. In Act III, scene v, he contrives to view his treachery to
Gloucester as loyalty to Cornwall: the new allegiance he pretends is
good, whilst the old allegiance to his father becomes evil. The situation appears more simple than it really is, for this is not a case of a
moral polarity with the concepts reversed and renamed. Certainly
Edmund's commitment to Cornwall is evil – one may say for con-
venience that Edmund calls this evil 'good'. What then is its opposite,
what is the polarity's other term, now to be called 'evil'? The concept
that offers itself to Edmund is nature: nature is 'evil' because it is
good. Or rather, Edmund seems to think it good, and for that reason
is uneasy as he labours to pervert the truth into its new form. 'How,
my lord, I may be censured,' he says to Cornwall early in this short
scene, 'that nature thus gives way to loyalty, something fears me to
think of.' The fact is, however, that nature cannot be regarded as
straightforwardly good – rather it is good only if bound within the
total moral order of which it should comprise a part; otherwise it is
evil. This evil aspect of nature was once, at the beginning of the play,
very much to Edmund's liking, and it seemed to him 'good', for he
was intent on establishing another of his moral polarities with
reversed names. We remember the speech on legitimacy (I, ii) beginning 'Thou, Nature, art my goddess; to thy law/My services are
bound', and ending with the striking invocation 'Now, gods, stand
up for bastards!' If Edmund in the later scene with Cornwall is determined to reject good nature (and presumably this is the case) he
nevertheless rejects a goodness which is peculiarly fallible – his own
bastard behaviour shows just how fallible nature can be. There is the
impression, somehow, that Edmund has become worse than he was,
that he is a step further away from good: doubly removed from it.
Consider the two polarities, early and late. In the first, nature was a
bad pole and was therefore called 'good'. In the second it is the good
pole and is therefore called 'bad'. Nature's lack of moral obligation
which originally recommended itself to Edmund, now constitutes a

degree of obligation which is too great: so that nature, having been embraced for evil reasons, must now be rejected for reasons still more evil, still more lacking (this is the impression) in morality. It is true that Edmund, as I have remarked, now recognises the better side of nature, where before he insisted on its worse side and called that 'good'. Yet this increase of moral awareness, what is it but the necessary means to greater corruption? – the reward for which is the earldom of Gloucester. The Edmund who now betrays, in order to usurp, his father, is more evil than the Edmund who sought to become his father's heir in place of Edgar.

Edmund   I will persever in my course of loyalty, though the conflict
          be sore between that and my blood.
Cornwall I will lay trust upon thee; and thou shalt find a dearer
          father in my love.   (III, v, 21–3)

Human error and sinfulness lay claim to goodness. In some ways this moral perversion may be detected most easily when a man's evil is least in doubt; for juggle how he will, the tendency of his mind can be counted on – we can treat him like a puzzle whose answer is known beforehand, but which has to be correctly worked out. People who are not wholly committed to evil, morally mixed characters such as Lear and Gloucester, may be harder to understand. We do not know at any given moment how perverted their views are, we may not even know whether their views *are* perverted. Our morality is at issue as well as theirs. Perversion corrupts us, to what extent? – certainly we are not wholly committed to evil, surely. Perhaps we would be better able to assess ourselves and mankind generally, mankind within the universe, if the moral disturbance which everywhere exists were less problematic in its meaning. We believe that the universe ought to be, intends to be, possibly is, good. We want to believe in the omnipotence of the good God, at least we often do. But we have to be realistic. Is it not the case that God's omnipotence has been challenged – we thus define evil – and can we possibly deny the presence of evil? We may wish to support God (at times) and to be his instruments, but such is the fact of evil that we must wonder whether some central disaster has occurred – are the satanic powers triumphing? A huge battle is joined, whose intensity does not appear to consist with the notion of God's omnipotence. Will God or the Devil win? Evidently God has not won

yet, even if he is going to win in the future: for if he had, goodness
would reign. On the other hand, perhaps the Devil has already won,
in that, patently, goodness does not reign. The moral disturbance of
the universe, which we recognise all around us, and in which we par-
ticipate, is susceptible of a double interpretation. Imperfection can be
regarded as faulty good, alternatively as the faultiness of evil. Good
manages to maintain itself, but is severely strained: or else the disturbance is the mark of evil, very evil itself. This problem of double
interpretation can hardly be unconnected with the problem of our
own moral status. How – since evil in some sense exists – can we as
observers distinguish a proper identification of it (the result of our
sound judgement) from a false identification (arising from judgement which is unsound)? Like the characters in the play, and more
especially like the morally mixed characters, we are in the dilemma
of mortal men: with the best or the worst intentions (and we are
confused about which is which) we cannot tell whether moral
disturbance is compatible with ultimate good, or proves ultimate
evil. The fallen state is ill-suited to the resolving of its own dilemma.
Gloucester's speech in Act I, scene ii (107–23) seems full of obscure
possibilities:

> These late eclipses in the sun and moon portend no good to us:
> though the wisdom of Nature can reason it thus and thus, yet
> Nature finds itself scourg'd by the sequent effects. Love cools,
> friendship falls off, brothers divide . . .

Gloucester then elaborates the ills of the time. It is to be noted that in
some of his specific judgements he is right (the King *has* fallen from
the bias of nature, there at least the father is against the child), but in
some judgements he is wrong (Edgar does *not* come under the pre-
diction, that particular son is not against the father). Again, the
general indictment of 'machinations, hollowness, treachery' could
well be applied to himself ('Find out this villain, Edmund; it shall
lose thee nothing: do it carefully'), but he shows no guilt, rather
implies that he is like Kent, whom he rightly knows to be good
('And the noble and true-hearted Kent banish'd! his offence, hon-
esty! 'Tis strange'). The ills of the time are certainly related to the
eclipses, but obscurely so. It is possible to regard the heavenly system
as distorted from its proper state, yet as still intact: that is, in the
final analysis the true system is prevalent. The evil of mankind has

conceivably led to this distortion, and we shall be punished as part
of the process of restoring the system. Alternatively the eclipses,
being abnormal, are themselves evil like men: and in portending us
no good they are giving notice, not of a just punishment, but of
malignant destruction; possibly the eclipses are actually the cause of
the human evil they are about to destroy.

The notion of man's undergoing a fall, though traditional and
highly emotive, is misleading in some respects. Man fell lower than
he was before, but he did not fall all the way, as Satan did. Fallen
man can never be other than fallen: yet the image, considered as an
image, makes difficult the registering of our tendency to do good (if
we stay fallen we cannot properly be said to rise), and equally our
tendency to do evil is not recognised (if fallen already, we cannot
fall any more). We continued to have strong affiliations with God
despite new affiliations with the Devil. Our state is ambivalent,
ambiguous. Moving betwixt good and evil are we not as yo-yoes in
this vale of tears? The string of Gloucester's yo-yo has got tangled,
and besides, his standing is uncertain between head and heels ('Nature
finds itself scourg'd by the sequent effects'). The Fall is our traditional image. But here are two further images of moral ambiguity,
taken from the play:

(1) *Lear* Deny to speak with me! They are sick! They are weary!
           They have travell'd all the night! Mere fetches, ay,
           The images of revolt and flying off.   (II, iv, 88–90)
(2) *Lear*   ... O most small fault,
           How ugly didst thou in Cordelia show!
           Which, like an engine, wrench'd my frame of nature
           From the fix'd place.   (I, iv, 275–8)

These images, which the King summons up to endorse his point of
view, may not entirely convince the audience – possibly he is not
entirely convinced himself: the intricate confusions of our moral
being seem to find expression, more adequately than in the image of
Fall. For with regard to the first passage, are good and evil distinctly
identified? 'Revolt' suggests the loss of ordered government, and of
course this is bad. Yet Lear himself has created the government which
Regan and Cornwall now represent. If their authority is legal, they
cannot raise revolt. If it is not, they are revolting against a government (Lear's) which has proceeded illegally, hence they are on the

side of order. The theory of Kingship is elaborate, and I am over-simplifying. But this image of revolt, in context, makes obscurely for good. 'Flying off' (perhaps the heavenly bodies break their orbit?) undoubtedly makes for evil. Yet is Lear right to assume that the Duke and Duchess initiate the flying-off process? Rather Lear himself initiates it: he causes true order to disintegrate by his original actions, and thereafter only further disintegration is possible, regardless of claims and counter-claims. Are good and evil fully distinguished in the second example? Engine and frame are the two elements of the simile, but there is some difficulty in deciding between the morality of the thing wrenching and the thing wrenched. The engine, being a fault, was according to Lear evil: the frame was good, at least until it was dislocated. On the other hand the audience must doubt whether Cordelia was really at fault. If she wrenched Lear by her behaviour, this may have been because his evil nature strongly resisted her good influence: thus although the engine is called a fault we easily suspect that the fault lay in the frame, in which case the moral interpretation has undergone reversal. Possibly Lear himself hardly believes any longer in his daughter's faultiness. 'O most small fault', he says, as though he could almost find it in him to say instead, 'O no fault at all'. The word 'which', introducing the image, refers a long way back to its noun 'fault': and such is the syntactical stretch here that we feel ourselves groping for an easier connection. The King's near-admission that Cordelia was not at fault whereas he was, prompts us to experiment with the entire phrase 'How ugly didst thou in Cordelia show' as though it were a sort of noun, developed from 'fault', but perhaps the true subject of the pronoun 'which'. The ugly showing, the appearance of faultiness (Lear does not quite say, or quite mean) was an engine which wrenched his frame: the faulty perceiver wrought evil upon his own better self. The engine is again evil, as it was to begin with. All the same, it could be said to take on an opposite meaning, for its office was formerly to imply Lear's goodness, through Cordelia's evil, and now it directly implies Lear's own evil. Apparently the frame is still good, constituting as it does the perceiver's better self. Yet can it really be the case that the engine is not the frame? Somehow the wrenching and the being-wrenched are one thing. Lear's worse nature did not pervert his better nature, his nature acted as it did because of what it already was. The frame displaced itself with its own engine. If the displacement

can still be seen in reference to a 'fixed place' ('Wrench'd my frame of
nature/From the fix'd place') this is to emphasise again the double
interpretation to which moral disturbance is susceptible: is the disturbance goodness wrenched, or is it verily evil? All this Lear does
not see, when he remembers Cordelia's 'O most small fault': but
does he, therefore, see none of it? Something of it he does see, in that
he is registering with anguish a change of heart: the small fault, when
it seemed huge, once made him vow in his wrath:

> . . . The barbarous Scythian,
> Or he that makes his generation messes
> To gorge his appetite, shall to my bosom
> Be as well neighbour'd, pitied, and reliev'd,
> As thou my sometime daughter.   (I, i, 116–20)

There was the wrenching engine, the wrenched frame: and there the
precondition of his subsequent change. Can one not say that Lear's
distorted vision, evil in itself, has brought about an advance in goodness? It is as though his evil nature was wrenching, was wrenched by,
his evil nature rightly, as though his real evil has qualified itself into
his real good, hence, surely was not evil after all. One does not doubt
that the place of human nature in the scheme of things is important,
but was the proper place occupied by Lear to begin with (or not),
was it in process of being occupied (or not), is it, or is it not,
occupied now? Fallen Lear, who can never be other than fallen, is
perhaps in some sense rising.

The Fall, being itself an image, invites comparison with other
images of moral crisis. But the ambivalence of our state, also the
double way in which we interpret moral disturbance around us,
these things associated are conveyed by various available means
besides imagery. They are hinted at, for example, in the curious
encounter between Lear and Kent, Act II, scene iv. If the mode of
presentation seems oblique, perhaps this is because imagery is
critically more familiar to us (it is, however, equally oblique). The
passage develops a sort of banal ritual: *reductio ad absurdum* is felt
simultaneously with moral significance. The King finds his servant in
the stocks, when the following exchange of basic alternatives occurs:

Lear   What's he that hath so much thy place mistook
           To set thee here?

Kent	It is both he and she,
	Your son and daughter.
Lear	No.
Kent	Yes.
Lear	No, I say.
Kent	I say, yea.
Lear	No, no; they would not.
Kent	Yes, they have.
Lear	By Jupiter, I swear, no.
Kent	By Juno, I swear, ay.
Lear	They durst not do't,

They could not, would not do't; 'tis worse than murther,
To do upon respect such violent outrage.   (12–24)

Kent the good man (as humanity goes) affirms the existence of evil;
his positiveness serves to define and enforce negation. The King, on
the other hand, would deny to be evil that which he is appalled to
find is not good; he is a worse man than Kent, and his language here
consists of negatives, yet arguably he promotes a more positive point
of view. In this play are many negatives for critics to ponder; Lear's
threat to Cordelia being the first that alerts us, 'Nothing will come
of nothing' (I, i, 90); we find the last of them, emphasised, reiter-
ated, in Lear's dying speech, 'Never, never, never, never, never'. I think
it unlikely that a dialogue of negatives alternated with positives is
merely trite.

When he discovered the indignity that had been done to Kent,
Lear of course became angry – in a many-sided way, or so it seems to
me. He was angry at the idea that goodness could be faulty, and
angry at having to recognise that it might be: angry at the idea that
faulty good could be evil's faultiness, and angry, finally, at the enormous possibility that evil might be ascendant. His anger in this
episode is evolved dramatically from the anger of Kent, who was
stocked for attacking Oswald:

Cornwall	Why art thou angry?
Kent	That such a slave as this should wear a sword,
	Who wears no honesty. Such smiling rogues as these,
	Like rats, oft bite the holy cords a-twain
	Which are too intrince t'unloose. (II, ii, 72–6)

There is nothing more characteristic of Lear than his great anger, unless it be the madness with which that anger is so closely associated (and is the anger of Hamlet, frequent with him, perhaps connected in some way with his problematical madness? – Kent's expression, 'Such smiling rogues as these', recalls the words of Hamlet spoken just before he hints at 'antic' madness: 'O villain, villain, smiling damnéd villain!/My tables, meet it is I set it down/ That one may smile, and smile, and be a villain', I, v, 106–8). Lear's anger does not disappear even in the latter part of the play, whatever may be the new elements which begin to be evident alongside it: his last speeches over the body of Cordelia certainly have anger as an ingredient.

Anger is a morally interesting emotion. Can we say of it that it is sometimes good, sometimes bad? Traditionally it is a deadly sin: nevertheless on occasion it closely resembles militancy, and perhaps in this aspect at least anger deserves to be called good. We are back on familiar ground, for militancy appeared to be a crucial issue in *Hamlet* too (see p. 19 et seq.). It may well be that militancy is necessary in the world, although even at its best it is a contaminated virtue, partaking too much of the nature of the evil it sets out to destroy; at its worst, when the righteous fighter mistakes himself and his cause, one may say simply that it is not true militancy. True militancy becomes necessary, despite its faultiness, perhaps because the superior sacrificial solution – Christ's sacrifice – has reference most of all to the interior condition of mankind, not to the exterior: less effectively (at any rate less immediately) does it bear upon the fact of evil loose in the world, perpetrated and promulgated by men who do not care to be redeemed by god incarnate; or who, redeemed, revert as all men must to a measure of evil – until redeemed again by Christ's sacrifice next week. Our inward moral state is a sort of middle term between the physical world which we inhabit, and the supernatural region which we also inhabit. Theologians will believe themselves able to notify me here of the right formulations and answers, but I do not believe our moral life is ever solved. Its reality is conflict, uncertainty, struggle, defeat. Christianity, committed to dealing sacrificially with evil, has nevertheless not eschewed militancy. I do not mean merely that human weakness and imperfection, found in Christians as in others, and rather Christianity's raison d'être than its indictment, have perverted a religion of love into its opposite: this has in part happened. I mean that militancy, notwithstanding its grave moral inadequacy, has been recognised as contributing to true Christianity. Strangely (in view of the risk we run of contamination) militancy was not unknown in heaven itself. In heaven there was a war, which preceded and led to the creation of man, and led also to man's fall and the need for redemption – I am willing to speak mythologically: the war was nothing if not a militant opposing of evil by good. The prince of light, supporting and supported by his father, won. No forgiveness, no sacrifice. Those were matters which gained primacy later, having to do with humanity – the victorious prince incarnated himself, was sacrificed by and for man: man, whose psyche reflects the battle in heaven, yet who lives in the world of matter: man, rather, and woman – woman being in some ways especially associated with matter, through that (obscurely) with evil, though she is not more evil than men; perhaps the Oedipus complex begins at the moment of the Fall. Militancy at its best, i.e. true militancy, must be accounted good up to a point, and militant anger with it; these cannot be dispensed with in the world. Kent's attitude towards Oswald was militant, angry – surely Kent is a good man, loyal servant to Lear. He was punished in the stocks, but punished by evil Cornwall; was he rightly punished, in some indirect fashion? And Edgar, another good man: militantly he kills Kent's victim, Oswald: this action leads to the greater militancy of the challenge and combat, when he kills Edmund his evil brother. Edgar in the end becomes a ruler of the land: Kent would have been one, too, had his heart not broken.

However, militancy fraught with all its unavoidable problems is not wholly synonymous with anger, for where militancy always begins in good, anger may not. If angry militancy, beginning in good, is perhaps doomed to contamination, anger of another sort is wholly evil. Evil anger will probably mistake itself for goodness: true goodness will then be dubbed evil and attacked by a militancy which is altogether false. Even if this thoroughgoing mistake is not made, anger can still fall short of proper militancy. For so obsessed may the angry person be with the (true) evil he opposes, that he assumes a universe of evil. Against it he can only pit his rage, which is helpless, for he feels the odds are overwhelming: what was good in some degree (angry militancy) is vilely distorted by the belief that goodness exists nowhere else but in himself, or at most is found not

among the gods but thinly among humanity. But for his obsession
he might have detected forces of goodness in the larger universe:
and the forces directed against him may be these very same forces,
not unjust but just – for has he not evilly denied all good beyond
himself?

The anger of Lear is perhaps of every kind. At the beginning of the
play it is at its most deceived, by the end it may (I am not sure)
approximate to true militancy. In the middle, especially during the
storm, there are intricately organised variations and transitions. I have
in mind the three big speeches of Lear in the earlier part of Act III,
scene ii: the first beginning 'Blow, winds, and crack your cheeks!
rage! blow!' (1–9); the second 'Rumble thy bellyful! Spit, fire!
spout, rain!' (14–24); and the third 'Let the great Gods' (49–60).
He perhaps sees the storm as goodness (disturbed at present in its
effort to throw off and destroy evil) and also as evil itself: the double
way of looking at things – already familiar to us – is further related
to Lear's own moral position. A sort of reciprocating system makes
the angry King simultaneously tyrant and victim. Each of these two
aspects implies the other, though the knowledge that this is so
impinges on him most uncertainly: each aspect tends to penetrate
the other. Such assertions on my part need supporting. Detailed
sequential analysis may be called for – though I doubt its being
called for vociferously. I prefer to move through the speeches in a
somewhat impressionistic way; even to move backwards and forwards between them.

Lear's desire in the first speech to destroy ingratitude, he con-
ceives to be the storm's desire too. He urges the storm on, its anger
is his own. He may fancy that he is being militant, and that he
participates in good's eternal struggle against evil. By the end of the
second speech, however, he has apparently reversed his position,
except that he still adopts a militant stance. The storm's anger is
now his no longer, rather it is totally opposed to his own. The storm
seems to have become evil: it is the agent of ingratitude, not ingratitude's enemy. A transition occurs in the earlier part of the second
speech. There he seems to detach his own separate identity, contriving to maintain something like an alliance with the storm whilst at
the same time not taxing it.

It is difficult to avoid the conviction that Lear's anger in these
two speeches is directed principally at his evil daughters – first he is

destroying them with the storm, then they with the storm are
destroying him. Goneril and Regan are what Lear *means* by ingratitude: against their evil his militancy is deployed in contrasted forms.
And yet, strangely, not altogether strangely, he seems to include himself among the ungrateful objects of the storm's anger – 'Singe my
white head', he commands, half-way through the first speech. At that
point he feels, perhaps, generalising from the behaviour of his
daughters, that all mankind is ungrateful – he seems to say as much:
Lear may hardly intend the indictment to apply to himself: and yet
he does inadvertently apply it, and it is applicable, for in regard to
Kent and Cordelia he was guilty enough. Another possibility, and it
is prejudicial to what I have just been arguing, is that already (in the
first speech) he is moving towards the position he will arrive at late in
the second speech, when he ceases to generalise, and when he heaps
all the blame for ingratitude on his daughters: surely nothing of
guiltiness is by then discernible, so the attempt to interpret guilt in
the first speech is presumably mistaken. Late in the second speech
the storm becomes the slave of the daughters: however, before that,
at the half-way point in fact (corresponding one might think with
the halfway point in the first speech, i.e. with Lear's demand to be
singed) the storm is rather presented as itself a master, for 'here I
stand, your slave'. The storm-master is vindictive, letting fall a
horrible pleasure on Lear the slave, who does not hint at loyal
following: moreover, the status of the storm is here particularly
uncertain – guilty in a moment's time, a moment ago not guilty (not
'taxed'): all the same, these are concessions which do not entirely
preclude culpability on the part of the King, expressed by himself, or
rather acknowledged in his words.

Lear's awareness of guilt is less than that. He stumbles on the
truth as though accidentally, and is inclined to take it for a different
truth, or for different conflicting truths. His culpability such as
it is, and his inadequate acknowledgement, could be distorting his
moral vision of the storm. Possibly he was right to see the storm in
the first speech as good, as destroying ingratitude (even, it may be,
his own). Why, then, are the terms in which he describes it inconsistent with its actually being good? – 'sulph'rous' is among the
adverse indications. Is the moral imperfection of anger (his own and
the storm's) apparent in the imagery? Is Lear's anger not even true
militancy, causing him to represent the good storm as less good than

it is? When he openly describes it in the second speech as if it were evil, his anger may be more falsely militant still. He there feels himself tormented, not merely singed. Conceivably this might be due punishment for his ingratitude, not a horrible supernatural pleasure to be resented by the sufferer: conceivably the storm might be vindictive and still perform a requisite moral function: Lear even knows something of all this (as we have seen) and chooses not to know it. The storm which is represented by him as good in the first speech, though it appears in some underlying sense bad, is in some sense good in the second speech though represented as bad.

In the third speech the mad King angrily exhorts the gods who are the storm to find out and punish concealed crime as it deserves to be punished. The confession or otherwise of his own guilt having been at issue in the preceding speeches, this third speech must seem to bear not only on other criminals, but experimentally upon himself. The criminal daughters are condemned: 'I am a man/More sinn'd against than sinning'. He admits, then, that he is a sinner: seems therefore to call down his own punishment in the general punishment: yet seems also to excuse himself, angry at having to suffer as much or more than supposedly worse sinners. The note of great suffering runs through all three speeches, no less than the note of anger. Lear is to be pitied, but why? Because he is good, or because he is bad? Perhaps self-destroying evil suffers into goodness: the bad in Lear is being painfully destroyed by the bad in him, which established tyranny and ingratitude. The good in him is being destroyed in like manner – it too suffers: possibly the self-sacrifice of original goodness tends to the painful destruction of the evil which inflicts. Somehow both these propositions are true of Lear's morally mixed and slowly improving human nature. Between good and bad there is intricate reciprocation: yet anger enters deeply into the process, and one may wonder whether anger is either self-destroying or self-sacrificing; one hesitates. Anger at its best is an evil emotion in part: at its best, therefore, is it not good? It hardly seems to be two things yet it hardly seems to be one.

11

It seems to me as much a characteristic of *King Lear* as of *Hamlet* that moral issues are explored with peculiar intensity. Reactions to this vary, apparently: we may try to make out that everything is morally simple, alternatively that it is utterly confused. Perhaps both reactions attest to our being roused. If we belong to the former group it is because (it could be because) we are determined to preserve our moral defence-lines – our determination measures our danger; we may belong to the latter group because we find ourselves beaten out of the old positions, but none the less do we desire to regain them, or to regain at any rate some comparable certainty. In these plays we probably all recognise, after our own fashion, a mixture of certainty and uncertainty.

The artistic movement of the plays – this is what controls us, by this we are guided through a maze of morals towards the dramatic ending of tragedy. But in life-situations there is no control, no authorial manipulation of that sort. We experience moral ferment in a less organised way, and without any pre-ordained ending stored up for us in the future. Possibly the really important moral situations in life are those in which the ferment is upon us. Codes – moral codes – are necessary: yet they remove responsibility from us, or rather they make us responsible in a different and less primary sense. They lay a duty upon us to do what is prescribed as right – failure on our part is only a failure of moral courage, a yielding to temptation, an embracing of evil. Bad enough: yet our powers of moral apprehension are scarcely exercised. When the ordinary code seems inadequate to the situation – seems not to work, or how it applies is not clear – that is the time when the meaning of morality must of necessity be approached, and our moral faculties must be fully exercised; often with reluctance, and I think always with some pain. The code of everyday is grappled with: or (to be more accurate) something else is grappled with, of which the code is a convenient but gross simplification.

With moral values, aesthetic values are connected – the two types will overlap and interpenetrate. The broad issues of progress and learning, which surround university English, demand moral activity from us who staff the departments: and, not surprisingly since literature is our concern, this activity tends to occupy an aesthetic context – whether directly, in that our own literariness is involved, or less directly (perhaps) in that the fostering of literariness among students is our objective. Now, I may have given the impression that criticism, for me, is a clear positive, associated in some ideal fashion with the experience from which literature springs, and to which it gives expression: a positive – and hence morally preferable – by whose means the negative influences of progress and learning will be combated. It may be true that progress implies an alien attitude; that learning, though certainly not so alien, gives a false emphasis: but is criticism other than alien, is its emphasis other than false, are its aims and interests identical with those of literary appreciation? Within the morally sensitive aesthetic context must not criticism, especially, be enquired into? – although, if criticism too were rejected, what literary standpoint capable of adoption within a university would remain? The relationship of criticism to literature nevertheless cannot go unchallenged.

Criticism, so far as it is unlike learning, differs from it by relying (to a large or a limited extent as the case may be) upon a modern response to older literature. The statement seems to me true as well as incautious. Criticism treats the past as being in some essential way accessible to the present: old literature is (a) largely self-contained, (b) largely self-sufficient, able to function as art unaided, despite lapse of time. Not that a learned approach is quite incompatible with subsequent aesthetic experience, though the mental preoccupation which is involved is all too likely to persist into an aesthetic hindrance: and not that a critical approach, in practice, is ever unindebted to some learning: on balance, however, a critically orientated approach has at least as much chance of coming to terms with art as a learned approach – at least as much chance, and therefore probably it has a better chance. The continuity of literary appreciation (I went into this at somewhat greater length in Chapter 7) lends itself to basic critical assumptions. Yet criticism and appreciation are not, surely, synonymous terms: they are not synonymous even though (perhaps more obviously) learning and appreciation are not synonymous either. What has to be considered is that criticism, apparently so unlike learning, is like it in one key respect. Criticism and learning rely on the same mental operation. They both think.

The word 'think' can without absurdity be applied to pretty well any mental phenomenon: when so used, however, it is felt to be used loosely. It is also applied, with more deliberation if still without much exactness, to one part of the mental totality, all the other parts being then ruled out, and indeed set in contrast. That was the sense, the more deliberate sense, in which I wished to be understood – criticism (like learning) thinks. However, there appear to be attendant suppositions. Thinking is regarded as a very superior mental activity possessed of organisation and awareness. From such a view I do not, in one way, dissent: yet the presence of these qualities in thinking seems to contribute to a down-grading of other mental activities, i.e. non-thinking activities, which in point of organisation and awareness are deemed deficient. Here my doubts spring up. Literature may have to be designated a non-thinking activity: the implication which then arises, however, seems in practice to be rejected. Critics obviously do not treat literature as inferior; for they are concerned to show how well organised it is. And yet, undeniably, this concern of theirs has to do with the fact that literature is not aware in the way that criticism is aware. To my mind (perhaps merely in my mind) confusion surrounds such points as these. Criticism is justified, or not justified, by the belief that its thinking activity is a worthwhile process somehow adding to or improving literature. Reluctantly, because the effort is considerable and probably futile, I must try to disorder this confusion by passing a few costive and ill-starred comets.

For the moment, though criticism and literature remain central, I set them aside in order to consider what thinking and non-thinking are like without the additional complication of language: what they are like when they occur wordlessly. As far as possible this state of affairs must be imagined. I don't know how far it *can* be imagined, since both writer and reader must necessarily be preoccupied with the verbal medium which is here employed. On the other hand there are more things in heaven and earth than the word; if we are to talk about them we must do just that – *talk*. In this imagined condition of wordlessness, not real now but no doubt sometimes real, thinking and non-thinking may still be compared as to status; organisation and awareness will still be relevant criteria.

How are we to describe the experience of a man rapt in a dream, or a man driving a car fast, or a man who loves his wife? I believe we would hesitate to say of any of these instances that they illustrate thinking – we would hesitate because thinking may enter into them, but we would be clear that their essential identity was not conferred upon them by their thinking element. Clear, at any rate, so long as we preserved a notion of thinking which left it more or less equivalent to powers of reasoning and analysis: and surely, if we adopted the alternative, looser definition of thinking, which leaves it equivalent to any mental phenomenon, we should merely fail in what we set out to do – characterise certain experiences sufficiently to distinguish them. Dreaming, driving, and love (I appeal to them merely as examples, and suggest, too, that the three activities are best carried out separately) do not involve much thinking in the stricter sense. That they involve or can involve highly organised states of mind I nevertheless find myself unable to deny. They are not organised in accordance with the principles which govern the organisation of thinking – this at least seems probable – but they are organised as highly. And what of awareness? Organisation and awareness may be quite different things – or, again, they may be the same. At any rate, I find I can't convince myself that the dreamer is *unaware* of his highly organised dream (if he is unaware of it, how can he be said to have it?), the driver *unaware* of the rapidly changing situation which he controls (if he were unaware of it wouldn't he crash?), the husband *unaware* of the wife of his bosom (why did he marry her, and does he not notice that his life is a married life?).

It is necessary to insist so much that non-thinking is or can be possessed of organised awareness, because the tendency of our language works rather against this idea. 'Meaning' – and other words of a similar kind such as 'knowledge', 'understanding' – seem somehow to assume and require the thinking context, or at any rate greatly to prefer it. We ought perhaps to realise that thinking is often feeble – we cannot pretend it has a high record of success: but so eager are we to throw in our lot with it that we concede the meaningfulness of non-thinking, if at all, only by allowing it to function in a sort of Indian reserve. We are partly right in this, hence wrong. We do it because we have no intention of letting non-thinking ever seem to challenge thinking. Of course non-thinking is different: but in terms of the generalisation *organised awareness* it is on a par with thinking. The real difference between them is found in the degrees of interior distancing or separation. I suppose I am really approaching the problem of *self*-awareness, as opposed to awareness of another sort.

Non-thinking is, so to speak, all of a piece. Its awareness is autonomous: the non-thinker feels no particular separation from the various perceptions of which, at that time, he is composed: their autonomy is his own. Not that he is merely the passive victim of whatever perceptually happens to him: on the contrary, his will seems more or less integrated into his awareness, so that there is a chance of managing and manipulating complex experience. Meanings assemble and connect flexibly for the non-thinker (I mean, for anyone who at a given moment is occupied with non-thinking): they are not subject to rule or system. The non-thinker and the meanings he perceives are at one, he is not separated from them: but the thinker is, being self-aware. Now, separation is not exclusively a characteristic of thinking, as I hope to show when I discuss language as a medium. It is not exclusively a characteristic, but it is a characteristic. Thinking is detached from that which it thinks about – and I am still assuming that thinking is wordless, so the special problems associated with language do not arise. The thinker feels himself to belong with the thinking activity rather than with its separated object. Awareness exists in two mental areas, halves of the thinker's mind. He locates himself in the thinking half, not in the (large) Indian reserve. If the image is liberal and enlightened, perhaps it thereby reveals a brutal alternative. Thinking aggrandises itself (and hence the thinker too) like conquest, enslavement, administration. The indigenous race is in some sense absorbed, and weakened as thinking is strengthened by the absorption, yet non-thinking retains some of its identity, dangerous, kept in check, made safe by a kind of intimate social distancing. The dominant and favoured system, i.e. thinking, has as it were taken over everything, nothing happens (or nothing much) which is not contained within its mode of operation. Thinking is a master-system, or so the self-aware thinker persuades himself, who is able to feel that he is master of that master scheme. He may enjoy an almost god-like sense of control; thinking is very open to pride,

which sometimes destroys intellectual people. Despite his identification with the thinking system, he perhaps believes that it has an
existence beyond him, in which case he is no more than a privileged
user; to be privileged is to be humble, as well as proud.

The notion that meaning is a matter of thinking, dies hard:
meaning is held to be *really* meaning, only if it is thinking meaning:
or, if there is other meaning, it somehow aspires to thinking; it is
non-thinking in itself, yet it may (thus showing its value) conduce to
thought. We may presumably consider if we wish the case of a man
who wonders whether to buy himself a hand-woven woollen tie.
He sees it in a shop window and likes it: he is caught up for a
moment in his awareness of a situation which is meaningful. One
could say that this meaning is the meaning of craftwork in our
society – to some extent hand-weaving is an absurdity, yet if it is
judged and found wanting from an industrial standpoint, it also
serves as a standpoint from which industry may be judged. One
could say that the meaning is the meaning of wool contrasted with
artificial fibres – this extends the former implications more widely,
includes farming, sheep-farming in particular, importance of sheep-
farming in the industrialised Britain of today, and in the Britain of
the past; importance of, in Australia; how Britain related to
Australia (a) now, and, in order to assess this (b) historically;
employment for sheep-farming communities, wherever; unemployment for fibre industries, wherever (Japan? implications for China,
for America?); unemployment, solving of, by buying tie – solving
of, *somewhere*; worsening of, elsewhere; cost of tie; personal financial
implications; not unconnected with broader financial implications.
Will other people admire the tie; what is the man's image of
himself; what is his social outlook, his sexual outlook; why are these
as they are; genetic considerations; environmental considerations;
etc. Such matters, one could say, are hardly subordinate to, because
hardly separable from, more obviously aesthetic issues: a tie, though
not the most complex of artefacts, is not the simplest either; issues
such as colour; whether more than one colour, and if more, their
pattern; gauge of strands and degree of finish; appearance of under-
side ('wrong' side); width of tie; taper or lack of it; length; square or
pointed end; sleeve form or single thickness; etc., etc.

All this one could say, but it would all be thinking interpretation,
and consequently a sort of translation, hence in some measure a

distortion. It would not actually be, though it might correspond with, what the man experienced as he stared for a few moments at the tie. My reason for rejecting the proffered meaning is not that it is heavy-handed nonsense. On the contrary, as a thinking translation it is credible. Nor am I merely adopting an anti-intellectual approach, whether with the support of bluff commonsense or emotional sensitivity. I am suggesting that awareness of the tie is different in kind, being non-thinking rather than thinking: but that the awareness is a meaning which, far from being unorganised, depends upon organisation entirely. Isn't the man just aware of the tie, says the reader whom I have paid liberally to ask this question. Yes: but the distinctiveness of his perception is itself a complete registering of meaning. It is a product of all the factors that have wrought upon it, a formulation of other things which, besides being what they are, have also become. We are dealing with meaning as effect, not cause. We do not apprehend the causes themselves in perceiving the tie, for they have changed their nature in realising their causative potential. We do nevertheless experience, even when our awareness is limited to the tie alone, a causal context which is gathered uniquely into the present. The perception is essentially, powerfully, and finally, itself, neither surrogate nor germinal: not the outcome of something more true though unknown, not something awaiting truer embodiment in another form, a thinking form. Nothing lies beyond it – in short it is simply the last word in neckwear. A thinking account renders causes: these (in the unlikely event of their being correctly assigned) reach out towards their effect in a meaningful manner, but not in a manner more meaningful than that in which their effect reaches back (though without overt specification) to them. Meaning of the thinking type, based upon causes distantly observed, is a complete meaning (ideally) and so is the non-thinking appreciation of effects a complete meaning. Whilst it is true that thinking, in knowing causes, knows effects too in its own fashion, and hence may seem to enjoy a double advantage – for non-thinking does not directly apprehend causes – yet doubt must remain as to whether any meaning which is complete is susceptible of doubling.

They have taken William of Occam's razor away from me, but I refused to give up the tie even when I came in here. I shall hang myself with it. Meanwhile I scatter a few more terms, like oaths. The tie, as an object seen, is invested with the light of the eye. It is literally in the light. Perhaps hardly distinguishable from this light is the mental light of meaningful perception, the tie is awareness, is form. I seem to have argued that the tie *becomes* from causal darkness, for the tie alone is perceived, and is the product of what has wrought upon it and been transmuted into it. But does not light enter causally, as well as darkness? This is difficult: one somehow has the sense that the eye's light, and mental light too, were already in existence, already there *before* the tie took possession of the attention, or *while* the tie was coming into meaningful realisation. One wonders why this particular tie acted as a focus of interest, other ties in the same window being (so to speak) seen and not seen. The light seems to have found out the special form which it can use – less interesting ties could of course be looked at, but the light of perception would be an inferior experience, not so meaningful.

Perhaps (who knows?) the basic condition for engendering meaningful new awareness occurs when causal darkness and causal light come together. These combine to produce what is both of them yet neither. The result of their interaction is not to be imagined a mere compromise between them, or discovery of elements held in common. The image of parents and child inevitably suggests itself: the child is a quite new being, nevertheless derives equally from both its progenitors. Unfortunately this image, or model, is rather misleading. Genetic conception is intricately physical, cellular: and presumably is unlike the conceiving of perceptions, which are mental phenomena. More important, since the defect occurs at the meta-phorical level, the image cannot show one of the parents as bodiless – as darkness. Has even the light parent a 'body'? Certainly the child has; being the new perception. It is difficult to resist a conviction that light implies or accompanies a kind of mental *somethingness*, infinitely diversified or generalised, whereas the dark is nearer to, though not, nothingness. The dark cause is striving for an embodi-ment which the embodied light cause seeks to change into. One would have to turn the sexual metaphor in some such manner. A better course might be to say that the light of new perception is caused jointly by *darkness* working towards light and form, and *light* extending itself into forms which also suit the evolving darkness.

The light which enters into apprehension of the single tie will already have some affinity, necessarily, with fact and form. It appears to have existence as well as potentiality, whereas the darkness is potentiality. Yet if the man is aware only of the lambent light of the tie, or grail: that is to say if the causes of the tie, including the light cause, are apprehended only in their effect: in what sense does the causal light exist separately for him? It has a status not unlike that of forgotten things, it may actually *be all forgotten things*, which can be remembered at any time, but which are not remembered now. Forgotten things lie in the darkness, they *are* darkness: yet theirs is not a darkness that has never attained to light. It seems possible to speak of causative light, but to locate it beyond the immediate field of attention. The word 'forget', however, normally implies mental failure – the question of failure in this case does not arise.

Of the huge number of forgotten things whose light exists in absence, some few will be causally important; though perhaps none will be totally irrelevant, in that all are of the light. Now, what if the man was *not* aware solely of the tie? When non-thinking prevails, our field of attention may often be large: it may include more than the one item of principal interest, or the focus of interest may shift from item to item within the field, or there may be some fixed distribution of interest among many items. In such cases additional light is present, perhaps in the form of things now *remembered*, perhaps in the form of *new perceptions*. There may be some degree of causal inter-dependence between the several components which make up the field: they may be contributing to each others' existence: each may be simultaneously a cause and an effect. Causes of this kind, though not specifically identified as causes by the non-thinker, are not in mental darkness at all, they are in full light. However, beyond these (and no matter how far the field of attention is extended) there will always be causes that *are* dark; whether dark in the sense of being absent causal lights, or dark in that they have never (until now in being causative) attained to light.

Awareness, as perhaps I have already implied, consists in its mediating function. New awareness belongs to light, and this is so for single or multiple perception. The light from the past which is in it – the causative light whose own existence likewise has something to do with darkness – is currently re-engaging with the potential of the dark. The causative light does not lose or give up its separate form – rather, this persists: the darkness has no form to lose: between them they produce that new form (in its totality it is new, though perhaps containing familiar features) which mediates them – a form in which each (the light, the dark) can be true to itself without being untrue to the other. Some people, opposing the notion of causal darkness, will presumably wish to argue that *all* the causes of new awareness must belong to the light, that light only was original, that mediation is between light and light. I do not believe the light of awareness, though original, was or is wholly self-evolving. On the contrary, I believe the growth of awareness is impossible without intervention from darkness.

Although the single, exclusive perception of the tie appears to differ from the broader non-thinking awareness of simultaneously grouped components, the difference is perhaps in some ways illusory. For one thing, how often is the field of attention truly identified with only a single object of contemplation? More important, is any object really single? And if every object is necessarily composed of a multiplicity of parts, does not this tend to a comparison with the multiplicity of broader non-thinking awareness? Both types of non-thinking awareness are wholes, the apparently confined and the apparently extended. Nevertheless I prefer to describe the latter as a second stage of non-thinking; despite the exaggeration of differences which is all too easy, some real differences do exist. Whether second-stage awareness is at issue, or (not inferior) first-stage, the organisation of non-thinking reaches between light and dark: within the confusions of the light an alliance can occur suddenly, made possible by, and making possible, a related alliance of potential occurring within chaotic darkness: a precise complex of causes is fixed through its effect, when all causes are mediated as only they can be, they only, by a form. Non-thinking's degree of meaning varies with the degree of organisation (as is the case with thinking).

Thinking is thinking *about*: it presupposes and needs non-thinking (which, by contrast, has no need of thinking). Thinking is a kind of third stage, in that an additional light-cause is introduced. The tie, single, seemed to involve no direct and separate perception of causal light, though this impression may have been somewhat deceptive: in another and possibly broader kind of non-thinking aware-ness, which I called the second stage, causal light was certainly present, but seemed to take the form of single perceptions which were contained within the whole. The first and second stages were homo-geneous. The third stage, however, is exposed to and dominated by

the light of system – a different light entirely, this, since non-thinking
is essentially unsystematic, its organisation being opportunistic and
transient; there is no demand made upon it to conform invariably
with a particular model of order already established. As a word,
'system' admittedly fails to express quite the meaning I wish to convey. Thinking is not exactly *a system*: it is the mother of innumerable
systems, or of partial systems, which can all be referred to principles
of reasoning. Even 'reasoning' may be too limiting an expression,
too inflexible. The best way of referring to that which results in a
well-recognised and characteristic *type* of organisation eludes me: I
must fall back on the idea that it is systematic in a certain way. In
thinking, then, the light of system plays its part as a cause, alongside
the light of the complete non-thinking perception which is brought
into contact with it: and this joint light-cause, together with causative darkness, gives rise to thinking awareness, thinking form, which
mediates all the causes. With regard to the darkness, in part it operates
through the non-thinking awareness which is being thought about:
that which lightened into non-thinking's effect is now among the
light-causes of thinking, and still works out the original dark
potential. But the light of system also connects with a different
darkness, in a sense its own special darkness; for the system must
once have mediated its causes, some of them dark, in order to exist as
light.

Thinking can organise itself in endless ways, but only in accordance with the system, i.e. in accordance with one set of principles.
It is not homogeneous with non-thinking; as we have seen the latter
is in large measure free to create different organisations *and also*
different principles of organisation. As long as thinking continues it is
characterised by a certain conflict – a one-sided conflict in which
causal system goes on winning; for the other cause of thinking is
non-thinking, whose modus operandi has to be continually dis-
qualified. I repeat, though, that thinking is of course a genuine and
powerful mediation of all its causes. The thinker *uses* that part of
himself which is the non-thinker. Does he? Self-aware, he rather
makes use of his non-thinking experience as something lying
beyond himself. *He* is the thinker. But I have dwelt on the two wordless categories long enough at least. How are they related to the
medium of language? I believe that language, like non-thinking and
thinking, is a mediating awareness. Many of the considerations bear-

ing on the wordless categories can be modified or developed to take in language.

Is there any reason why language, without further ado, should not be classed as thinking or non-thinking? – to have set up these categories in such a way that words are expressly excluded may be permissible, but it is another thing to justify the exclusion on grounds of reality. Now, one comes to see that language cannot be allocated to thinking (supposing the possibility of allocating it is admitted) only because it seems partly to be non-thinking: and vice versa: it seems to lie somewhere between, to be like both categories and hence like neither. Certainly language is comparable with word-less thinking to the extent that system is involved in each case: and thus perceptions that are verbal exhibit something like the typical third-stage awareness, in which system is separated from perceptions of another type, but nevertheless combines with them (and with darkness) to cause an effect within the system. Moreover, features of the language system can be selected and emphasised so as to enhance an affinity with thinking. The systems are comparable or perhaps they overlap, but they are not the same. It is this fact which makes for an alternative connection with non-thinking. Although the language system – being a system – aggrandises non-thinking to itself, it allows of something like accommodation. A language is nothing if not systematic, yet one has to say paradoxically that it is also a con-fused affair. It is many laws which conflict, yet which do not finally conflict, because the language can be used properly. It looks like, and is, a mass of accretions, the outcome of many necessities and many principles yet it is adjustable into order, is governable, governed, self-governing. The thinking system is sanctioned by one aspect of our humanity, and we have seen that language can be brought into a significant relationship with that system. However, the system which is language reflects aspects of our humanity besides thinking. Its innumerable observances allow some affiliation with wordless non-thinking. Language can organise itself in ways which owe little to rational process, there is an opportunity for freer form and meaning. The actual presence of words, of their system, works against full comparability, but I am inclined to admit a category of non-thinking language, as well as thinking language.

A verbal form of either sort mediates linguistic causes and other causes which are wordless: it mediates these various light-causes and also still others which are dark. 'Mediates': 'medium': the medium of language. Anyone commenting on the latter expression makes his way through an ever-familiar, ever-baffling maze, and I suppose is entitled to follow what route he pleases.

It seems to me that a verbal form (again of either sort) necessarily incorporates wordless elements, i.e. elements which are, or *were*, unlike itself. The verbal form is of course a particularised instance of the general language system: in claiming a transmuted wordlessness for the form, I am therefore claiming the same thing for the system. I am suggesting that even the linguistic cause of a verbal form contains transmuted wordlessness: and there are in addition wordless causes which lie outside the linguistic cause; for a man experiences non-thinking or thinking awareness, and desires to bring this awareness into contact with speech. Surely, language has always had to render the state of things beyond itself – things separate, yet not separate so far as they *are rendered*. To do this it has had to manipulate its unique nature, its difference from everything else, its speechiness. It has offered itself for training (if metaphor helps us here) but the fact that it belongs to another species of being has posed a problem, for all idea of copying the trainer is ruled out from the start (language cannot imitate the wordless states): not a dog dressed up in frills and pushing a pram, but a friendly genie who creates the magical fulfilment of a wish in order to make the wish known.

The genie did a little more than I expected him to when I rubbed the lamp. The causes of a verbal form always include both wordless and linguistic elements: their effect, being verbal, is an extension of language, an assimilation of the wordless (this at least is true of the more meaningful verbal forms): and yet the proportional influence of these two distinct sets of causes may seem to vary. I mean by this that non-thinking or thinking awareness (wordless) may be separately present in a highly organised way, as cause which is mediated into language. Alternatively it may not, it may be only slightly present, in which case the linguistic cause of the final verbal form will predominate. However, the wordless awareness which entered into the making of that predominantly linguistic cause (I repeat, entered into the making of the *cause*) finds its way also into the eventual wording: and because a verbal form can be accepted as the rendering of a wordlessness which is separately present, it can be felt also to render a wordlessness which is not separately present, whose transmutation only is present. The pursuit of words will lead us to the experience of a verbal form which might have been produced had we first pursued wordlessness; that is, had we attained to a significant degree of non-thinking or thinking awareness before attempting a connection with language. When, through us, the genie transmutes predominantly linguistic causes into verbal form, he saves us work of a wordless sort, perhaps even work beyond our powers: he is enabled to do this because, basically, our forbears performed that wordless work in the course of creating the generalised language system used by the genie. They did not perform it quite directly, however: the diffused totality of their wordless awareness, so far as it contributed to the formation of the language system, is explored by the genie's responsiveness to purely linguistic causes, and thus do we discover the result of our own wordless might-have-been, find out our darkness as light. For we have always to reckon with darkness – much that is dark enters into new verbal form, as into any form, verbal or not. Even the language system, though essentially of the light, comes only partially within the field of attention at any given moment: this light (quite apart from the darkness which has been transmuted into it) is therefore some of it 'forgotten' light, a kind of darkness. All causes of a verbal form are mediated (Refrain); light and dark, whatever the degree of light or the degree of darkness.

When we experience verbal awareness, are we self-aware? The answer to this question turns on the distinction which was made earlier between non-thinking language and thinking language. Yet what seems to be a possible answer based on this distinction must be firmly rejected. The answer is false which argues as follows: Thinking is self-aware, non-thinking is not, so thinking language is self-aware, and non-thinking language is not. We recall that the thinker identifies himself with a system. The system engrosses a separated variety of experience (viz non-thinking) and the process brings about self-awareness. Thinking language transmutes the thinking into something like a verbal equivalent: nevertheless language, which is a system in itself, is not wholly comparable with thinking – rather it has exploitable characteristics which allow but do not predicate the development of the thinking mode. My point is that the self-awareness of thinking language occurs not only because thinking is a system, but because language is a system as well: the two systems work together, although the immediate outcome is of course linguistic. In the case of non-thinking language only one system is at work, the language system, but it is enough. The operation of any system, engrossing a separated variety of experience, is all that is needed to produce self-awareness. Whoever is aware of non-thinking language is self-aware. His experience owes comparatively little to thinking, but his self-awareness does not fall short of that which accompanies thinking language. The two forms of self-awareness, each inseparable from the operation of the language system, are different in that the one has certain affinities with wordless non-thinking (despite the new element of self-awareness), the other with wordless thinking.

The question of self-awareness in the experience of non-thinking writing is especially important where literature is concerned: at any rate, criticism thinks so. Literature can be regarded as a highly developed version of non-thinking language: and one of the assumptions made by critics (I suppose) is that literature may fail to arouse a sufficiently self-aware response in the reader. It is difficult not to feel, in fact, that critics believe literature to be defective in this respect, although they choose to blame the shortcomings of readers: literature, they seem to say, cannot count on finding fit perceivers – for the only fit perceivers are self-aware critics. Surely criticism is confused here; I willingly grant that *some* readers may lack the fitness to perceive. Criticism supposes, mistakenly, that self-awareness can only be associated with thinking and thinking-writing. Apparently in order to introduce thinking into literary experience, which will thus become self-aware, critics have rendered literature into criticism. But literary experience is *already* self-aware, as we have seen, though its self-awareness has few if any affinities with thinking.

Now, criticism is also concerned with another problem, one that perhaps should be partly identified with the problem of self-awareness. I refer to the relationship between the public nature of a verbal form, and the private experiencing of it. With this same dichotomy the age-old notion of communication is involved – full of traps and pitfalls, especially where literature is at issue. Critics say that what is *there* in literature may not be what the writer saw: true, they sometimes argue from the author's 'intention', but on the other hand they often proceed as though they had concluded that a typical author is in a curious way not responsible for his actions, does not know what he is doing: a proof to critics that their activity is necessary, since they are rectifying the author's failure. But readers who are not critics are perhaps also aware of verbal form in another way than the author, though innocent of any desire to render literature in terms of thinking writing. As an explanation for the possible or probable divergence of experience between author and reader, therefore, the argument previously advanced – that critics are trying to impose a thinking type of verbal awareness on a non-thinking type – seems only valid up to a point.

The publicness of language is a materiality which exceeds private awareness; this is true of all language, but we can continue to have literature especially in mind. At one and the same time that it exists materially, and seems only thus to be complete, language exists as the interior awareness of individuals, without whom it seems to have no final reality: language is both more than the individual, and not more. Something of this I have already had occasion to mention (p. 32) – the subject seems full of obscure implications, possibilities. Language, perhaps, ought to be seen as the sum of language-in-use. Any one user – I mean here author – who makes sufficient contact with language is doing all that one person ever can. In not being the public, he is not failing: in not anticipating every legitimate reaction to the verbal form he produces, he is not failing. For these verbal forms of his will engage with people whose linguistic identity must be other than his own, yet in electing to utter publicly he is releasing the forms and detaching them from dependence on himself: he is relinquishing further control over them. The awareness with which the forms will come to be associated in different people cannot altogether be his, but this is not to imply that he produces the forms without awareness, without self-awareness, irresponsibly. The language he employs seems to him right at the time of producing it, he is conscious of exercising choice. I am not as it happens suggesting that only he writes well who is widely misunderstood. The creation of forms which involve complex verbal awareness cannot be accomplished at all, I believe, unless the complexity is potentially greater than it actually is for any one person; the road would not have led so far unless it led on.

Literature, which is non-thinking writing of a high order, has already done what criticism, as thinking writing, sets out to do for it.

Literature is in every appropriate way aware: its organisation beyond the author's awareness or any person's own awareness (including that of critics) is consequent upon the materiality of language, which makes literature possible. Criticism is superfluous, arguably.

12

However, I turn once more to discussion of *King Lear* in thinking terms, lest criticism should not be superfluous. I could have wished that the argument I turn from had culminated in something more decisive than that word 'arguably'. My arguments seem regularly to rouse a wayward force which, until I have reckoned without it, does not exist. Perhaps I hoped to show that criticism was a very inferior thing, yet I have hardly done as much as show that literature is not inferior. I have indeed come to believe in what it was found necessary to say, but the belief is of the peculiar kind which one can call unreal; as though it might all be a hallucination. If I cannot believe that criticism is actually necessary, I cannot deny that I hold a critical point of view: inevitably the latter is part and parcel of my response to the play. I have no power now to unremember my critic's outlook, the habit of years. I am bound to confess, as a smoker, that I cannot seriously contemplate giving it up. Of a truth, your pipe-smoking critic is the very flower and caterpillar of cancer in the bud. Unfortunately I seem to have chosen to organise my experience in the thinking way, by criticism, rather than in the non-thinking way, by literature alone. It is odd, is it not, that beset as I am by vacillation over the status of criticism, I should allege a structure of vacillation in the work which I criticise? For I pretend to discern vacillation in *King Lear* of a peculiarly positive sort: and vacillation, though of a pitifully negative sort, is a feature of life as I know it. My vacillation in the face of professional issues is a matter of concern to me, because it demands a structuring which I seem unable to provide: alternating beliefs conflict painfully and I cannot reconcile them into a new whole. It appears to me that the play, on the other hand, deals with the bogey of vacillation by establishing vacillation as a principle of control.

Lear, I think, is a morally ambiguous character. This does not mean, of course, that in him moral forces have struck a balance;

found a compromise; been averaged out. True, he is representative of fallen man, and inhabits a middle world between God and the Devil. But this is not inconsistent with the fact that good and evil are co-present in him: his ambiguity is a containing of moral extremes. A simple diagram of Lear's state might look like this:

GOOD

AMBIGUOUS

EVIL

All three terms together are his ambiguousness, the upper and the lower being comprised within the meaning of the middle one. In case anyone should object to the use of diagrams in this chapter, I undertake to make them optional, offering them simply as a gloss (perhaps helpful to some people) upon a verbal analysis which I hope could suffice alone. So I have just discussed Lear's ambiguity in a way which does not culminate in the necessity of the diagram. The diagram itself, on the other hand, is less than self-supporting – it requires assistance from the critique to make its modest contribution.

Although Lear's middle world, and ours, partakes of good and evil; *because* it partakes of good and evil; the King can choose a better or a worse course of action, by emphasising the good which is within him or the bad. Sometimes his choice goes one way, sometimes the other. No doubt he is intrinsically a variable character, but in practice he is surrounded by forces and circumstances outside himself which he must respond to: he is influenced not only by the extremes within him, which exist there in a state of connection, but by the same extremes beyond him where they are entities distinct from each other and apart. He may react favourably to a good force, align himself with it in a joint reaction against evil, or he may do the reverse, joining with evil against good. In the latter case, when he is associated with evil, he may be deceived into thinking himself good, and thus he will tend to imagine that true goodness is evil. When he takes up with goodness, on the other hand, evil will appear evil, and of course will actually be evil. Either way he will see much evil to oppose. In a diagram, one could depict Lear's middle state as before, and show on each side of him the good and bad forces which respectively influence him. Thus:

	GOOD	
EVIL	AMBIGUOUS	GOOD
	EVIL	

I have said that the external elements are distinct from each other. So far as the forces involved are supernatural, surely this is true in some final sense. But even under these circumstances much confusion can come out of the conflict between them: moreover we know that good and evil, though distinct and apart in their opposition to one another, are dependent conceptually, mutually dependent. What of the external influences upon the King which are not supernatural? Lear, possessing the general ambiguity of fallen man, is more particularly a man who chooses evil as often as he chooses good (though deluded by the belief that he always chooses good). Clearly he can be influenced by men who are better than himself, who choose good more often and more successfully than he does: and he can be influenced from the opposite moral pole, but still non-supernaturally, by men who are worse than himself. The supernatural and human influences tend to mingle: beyond Lear is the good man whose goodness, like Lear's own, finds its source in the external supernatural – and correspondingly there is the influential bad man, his evil supernaturally derived from outside himself, as is Lear's. Diagrammatically, the single terms on each flank, 'Good' and 'Evil', could become items in the same scale of human values which defines Lear in the centre:

GOOD

AMBIGUOUS	GOOD	
EVIL	AMBIGUOUS	GOOD
	EVIL	AMBIGUOUS

EVIL

Lear is morally fallen, mixed: and in this he is like all the characters who surround him, for they are human too. Some are good, I have suggested, as people go – better than Lear: some are worse. And one at least is neither better nor worse than Lear, but morally identical. Gloucester is ambiguous in precisely the same way. Influenced by his bad child he penalises his good child, then is himself penalised by the bad child. One could say that Gloucester's case is Lear's. Why are matters reduplicated in this way, why does the sub-plot exist at all? It seems somehow to exist for the benefit of the main plot. The King escapes his enemies when Gloucester has him conveyed away to Dover from the heath: the two sons of Gloucester, Edmund and Edgar, likewise modify the course of Lear's life, if less directly. The shaping of the main plot by the sub-plot is important – conduct of narrative is always vitally important. But Edmund and Edgar (perhaps more than their father) contribute to the main plot in another way than by influencing its narrative form. They provide a means for judging the King's behaviour. They sway our assessment of him. The brothers in the sub-plot seem to lend a meaning to his actions. Lear inflicts injustice and so does Edmund. Gloucester inflicts injustice too, one may say: however, his tyranny derives in a sense from Edmund, the primary inflictor. The King's crime can ultimately be referred to Edmund for this very reason, since only thus will it be seen for what it is, unmitigated and inexcusable, separated from our pity. The victim in Lear, on the other hand, can be referred to Edgar, the good brother in the sub-plot. Not (again) to Gloucester: Gloucester's victimhood, like Lear's, is complicated by the associated fact of his tyranny; this detracting from, or at least confusing, our pity. Edgar's victimhood is pure, and seen for what it truly is. So the goodness of the King is registered by a comparison with this brother, no less sharply than his evil is registered by a comparison with the other.

Now, when one considers either brother, one does not consider him merely as an isolated figure. One is aware of him as being a brother, aware therefore of his having a brother. And one is necessarily aware of the father whose sons they both are. In short, to concentrate on Edmund, or Edgar, or Gloucester, is in each case to be automatically aware of the other two, arranged in the family relationship. If Lear is associated in some respects with the evil Edmund, and in other respects with the good Edgar, one ought perhaps to identify the external human influences that bear upon him with those two characters especially. The left-hand column of the previous diagram would then be equivalent to Edmund – sufficiently human, i.e. morally ambiguous, yet thoroughly committed to the pursuit of evil: the right hand column would be equivalent to Edgar, human also and hence ambiguous, yet committed to the principle of good. However, I have urged that in giving our attention to either brother we invoke awareness of all three members of the family. I am struck by the fact that the ambiguity of Edmund, who is dedicated to evil, seems to be as it were shadowed out and completed by the remaining members of his family: and good Edgar's ambiguity is completed in a similar manner, though in reverse. If for convenience the previous diagram is set out again, another can be placed below it which is curiously similar:

(1)   GOOD

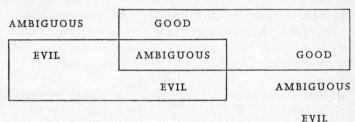

	GOOD	
AMBIGUOUS		
EVIL	AMBIGUOUS	GOOD
	EVIL	AMBIGUOUS
		EVIL

(2)   EDGAR

GLOUCESTER	GOOD	
EDMUND	AMBIGUOUS	EDGAR
	EVIL	GLOUCESTER
		EDMUND

Indeed it is less than surprising that a play's abstract moral organisation should be reflected and supported by the moral organisation of characters among whom the hero moves. There has to be a structuring of dramatis personae: it is a fixity which makes narrative movement possible. Not that a play's abstract moral organisation and its organisation of characters need be precisely identical; for there are innumerable compromises to which drama must adjust itself – which it can even exploit to advantage – in pursuing the art of stage illusion. Thus Gloucester and Edgar are subsumed within the evil of Edmund: but Gloucester and Edgar do not forfeit themselves wholly to the presentation of evil, their goodness is more than an adjunct necessary to show the nature of evil. In the same way, Gloucester and Edmund are not forfeit to the presentation of good, their evil is no mere adjunct to Edgar whose identity subsumes those of father and brother. The two alternative schemes are inherent in each other. And Gloucester, too, can be central: the realisation of his midway moral status requires the subsuming, into his own dramatic identity, of his sons. This latter circumstance, Gloucester's centrality, raises further points about the relationship of sub-plot to main plot. Since Gloucester is wrought into the structure identified, and since he is in a sense Lear's double, a natural course is to test whether the personages of the main plot fall into some comparable arrangement. Conditions similar to those which define Gloucester seem to define Lear. The characters nearest the King are arranged so as to render that interfusing of good and evil which we have seen constitutes his basic ambiguity. Who is Gloucester wronged by? – His son Edmund. Who is Lear wronged by? – His daughters Goneril and Regan, with their husbands. Whom does Gloucester injure under Edmund's influence? – Edgar his other son. Whom does Lear injure under the influence of his evil daughters? – His good daughter Cordelia, and also his liegeman the Earl of Kent. The hierarchy of the main plot, corresponding with that of the sub-plot, would therefore show Lear in the middle, Kent and Cordelia being morally above him, and below him being the evil sisters and their husbands. Perhaps Cordelia should be accorded a higher position than Kent, if only because of her remoteness from the hurly-burly of the principal action. For the Dukes, at present I assume that they are as bad as one another. (Cornwall, certainly, is unequivocally evil, but Albany is not. His case is of some interest and I propose to refer to it in a later chapter.)

And yet I insisted earlier that Lear is comparable with Edmund and Edgar. The parallel moral hierarchies which I have just described

emphasise again that he is comparable with Gloucester. Is there not a
conflict here between two theories, though separately these may seem
all right? We need to recall that, as an ambiguous character, Lear
already has in him the extremes which the brothers come to represent: in him the extremes are contained and restrained by the nature
of his ambiguity, whereas in the persons of the brothers the extremes
are separated and externalised (although, as I have argued at length,
the identity of each brother is humanly completed through the
father and the other brother). In equating Lear with Edmund and
Edgar we are not denying to him that ambiguity which makes it
natural to equate him also with Gloucester. By the same token it is
possible that Gloucester is comparable with the moral extremes
existing in the hierarchy of the main plot, although he still, like
Lear, remains ambiguous. For could not Gloucester, the inflictor of
injustice, be compared with Goneril, Regan, and their husbands, and
could he not, when injustice is inflicted upon him, be compared
with Kent and even Cordelia? If I were to express these points
in a further diagram, I would write the names of the main plot
characters in the place of the previous abstract scheme which represented Lear's ambiguity (adding Cordelia to the top who, in Tate's
once-popular version of the play, marries Edgar). I would retain the
sub-plot hierarchy in the same relative position as before; thus Lear
himself (assigned to the term 'ambiguous' – so to speak his central
category) would be level with Edmund and Edgar respectively, and
Gloucester would be level both with the good Kent, and with the evil
Dukes and Duchesses. Thus:

EDGAR   (CORDELIA)

GLOUCESTER   KENT

EDMUND   LEAR   EDGAR

        ALB./GONERIL – REGAN/CORN.   GLOUCESTER

                                     EDMUND

Gloucester is located in a moral hierarchy, so is Lear. Now although Gloucester, like Lear, takes meaning from his association with good and bad characters who belong to the hierarchy which is not his own, the importance of this fact is rather for the main plot than the sub-plot. For it is through Gloucester's varying associations that Lear's parity with Edmund and Edgar is manipulated. The King's likeness to the brothers must be distantly felt, and will actually be felt, because circumstances serve as reminders: e.g. Lear inflicts injustice on Kent and Cordelia, Edmund inflicts injustice on Gloucester and Edgar: Lear is banished by his daughters, suffers in the storm with Edgar, banished by his father. But these instances and many other basic reminders of circumstance need to be brought under control, and Gloucester is the chief instrument by whom control is effected. Whenever Gloucester is associated with Kent, and felt to be like him, a train of necessary connections is verified. For the similarity between the two men arises out of the fact that both are victims – Gloucester the victim of Edmund, Kent the victim of Lear: therefore Edmund and Lear are equivalent personages. That Lear in another aspect happens to be a victim, is not keyed in (if one may use the expression) by the Gloucester/Kent relationship. Lear's victim aspect is felt whenever an alternative and equally necessary train of consequences is conjured into being – this time by associating tyrant Gloucester with the evil Dukes and Duchesses, who are also tyrants. Gloucester tyrannises over Edgar: the Dukes and Duchesses tyrannise over Lear: therefore Edgar and Lear stand equivalent. Again it must be remarked that Lear's other aspect is not keyed in by this form of association – that aspect (i.e. the tyrannical) being summoned up by the association with Kent, as has just been seen. One may conclude, then, that Gloucester's leaning towards his own separated and good extreme in the main plot results in our connecting Lear (though he is not a worse man than Gloucester) with that bad extreme of the King's which is located in the sub-plot. And conversely, Gloucester's tendency towards the main plot's bad extreme makes us connect Lear (who nevertheless is no better) with the extreme in the sub-plot which serves to figure forth the King's goodness. These patterns will be evoked by the handling of Gloucester, whether or not Lear is present on the stage. Lear's status is assessed by what he is and does, but it is also in continuous adjustment from the sub-plot.

The ways vary by which Gloucester is associated with good or bad in the main plot. Often comparatively straightforward methods are used. The play's opening sequence, for example, consists of discussion between Gloucester and Kent. They are seen to be friends; and Gloucester specifically tells Edmund, when introducing him to Kent, 'remember him hereafter as my honourable friend' (I, i, 27–8). In Act II, scene ii, Gloucester comforts Caius (Kent in disguise) who is in the stocks:

Gloucester	I am sorry for thee, friend; 'tis the Duke's pleasure,
	Whose disposition, all the world well knows,
	Will not be rubb'd nor stopp'd: I'll entreat for thee.
Kent	Pray, do not, Sir . . .
Gloucester	The Duke's to blame in this; 'twill be ill taken. (152–9)

Of course, Gloucester does not realise here that he is addressing Kent. Nor does he realise it during the heath scene later, although he actually refers to Kent in the course of an exchange with Caius:

Kent	Importune him once more to go, my Lord;
	His wits begin t'unsettle.
Gloucester	Canst thou blame him?
	[*storm still.*
	His daughters seek his death. Ah! that good Kent;
	He said it would be thus, poor banish'd man!
	(III, iv, 165–8)

The castle of Gloucester is an important venue of the action; in it he receives Cornwall and Regan, is their host, and this broadly serves to emphasise his association with the Dukes and Duchesses who tyrannise over Lear. Interestingly, Cornwall's power is engaged by that tyrannical Gloucester who seeks the life of Edgar:

> Let him fly far:
> Not in this land shall he remain uncaught;
> And found – dispatch. The noble Duke my master,
> My worthy arch and patron, comes tonight:
> By his authority I will proclaim it,
> That he which finds him shall deserve our thanks,
> Bringing the murderous coward to the stake;
> He that conceals him, death. (II, i, 56–63)

Yet the manipulation of Gloucester, and through him of Lear, is often far more intricate than these selected illustrations suggest. The duality of Gloucester tends to become simultaneously apparent. Furthermore, the Earl's association with good and bad extremes in the main plot can be felt without explicit reference to those extremes: the associations are felt, and their implications for Lear are felt too. Form is exploited as if it were metaphor. I will analyse a single example – many readers will wish I had confined myself to rather fewer. In Act IV, scene i, 21–2, Gloucester apostrophises Edgar (whom he does not suppose to be present) thus:

> . . . Oh! dear son Edgar,
> The food of thy abused father's wrath.

The speaker is aware of himself as tyrant, destructive in his wrath. But also he is aware of himself as victim – he is 'abused', Edmund having deceived him (his blinding by Cornwall and Regan is ultimately associated with this fact). Now, the principle is established in the play that Gloucester's case runs parallel with Lear's. Therefore, when Gloucester recognises the two conflicting aspects of himself, Lear seems to 'recognise' the same aspects in himself: we don't exactly attribute thoughts to him in *absentia*, but we feel that the dramatic current which is carrying Gloucester must be carrying Lear. At the back of our minds, and properly only there, occurs an experimental comparison, which is absurd when made too explicit: we know, nevertheless, in some sense, that Lear might have been speaking rather than Gloucester – 'Oh! dear daughter Cordelia', he might have said, 'the food of thy abused father's wrath'. Through Gloucester, then, Lear seems somehow exposed to the knowledge that he too is tyrant and victim both. However, much more than this kind of comparison is conveyed by Gloucester's words. If Gloucester is a victim ('abused') so is Edgar a victim, the dear son of whom he speaks. We are familiar with the idea that Edgar serves as the good pole of the hierarchy in which Gloucester is situated: Edgar is the goodness within Gloucester's ambiguity: and Gloucester's goodness is represented, separate and externalised, by the main plot figure of Kent. It is to be expected that Edgar and Kent, the embodiments of Gloucester's goodness, will be connected together at times, and they are: e.g. at the death of Gloucester, narrated by Edgar in Act V, scene iii; or when Edgar (Tom) describes himself as 'whipp'd from tithing to tithing, and stock-punish'd, and imprison'd' (III, iv, 137–9) – Kent being then present, a listener, recently freed from the stocks himself. So it appears to be the case that Gloucester's community of interest with victimhood, community with his dear son, implies indirectly an association between Gloucester and Kent: implies, that is, one of the basic control-patterns which I have described. This in turn means that Lear, victim though he is like Gloucester, like Edgar, like Kent, is comparable with the Bastard. Lear is tyrant: and we have come to adjudge him tyrant *because* we see him, through Gloucester, to be a victim: in a peculiar way his victimhood establishes his tyranny. These induced perceptions are inherent in Gloucester's calling himself 'abused', and in his identifying one aspect of himself with Edgar. The entire process is operated in reverse, and almost simultaneously, through Gloucester's awareness of his own tyrannical 'wrath'. Edmund is the evil pole of Gloucester's ambiguity in the sub-plot hierarchy. He (Edmund) is closely associated with the evil Dukes and Duchesses in the main plot. So the community of tyranny between Gloucester and Edmund directs us towards Gloucester's association with Cornwall and the rest: this is the other basic association by means of which Lear is judged. In accordance with this pattern Lear is adjudged victim, despite his being no less a tyrant than Gloucester, Edmund, the Dukes and Duchesses: moreover, he is so judged precisely *because* of that tyranny which is suggested by the comparison with Gloucester. The overt content of Gloucester's speech, therefore, by the play's formal structuring, is given an immensely amplified significance. And similar exploitation of form is frequent in this play.

13

Dull stuff? Criticism of the worst sort. 'Laborious, heavy, busy, bold and blind.' Is there a worst sort? Immortal Dulness, Divinity! That thou exhibitest within thyself two extremes, the factual and the manipulative, I attempted to formerly, and in a different, though not altogether so, perhaps, context, shew. I sing criticism, aspect of learning.

At the time of the Ancients v. Moderns controversy, criticism was part of the province of scholarship: criticism indeed seemed to belong there more obviously than did philosophy and science, whose position was open to dispute, because their independence could at least be claimed. Thus, if early criticism could move on occasion in either of two directions, away from neutral ground towards philosophy or towards science, this was hardly more than characteristic of scholarship, which itself had the same divergent tendency. In our later age this situation has changed to the extent that criticism has acquired an independence of its own. It has become separated from scholarship. Nevertheless it has developed according to the nature of its original, and has matured the 'philosophical' appearance and the 'scientific', both of them present from the beginning. Apart from the tendency towards divergent extremes it has also, though independent, retained in another of its types a close alliance with evolving (if in some ways narrowing) scholarship, so that to speak of 'scholarly' criticism is likewise possible. All three types are found in English departments today; of course, the existence of the basic types does not preclude the possibility of combination.

Do I believe thinking writing to be pernicious in all its varieties? Sometimes I should like to believe just that, but cannot. At other times, quite inconsistently, I neither believe it nor want to. These efforts at evaluation should doubtless be dismissed, falsely generalised as they are from particular cases. A bad example of thinking writing (that is to say) is apt to arouse the first response, a good example the second. The writing in question, being a form of organisation, does it, one wonders, organise *more*? If it replaces weak organisation by strong, then the fact that the writing belongs to the thinking type has presumably proved to be anything but a disadvantage. This criterion is prominent in the evaluative process. I should like first to apply it not to criticism, but to those three branches of learning which were discussed in Chapter 7 – scholarship, philosophy, science.

Scholarship thinkingly investigates the facts of our human past. The statement is suspect? Human history (including of course language-history) is the main concern: perhaps only some kinds of human fact are investigated, and only in some of their aspects, perhaps the investigation bears on many facts that are not human; valid qualifications, I feel, invalid disqualifications. Now, the prime humanness of the facts is diffused or distributed through an incalculable number of individuals: further, in any society, forces develop which must be called characteristically human, which yet are not so characteristic, or are not characteristic at all, of the human unit – society is a man who differs from the men in it. My point is that the flux of history is never wholly equivalent to an organised state of mind in anyone: equally important, it includes the more or less organised state of mind of every historical person. There is of course a sense in which history is available to its contemporaries, the reason being that people are to a certain extent aware, thinkingly or non-thinkingly, of the situation in which they live and have their being: but there are as many such awarenesses of history as there are people alive at the time. Scholars, who look at history after it has occurred, or rather who look at parts of it, are better fitted in some ways, in other ways worse fitted for the task, than were contemporaries. Scholarly awareness, scholarly organisation, is not of course unanimous concerning the past – there are again many variant and conflicting views. True, some formulations win their way to general acceptance, are treated as though they were definitive accounts of the historical flux: nevertheless, the historical flux was certainly no complete manifestation of *understanding*, nor did the past evolve in accordance with any requirement that *understanding* of it should even be possible. At its best scholarship (which is scholarly awareness evolved into thinking writing) attains to an increased degree of organisation within the present-day context: the organisation being of human facts, among them the facts of prior human awareness (whether thinking or non-thinking).

In its own way scholarship partakes of the humanness which it organises into thinking writing. There is so to speak a double quota of humanity: and this, philosophy exhibits too. I don't mean that philosophy's abstract and speculative urge is to express the human imbroglio. I mean that, as with scholarship, the element of understanding is human, inevitably, and so is the material understood (here I exclude natural philosophy, which leans towards, perhaps is, science). Considerable differences of emphasis appear: perhaps these are more easily felt than defined, but I did attempt some discussion in the earlier chapter. Philosophy is less obviously factual than scholarship, or rather it replaces one kind of factuality by another. For outward circumstances and events are distanced and/or generalised. Likewise mental phenomena, whether organised or fragmentary, are detached from the context they originally occupied, the philosopher seeking to universalise them. This tendency towards abstraction is a matter of degree, not of sharp distinction: still, philosophy and scholarship do usually look very different. The apparently unfactual concern of philosophy (really factual, however) may imply and even demand a freer play of the philosopher's understanding: he is obliged to create order by clearing away confusing accidentals — or obliged to re-create it. The scholar has to deal with accidentals in another way altogether: he must understand time by being loyal to its manifestations, he accepts the limitations of what happened. Perhaps the philosopher, despite the appearance he gives of free understanding, aims to conform with reality outside (because greater than) himself, but I feel that the scholar is the more strictly bound — he is the more directly obligated to external evidence. Not that either philosopher or scholar becomes thereby the superior being. In their different fashions they both may produce from human material, by means of thinking writing, organisation which did not exist before.

The scientist. It is true, he brings about an increase of organised awareness: thus he is like scholar and philosopher together. It is also true that he feels bound to conform his understanding to realities lying beyond himself: here he seems, if not finally unlike the philosopher, much more like the scholar, being subject immediately to the demands of evidence. But he is concerned — I refer to the scientist who traces matter – with exterior realities, which are not human: in this respect he resembles neither philosopher nor scholar. Science, of course, has not confined itself to inanimate matter, but has taken account of physical life including physical human life: how far it has taken human mental life into account also, and human behaviour, is open to debate. Perhaps the study of these latter topics tends to look scientific when informed by certain of the attitudes which are most readily recognised in the work of material scientists, and tends to look less scientific when such attitudes are not enforced (in that case, however, effective study remains feasible). At any rate I feel that material science has coloured all that appears to be scientific: it seems to me not absurd, in fact it seems right, to base the meaning of the word 'science' upon the model of material science. The scientist, then, or the material scientist, presents the organisation of facts external to himself and non-human. The double quota of humanity, which I said was characteristic of scholarship and philosophy, is absent from his work; for the scientist's understanding is human but, supposedly, what he understands is not human. However, this is anything but a liability as regards the degree of fresh organisation which is achieved: the liability if it is one belongs rather to scholars and philosophers. Where they strive to understand phenomena that are grounded in humanity – phenomena infused already with other men's understanding, or connected (at least) with the faculty of understanding – the scientist takes credit for assimilating into a human context that which (barring a debt to fellow scientists) was never previously within it. Before the thinking writing of scientists there was no science at all, only nature beyond man. But human nature knew something of scholarship and philosophy before either of these existed. The achievement of science is thus impressive. The difference between nothing and something is more impressive than the difference between something and something more.

Even so, one is left wondering about that half-humanity of science. Inhuman things are assimilated by science into a human context, there is a great gain in organised awareness. But does the assimilation much *affect* the context: is the awareness which is within the context an awareness *of* the context? I thought it likely that an unprejudiced evaluation of thinking writing turned on one criterion especially: it seemed best to begin by asking whether the writing organised *more*. None of the three branches of learning is deficient in this respect. Perhaps science offers the best prospect of wholly new organised awareness, but the other two have their full capability. There seems to be no theoretical objection to any of these kinds – at least if the quantitative criterion alone is applied. Can this criterion however, should it, ever be applied alone? We try to assess the amount of organisation: the character of organisation does not pass unnoticed, and is actually quite as important. In other words a further criterion applies in the evaluating process – *organisational quality*.

I want to look briefly at the place of non-thinking in the three types of learning under review, and I am not sure that 'quality' is the best term for my purpose. The relation which any kind of thinking has towards non-thinking appears to me crucial, and therefore the quality of thinking is at issue: the more effectively the thinking relates to non-thinking, the better. At the same time I can see that I have retained some notion of quantity – the supposedly new criterion makes use of the old. Perhaps I could go on referring to quantity, though in an awkward and complicated way: the quantity of non-thinking which is present in the quantity of thinking. My intention, in speaking of quality instead, is to take the less confusing course. The thinking which is science has only a low quality as regards the absorption of non-thinking awareness. The scientist's non-thinking – the part of it relevant to his work – is restricted. He devotes himself to a task that does not bring into play the fulness of his own humanity, much of which he puts aside in order to concentrate on the properties of inanimate matter. The non-thinking experience, converted into his thinking system, is limited: and furthermore, by the nature of his pursuit, no human considerations are introduced from beyond, from matter itself, which he studies. No stimulus from outside, human in origin, acts upon the human writer: no human stimulus, that is to say, except the thinking stimulus of other scientists, whose involvement with non-thinking is as deficient as his own. Science in short, though occupying a human context, evokes the human context very little, and would probably be regarded as worse if it did.

Philosophy and scholarship are less open to objection of this sort. Their contact with that large part of human awareness which consists in non-thinking cannot, of course, be directly expressed. Like science, they belong to thinking. In order to avail themselves

of the advantages they aim at, they must forego all resources of language connected with the expression of non-thinking, and depend on
other resources more suitable. Nevertheless, thinking's contact with
non-thinking, if indirect, is inevitable – something besides thinking
must ultimately be thought about: philosophy and scholarship do
not fail where science (which does not entirely fail) has no wish to
succeed. For, first, the identification of philosophy and scholarship
with human concerns is likely to call forth in the writers themselves a
good deal of non-thinking awareness (more than is the case with
science and the scientist) and this will be duly transmuted into the
forms of thinking writing – some of it at least. Second, the subject-
matter which is in process of being verbally presented by philosopher and scholar (though not that which is being presented by the
scientist) is entirely human, contains elements of non-thinking
awareness – besides generalised or mass effects which may hardly
have entered the awareness of contemporary individuals at all:
the whole serving to enrich further the thinking writing which
assimilates it, to the full extent that such writing is capable of
enrichment. Thus although science achieves a quantity of new
organisation which is likely to be more spectacular than that of
either philosophy or scholarship, it is qualitatively less convincing.
Philosophers and scholars, organising humanity, organise their
own humanity. They do as much justice to non-thinking as thinkers
can.

Of the three branches of learning only scholarship finds a place
in English departments: philosophy is not entirely unknown there:
science is. Criticism shares the possession of the scene with scholarship. Now, although philosophy and science as such are not our
departmental concern, they have a relevance for us which is considerable. This is because criticism holds within itself the same tendency
to extremes which characterises scholarship. Scholarly learning can
move towards its extremes: in one case it will then have affinities
with philosophical learning, in the other with scientific learning: of
course, it does not *have* to move towards either extreme. These points
have been noted. At the beginning of the chapter I suggested that
criticism as a major category could be sub-divided into three
prominent aspects. It is legitimate to speak of philosophical and
scientific criticism, which represent the developed extremes.
Scholarly criticism is the remaining aspect, and it keeps up a direct

alliance with scholarship (middle-criticism in alliance with middle scholarship). We can properly look to the branches of learning for clues useful in understanding the corresponding aspects of criticism. The general category within which the more detailed comparisons occur is still that of thinking writing.

Although scholarship – literary or linguistic in a department of English – has its own long-standing identity, it is set apart from that branch of criticism which must be called *scholarly*, rather by a zone of transition than by boundaries and frontiers. As far as scholarship itself is concerned there are no issues peculiar to art, or they are un-important, or examination of them is not obligatory. Scholarly criticism, on the other hand, does examine issues peculiar to art – these being regarded as important (at least up to a point) and obliga-tory. But it examines them in the course of establishing a historical context for literature, and this is so even on the rare occasions when it examines them in a thorough-going fashion. Historical facts predominate, art is history. Around this kind of criticism orthodoxy gathers, as though the assumption were valid that of all criticism it alone belongs to seats of learning and to literature. Its influence has been widespread, perhaps because the historical character of literature cannot finally be dismissed. The scholarly critic, as may be supposed, is so far from wanting to dismiss it that he develops his thinking to accord with the supposed organisation of the past lying outside himself.

Artistic issues of a certain kind are paramount for the *philosophical* critic, who, without being anti-historical or unhistorical, is little inclined to yield the autonomy of his thinking to the shaping of past facts. He too, in his necessary way, has been and is influential within departments of English. He believes that the art of literature involves universal and permanent processes, which are so to speak illustrated in the literature of each period: he feels that in some vital sense the general in art takes precedence over the particular – a position not in-consistent with the handling of minutiae, since these may be general in their character. It will be clear that I do not mean by philosophical criticism anything that has to do with philosophy in literature. I mean speculative aesthetic enquiry. Principles are alleged which are supposed to clarify the naturr of literature – what it is and how it works. There is a sense in which philosophical criticism looks inward to literary experience: the approach may take history as its starting point, or assume it: a sort of direct method, notwithstanding the tendency towards abstraction.

Scientific criticism grew up alongside the other two: all three have their up-to-date versions. However, scientific criticism has turned aggressive, and whether for that reason or because of some inherent appeal which it exercises, it has become the dominant force today – at any rate it chiefly accounts for 'modernness'. Scientific criticism has a circumstantiality, a factual insistence: to this extent it may seem like scholarly criticism, and not like philosophical criticism. Yet in a sense the scientific critic regards the facts as belonging to himself, for he confronts them on a footing of immediacy: here he shows something of the philosophical critic's reliance on direct apprehension, where the scholarly critic treats facts as belonging to people of the past, through whose eyes he must see. I do not wish to suggest that scientific criticism lacks identity of its own (for the opposite is true) – merely that points of comparison and contrast cancel each other out in a curious way. The text, the actual work before him, is paramount for the scientific critic: his independent and close experience of it he believes he can shape to its every precise demand, he will conform to its nature exterior to himself; again like and unlike the philosophical critic, like and unlike the scholarly critic. 'He is responding freely, he is his own man, and should not pretend he is only the object he perceives', the philosophical critic might say of him. 'He is rendering this past object, but cannot do so properly unless he knows what the past was', says the scholarly critic. It seems to me that the scientific critic's reply is essentially as follows: 'I am not concerned with response, or rather I am concerned only with scientific response. Nor am I concerned about historical context, for the work stands complete in itself. This thing before me, this text, can be described and objectively analysed: it is a functioning entity, answerable to its own laws of being: it reveals what I discover.' The scientific critic treats literature like matter. The analogy, which is cogent, impels him to become a scientist: either that, or he sees no reason for not behaving as if he were one, though recognising the analogy for what it is.

Is the thinking writing of criticism, then, to be judged in its three main forms much as the corresponding forms of learning were judged, scholarship, philosophy, and science – all of them likewise examples, in their different ways, of thinking writing? We assessed

learning first by a quantitative criterion – how much new organisation, we asked, was achieved by the various types. Criticism, by this
criterion, must be deemed inadequate. True, thinking organisation is
produced, but this merely replaces a degree of non-thinking organisation as high or higher. It replaces the non-thinking writing which is
literature. Here criticism in general, then, is superfluous, and I have
said so already: it is equally superfluous in each of its types. Of the
three, however, scientific criticism is probably most damaged by the
application of the quantitative criterion, by reason of the high
implicit (or even explicit) claims that are made for it. The analogy
with matter allows the scientific critic to believe that he is achieving
an especially large amount of new organisation, bringing into human
awareness for the very first time that which formerly was outside it
and beyond it: however, he is actually dealing with literature, so the
confidence he has in his own usefulness is misplaced. The second
criterion which we applied to learning was qualitative. It was then
found that all types of learning were subject to the limitations of
thinking language, whose paucity therefore affects all types of
criticism too. But we found that scholars and philosophers achieved
nevertheless a certain breadth of humanness, because their own
human preoccupation and the humanity of the material they sought
to organise necessarily made an entry into the system of thinking
writing: scientists, on the other hand, failed to achieve it. From this it
may seem to follow that scientific critics are inferior: however, they
are humanly concerned with human literature, not less so than critics
who are scholarly, philosophical.

The scientific critic achieves qualitative success in the face of his
own assumptions. His findings, he supposes, are not derived from
the subjective operation of the work of literature within himself,
but from the work itself: he presents a thinking organisation as
though it were his, certainly, but not him. He assumes he is dealing
with external entities, external truths, which confer infallible utterance upon him. Literature is essentially a thing. That human awareness (non-thinking or otherwise) is somehow present, that it may be
creeping into his thinking writing from outside, such possibilities
the scientific critic would deny, just as he denies his own influential
subjectivity. By his objectivity and absolutism he attempts to rule
out the human element altogether: and this, though it may not
detract from his actual critical achievement (if criticism of any sort

can be said to achieve anything) makes nonsense of his know-all air. There is an element of self-deception in his carriage, of a particularly dangerous sort. He has before him an ideal of literary education which he holds to be true though it is false. He believes he contributes to the ideal: he recommends his methods. But these contribute in reality to another ideal entirely, the true one which he would call false. It is a curious situation, which obscures the relationship of means to ends: the possibility even arises, of educators endorsing the scientific critic's approach without realising that they share none of his hopes. What is appropriate to an alien and externalised goal (the understanding of matter) can lend itself by chance to the analysis of more human, more inward states of awareness. So far as scientific methods fail to do what they are best capable of doing, scientific criticism is viable, but that hardly seems a reason for pursuing it ever more intently. Much the same comment might be made about the science-inspired drive for efficiency and progress in education generally.

14

With all its shortcomings, its varying degrees of illusion, the great industry goes on: criticism is produced and criticism is consumed. It is a literary phenomenon. Is it literature's evil, embraced like pride persisted in with joy, that must turn to ashes? The question seems a flight of fancy, for we don't as a rule ponder criticism morally. But moral implications are probable on three connected counts: criticism first is a human activity, and the rights and wrongs of a case enter into most human activities of any magnitude; second, it is concerned with literature, literature in turn is concerned with morals, so for good or ill criticism has to do with morals too; lastly, it is supposed to function educationally – whether it does so must be adjudged by educational criteria which include, or else are included by, moral criteria. The possibility exists that criticism is evil. But, even if that were so, the evil might be necessary to good; in Shakespearean tragedies, after all, evil can sometimes appear not only instrumental in bringing about good, but can even be (because of this) an aspect of good itself, for the process of good's greater becoming is perhaps inherent in whatever was the precedent state of affairs. Such uncertainty as this, far-reaching as it is, must raise the further question of whether *resistance* to criticism is not more evil than criticism. Of course, the uncertainty (ought it to be there anyway?) is hardly tragic: tragedy belongs to plays rather than to university daily life. The teaching of English to students is no doubt quotidian enough, on the other hand we are not called upon to educate dramatis personae.

What are we to think, critically, about the end of the tragedy *King Lear*?

Through a principle of vacillation – a structural articulation which allows sub-plot to be matched to main plot in differing ways – Lear is connected both with the persecuting Edmund and the persecuted Edgar. These two characters are of course connected with one

another, directly, as well as through their father Gloucester. Eventually the brothers, who have symbolised Lear's two reciprocally
connected aspects, meet and fight: the outcome of the struggle must
have a bearing on, must indeed be centrally related to, the moral
situation of the King, although at the time he is not present on the
stage. I suggest that the death of the Bastard necessarily affects both
of Lear's aspects, by reason of the sub-plot's double reference. For
the death of the persecutor is the death of that Lear who is a persecutor: so far as Lear has been comparable with the evil Edmund, all
such comparison is now at an end, Lear is a persecutor no more.
Hence the alternative comparison, which can be formed between
Lear and the good Edgar, ends also: Lear in his persecuted aspect, his
Edgar aspect, no longer exists – not that Edgar is dead, who indeed is
triumphant, but Edgar-the-persecuted has ceased to be (ceased, with
Edmund, to be). The King's fundamental moral dilemma (tyrant/
victim) appears to have been solved through this climactic action
within the sub-plot: solved not only for the audience, but in some
real sense for Lear as well. The symbolism is so much a part of the
real situation of the King that it cannot be detached from the
assumptions we make about his state of mind – the battle, we feel,
must have some correspondence within him. Despite this, the working out of the sub-plot is not quite the same thing as the working
out by Lear of his dilemma. Indeed the brothers' duel, so brilliantly
dramatised in its own right, seems almost to steal a hero's struggle
from him. The King lives on, his conflict resolved without his intervention. What is left for him to do? – all that could be done having
been done for him in an affair involving others. It is as though
his destiny passes into younger hands, and he survives into the
new age, briefly. Perhaps all this is true: but the last great emotional
outpouring must still take place, when Cordelia's body is in his
arms.

It is possible that Lear who resembled Edgar-the-persecuted now
resembles Edgar-triumphant – Edgar how changed! The Bastard may
be said to have died because, ultimately, his own evil returned upon
him, though the death-blow was administered by his good brother.
Was the death, then, the result of Edmund's evil and Edgar's good
working simultaneously? I am inclined to think not. For in Edgar's
action we can recognise a classic instance of militancy – at once

necessary, successful, and deplorable. The hitherto meek Edgar was a
good man suffering the inflictions of evil. Unavoidably – and one
feels obliged to add, rightly – he killed the evil steward Oswald, who
was attacking Gloucester. The letter which Oswald had with him suggests to Edgar the full extent of his brother's treachery: and thus he
comes to plan his brother's slaughter. Edgar does to Edmund exactly
what Edmund, on the battlefield and beforehand, would do to him.
The Bastard may be self-destroyed by his own evil, but if so this evil
of his returns upon him *via* Edgar: Edgar is possessed of Edmund's
evil, at least in part, and is thus not a wholly good and separate force
tending independently to his brother's downfall. Supposing that
Edgar is good at all, he is certainly not as good as he was when he
suffered at the hands of an evil which sought to destroy him. He has
learned from evil how to behave. Retaliating upon Edmund, he has
borrowed from him an evil which he cannot be rid of – he has made
it his own. True he destroys Edmund, but does this diminish or
increase evil's empire?

   Edmund is destroyed by his evil returning upon him via his
brother: in some sense at any rate this must be the case, though unless
Edgar has turned altogether evil – surely improbable – there must be
another sense in which the Bastard's death is attributable to Edgar's
goodness. The goodness (can we call it that?) of militancy: contaminated though he is in his attempt to root out evil, Edgar no doubt
is a better man than his brother, who embraced evil in order to root
out good. Nevertheless one seems to have to say, almost perversely,
that so far as Edmund is destroyed by evil (his own, Edgar's) he
becomes to that extent good; for evil, where it succeeds, succeeds by
definition against good. He is a sort of victim, notwithstanding his
being also obscurely the tyrant before whom he falls. Edmund actually *forgives* Edgar (V, iii, 166): and Edgar, replying to his stricken
enemy with the words 'Let's exchange charity', seems to recognise
(though from an inherently good point of view) that if his brother's
conduct has been vicious there is something in his own needing the
forgiveness which Edmund can apparently offer. ('Exchange forgiveness with me, noble Hamlet', says Laertes before he dies.) Edmund is
charitable before he hears about Gloucester's death, which moves
him, 'and shall perchance do good' (200). This prior evidence may
be held to work against the idea that his good intentions are solely

I AM NOT PRINCE HAMLET

the result of hearing the tale. 'Some good I mean to do' (243): in a limited way the Bastard actually does die a good man, 'despite of mine own nature'. The good which Edmund means to do is the undoing of his writ on the life of Lear and Cordelia. The attempt fails with regard to Cordelia, and hence indirectly with regard to Lear. Perhaps the reason for this failure lies in the fact that Edmund's goodness is superimposed on him against his will: he does not want to destroy himself, but cannot avoid falling victim to his own evil, as that is enfranchised in Edgar. One should argue that Edgar's militancy is the triumph not of a greater but a lesser evil than Edmund's: militancy is potent because of the good in it: its qualifying evil confers on Edmund the status only of a semi-virtuous victim – his attempt at goodness fails.

Lear gives voice to many conflicting thoughts when he makes his final appearance carrying the body of Cordelia. These include at one point a poignantly unjust rejection of those about him – yet despite the derangement of his wits there is in this rejection an element of justice too, for Kent and Edgar are both of them militant men:

Kent	[Kneeling]	O my good master!
Lear	Prithee, away.	
Edgar		'Tis noble Kent, your friend.
Lear	A plague upon you, murderers, traitors all!	

                                                   (V, iii, 267–9)

Throughout his last speeches the King is responding in a variety of ways to the existence and the power of evil. Now, the fight between the brothers seems to leave him in something like the militant position, through the survival of Edgar: Edgar's victory, one could say, puts the case for anger favourably, and we realise that as far as Lear's anger is concerned it has deviously and indeterminately approached the 'good' category. Yet anger is not the only thing he feels. Overwhelmingly aware as he is from time to time of Cordelia's death by evil, he sometimes seems to see that angry militancy is dangerous. Perhaps he recognises, perhaps he does not, that 'good' anger is altogether too like bad anger. At any rate, although Edgar's militancy promotes that of Lear symbolically, we find no fixed or settled state of affairs prevailing: often the King is centrally committed to his

militancy: but at times seems intent on repudiating it; at times he
falls short of it, relapsing towards that other anger which he has
always been prone to display. So far as Lear near his end assumes
Cordelia to be dead – I had better stress the reservation – there is discernible in his random and agonised encounter with evil a hierarchy
of attitudes, in which militancy occupies the middle position. Starting at the top: (a) He feels himself extremely close to the goodness
which has been sacrificed to evil. Uniquely so; for he feels that nobody else understands or is willing to understand the enormity of
Cordelia's death. This failure of people to grieve is perhaps a form of
the evil which has brought the sacrifice about. Nevertheless, close
though he is to goodness, he cannot achieve union with it: his grief
declares a separation. 'Howl, howl, howl! O! you are men of
stones', line 257: and in lines 307–8, 'Thou'lt come no more/
Never, never, never, never, never!' (b) His yearning after goodness
does not begin and end with hopeless grief. He shows himself apt to
replace this response by another, which puts the yearning and the
grief at one remove, i.e. he is then at two removes from sacrificial
goodness. Militancy, in short, seems to him a natural and desirable
course. 'I kill'd the slave that was a-hanging thee' (274). 'I have seen
the day, with my good biting falchion/I would have made them
skip' (276–7). 'He's a good fellow, I can tell you that;/He'll strike,
and quickly too' (284–5). To the extent that this kind of reaction is
not one of heart's grief, he is among the 'men of stones' whom he
has elsewhere shown himself able to rebuke. (c) He can include
Kent and Edgar in the fierce general curse, 'A plague upon you,
murderers, traitors all!'. But, as we have just seen, he can also praise
them, and praise himself, for militancy. There appears to be no link
between the attitudes. That militancy may tend towards, may amount
to, murder and treachery, he fails to recognise; or if he recognises
anything of the sort, he yet does not feel guilty personally; by turns
praising and blaming other people's militancy, but always praising
his own. Is it true that he refuses blame, sees not at all that he is
cursable along with Kent and Edgar? Immediately after the curse he
utters a lament charged with overtones, 'I might have sav'd her' (270):
he *might have* opposed them all: conceivably guilt presses upon him –
that he did not save Cordelia because he, too, was a murderer and a
traitor. Such a guilt would register, even as it deplored, the evil anger
which masquerades as virtuous militancy. Militant Lear seemed to

stand at two removes from goodness – unless he was deceived as to
the nature of militancy, unless militancy is not good at all: in that
case he was at three removes. Fleetingly he may know this now. The
audience has long known it. To the extent that Lear's grief ap-
proaches remorse there is awareness of the terrible worst which was
in him, perhaps is in him still. A man in remorse knows his
own evil. Lear grieving is not I think quite prey to remorse. But the
near-identity of positives and negatives, here at the play's end,
may well suggest that in not being a prey to it he very nearly is prey to
it.

Positives and negatives of one sort or another do seem present
in profusion, but, as is generally the case in Shakespeare, they
are not contrasted in any permanent or stable manner. Contrasts
seem to be implied – contrasts obvious enough. Every contrast seems
about to be verified, only to shift into something other than itself
instead; the new form being partially related to that originally
implied, but in a way that often includes effects of reversal. Whole
sequences of new contrasts are sometimes developed from an
older contrast in the course of its being brought into association
with other parts of the play, which were not at first – apparently not
– involved.

'I know when one is dead, and when one lives', says Lear (260) as
he carries in Cordelia: a statement which turns out to be strangely
false, for he alternates several times between believing her alive and
believing her dead. I cannot accept the view that Lear is never really
sure of Cordelia's life. I can see, however, that his beliefs when considered together make up a pair very different in appearance from the
pair which is life/death. Life and death: these are equal and opposite,
they are mutually dependent, mutually exclusive, they comprise an
obvious duality. Lear's beliefs, on the other hand, though they seem
to partake of the life/death antithesis, or seem somehow as though
they ought to partake of it, are yet not equal and opposite. If they are
equal and opposite, if they comprise a duality at all, it must be of
another sort. Thus there is the conviction of his daughter's death,
total unqualified conviction: and there is the certainty of her life,
realised with the help of evidence so tenuous as to have virtually no
existence, such evidence which in any case is hardly more than con-
ditional. The relevant portion of the last scene extends from 259 to
311:

(Dead)	(Alive)
(1) ... She's gone for ever ... She's dead as earth.	(2) ... Lend me a looking-glass; If that her breath will mist or stain the stone, Why, then she lives.
	(3) This feather stirs; she lives! if it be so ...
(4) I might have sav'd her; now she's gone for ever!	(5) Cordelia, Cordelia! stay a little. Ha! What is't thou say'st?
(6) ... No, no, no life! Why should a dog, a horse, a rat, have life, And thou no breath at all? Thou'lt come no more, Never, never, never, never, never!	
	(7) Do you see this? Look on her, look, her lips, Look there, look there! [*Dies.*]

I believe the confusion is dynamic: not disintegration, but a modifying whole. Two principles seem to be partly identified, partly to be played against each other. The first principle having the urgency of life or death (is Cordelia alive, is she dead? – what is the *case*, irrespective of belief?) we are unwilling to reckon with the disturbing inequality, or different equalness, established by the second principle. Reckon with it we must, however. Rightly, we try to eradicate the difference which separates the two principles, seeking to impose on the second principle the obvious parity of contrast which characterises the first – we do all we can, although it cannot be enough. To Lear's scarcely substantial belief in Cordelia's life we give an added emphasis, which is designed to balance his belief in her death. She is alive: the slightness of the evidence, his hard-won confidence, these factors seemingly so negative make immensely poignant the momentary joy of the father. Doubtless it is enhanced by the audience's suspicion that she is actually dead; we cannot in theory know that she is dead, except insofar as this is borne upon us by her not reviving – we cannot know until our suspicion, our increasing certainty, is confirmed at the end of the play by Albany's general command 'Bear them from hence', and then we see Cordelia's body carried off. Our suspicion, in practice of course our knowledge, enhances the poignancy, but Lear's experience we feel is poignant too.

She is really alive, instead of being dead. Yet should not the opposite of grief (the emotion experienced alternatively) be unmitigated joy, as the opposite of death is life? The underlying contrast between these equal concepts (death, life) prompts us to reckon with poignant joy as a positive which balances the King's negative grief, though we realise that poignant joy is not joy. Perhaps unmitigated joy can never be attained: the opposite of death is the triumph of life, but the opposite of grief is not joy. Grief is a form of love, it is love deprived of its object. The true opposite of grief is a love which has gained its object. Does love ever gain its object, quite? Love still yearns which is not deprived into the state of grief. The very nature of love registers a separation from the object, a desire to be wholly united with it: that the loved person lives can perhaps never quiet love's longing, at least while self endures. There is a sense in which the extreme difficulty of perfecting, within the play, the real form of the life/death antithesis (the difficulty, that is, of arriving at a perfect knowledge) expresses the unfulfilment of love (expresses, that is, an entirely different problem). The difficulty of the achievement, when Lear brings himself to believe in Cordelia's life, conveys both wonder and relief that the achievement, fleetingly possible, has been possible at all. The union of love has happened, which never can happen: that wonder, that relief, register the inoperant law of separation. The human condition of selfhood is suspended, life has ended, Lear dies. The positivity of life has seemed to be set against the negativity of death, yet by a subtle dynamic – a balance and a false balance and a new balance – the positiveness of love is presented as death-like. In terms peculiar to itself drama has rendered the progress of love, taking as a starting point the question of whether the King's daughter is alive or dead. The closing phase of the play can be held to make apparent the hero's condition. He undergoes a transition, with all that it implies for the self, from one kind of love which is separation to another which is union. Cordelia is the object of his love, and her actual fate is a connected issue. Yet it is finally distinguishable from Lear's experience.

The consummation of Lear's love, then, is equivalent to his

death. The achievement is surely positive in comparison with the
deprived negativity of grief. Yet the only comment Lear makes which
comes anywhere near a description of this love is as strangely
formulated as it is deeply moving. If Cordelia lives,

> It is a chance which does redeem all sorrows
> That ever I have felt.   (266–7)

'Redeem' is not a word which has to be used in a religious sense,
even though it does figure prominently in Christian doctrine. Clearly
it carries no religious meaning here, for the redeeming of Lear's
sorrows is associated with Cordelia's life, whereas Christian redemption is associated with a *death*, that of Christ. And yet the simple
rejection of religious connotations, correct as far as it goes, hardly
seems satisfactory. And the reason surely is this: the word appears in a
context charged with moral overtones which are broadly Christian in
kind. A death *has* occurred. It is Cordelia's, not Christ's, but
Cordelia is a symbol of goodness, and what is more she has been
destroyed expressly by the forces of evil. Perhaps a Lear unswayed
by the conviction of Cordelia's life ought to have been saying
(prevented by despair) that her death redeemed his sorrows: perhaps
some such obscurely confused notion on our part makes us feel that
in a reversed way this is more or less what he is saying. A passage in
Act IV, scene vi seems to prefigure the later speech, so I suppose the
difficulties we face are real and not the result of Shakespeare's inepti-
tude. The mad King spoke of his death in terms of fulfilled love.
Then a Gentleman, commenting, referred the situation to Cordelia's
redeeming of nature 'from the general curse': it is difficult to see
the Fall as redeemed by anything but the death of Christ, although
the achievement is given to the living girl. In a way, of course, the
assumption made by the Gentleman is unimportant. However, it
becomes important, it reveals its implications, when Lear adopts the
same assumption himself subsequently. Here is the earlier passage:

Lear   . . . I will die bravely,
           Like a smug bridegroom. What! I will be jovial:
           Come, come; I am a king, masters, know you that?
Gentleman   You are a royal one, and we obey you.
Lear   Then there's life in't. Come you and get it, you shall
           get it by running. Sa, sa, sa, sa.
                                    [Exit running. *Attendants follow.*

Gentleman   A sight most pitiful in the meanest wretch,
             Past speaking of in a King! Thou hast one daughter,
             Who redeems nature from the general curse
             Which twain have brought her to.   (199–208)

That the word 'redeem' is used in an opposite kind of way seems
to me symptomatic of the play's tragic achievement. The moral
world of good and evil, as Shakespeare has demonstrated through
the medium of the drama, is one in which goodness is destroyed: evil
seems victorious, but, by a central paradox, it thereby does the work
of good. For evil's purpose is to destroy good, replacing it entirely,
but in the moment when goodness – still true to its nature – is overwhelmed, evil's raison d'être ceases, and evil ceases: by destroying
good, evil destroys itself, in accordance with the requirement of
good. Lear inhabits the moral world and has contributed to its processes. He is a creature of the Fall, which brought sin and death.
These, the Fall's consequences, can never be undone in mortal life, yet
the terrible sacrifice of good, if understood in the right way, will
ultimately redeem our state. It will not, of course, make man
innocent as he was in the Garden, but it will purge the sinner, who
can be purged in no other way. Now, the great sorrows which Lear
knows, he knows have to do with evil. But how far he recognises the
evil as his own, and how consistently, are points that stand in doubt;
though what is not in doubt is that he recognises the evil as his own
to some extent and on some occasions. Throughout the play he is so
to speak exposed to the possibility of full knowledge – exposed to
the enormous pressure of it, which always increases. Yet he never
reaches the point of being able to declare it, and, that he does not, is a
fact making for King Lear the tragedy. He recoils from the knowledge
of the Fall and its consequences, feeling on account of that knowledge a grief too great to be borne. He longs for the impossible
pre-lapsarian alternative. The old man reaches back to grasp again
the innocence of childhood, when the Fall unknown was yet to
come. 'Why should a dog, a horse, a rat, have life,/And thou no
breath at all?' (306–7): the answer would have to be that they are
animals, whereas Cordelia is an incarnate spirit dead for fallen men.
'Pray you, undo this button', he says like a child (309), and sees on
Cordelia's lips, impossibly, life awakening into Eden. By coming

alive she redeem.s sin and death for Lear, buys them back with
coinage of innocence, the wrong way.

It is hardly likely that the climax of the tragedy owes nothing to
its larger context. The climax involves an illusion – Lear's. Lear
throughout has been seen in close relationship with Gloucester. An
earlier climax in the play involved Gloucester's illusion – he thought
he was throwing himself from a cliff. Lear was to say

> . . . she lives! if it be so,
> It is a chance which does redeem all sorrows
> That ever I have felt.

Gloucester had said

> . . . If Edgar live, O, bless him!   (IV, vi, 40)

It is quite typical of Shakespeare that comparison should here be
falsified by contrast, and contrast by comparison: the double principle sets meanings in motion. Each of the speakers seems capable of
believing that his child lives, but Cordelia is dead, Edgar is not.
Under pressure from the truth Lear has always been likely to substitute illusion for knowledge: Gloucester equally: that is the imperfect
way in which they make contact with truth. In an abstract and simplified sense Lear and Gloucester are one person, mankind – if their
responses are the-same-but-different, this is because both men
together convey the human predicament and its possible attitudes.

Cordelia is dead by evil. Lear sees only enough of moral reality
to make him turn aside: and he turns instead to face despair. Turning
from that, he dies in the context of illusory life, his union with goodness being a reversion to the first-created love which characterised
man before he became a fully moral creature – before he became
mortal. The illusion of Cordelia's life, though a triumph of love
when contrasted with despair's separation, is yet comparable with
despair in that moral reality is avoided. Both reactions are finally
negative: the primary reaction, despair, seems the more negative, and
the love which opposes it, the more positive – but paradoxically the
despair lies nearer reality than the love, for it belongs to fallen man,
and Lear's fulfilled love does not.

Perhaps there is a sense in which Lear's conviction of Cordelia's
life is not, or at least need not have been, an illusion at all. I must be
supposed here to mean something other than I have said, since

Cordelia is actually dead. I am struck by the circumstance that Gloucester, who is also capable of believing in his child's life, happens to believe rightly. In that respect at least he is under no illusion, although he makes the same claim that Lear does. Moreover, it is by this belief, this faith, that he avoids the illusion that does threaten him, despair: in dramatic terms, Edgar acts as guide in order to prevent Gloucester's succumbing to despair. Lear's illusion too is despair: the faith he attains to (that his daughter is alive) harks back to his despair's illusion. A sanction for faith is apparently to be found in the fact of Edgar's life, whilst faith is apparently rendered absurd by the fact of Cordelia's death: yet what has faith to do with particular facts? Faith is general, is moral understanding, is not faith unless it operates whether Edgar and Cordelia are alive or dead. Two faiths are thus presented in the closing stages of the play, and two facts, but the tendency of these four elements taken together is not to expose faith's necessity to doubt, rather it is to insist upon true faith's necessity. From the point of view of the audience, the faith which Lear has in Cordelia's life when he dies is neither a triumph of faith nor a vanquishing of faith, for it is not faith. It is not true faith, for true faith only exists in reference to moral reality. Lear deals with despair by denying moral reality entirely and reverting to what has become the unreality of innocence, Gloucester deals with it by accepting moral reality to the full. Lear reaches his denial via anger, Gloucester's acceptance is patience. When Gloucester later dies united with goodness, his moral love is as actual as Edgar's life: no illusory first-created love for an illusory life; his patience, however, was not dependent upon his eventually discovering Edgar to be alive. Like Lear in some ways, but for different reasons, Gloucester reaches a state of moral being which human life is unable to contain. The joy Gloucester experiences is so to speak after humanity, the joy of Lear is before it.

It seems to me that Gloucester functions dramatically as more than a criterion enabling us to judge the hero's end. King Lear is wrong, but through his tragedy we know the tragedy which is the play King Lear. The moral reality, within which occurs the hero's poignant victory, his tragedy finally negative . . . this moral reality is itself tragic in a positive way. For it involves a faithful recognition that evil at its most destructive means goodness. The sacrifice of Cordelia is to be endured as an affirmation, without despair.

I end by tracing the role of Albany, which is not without interest. In the opening exchange, Lear's attitude towards the two Dukes, Albany and Cornwall, is discussed:

Kent   I thought the King had more affected the Duke of Albany
            than Cornwall.
Gloucester It did always seem so to us; but now, in the division of
            the kingdom, it appears not which of the Dukes he values
            most; for equalities are so weigh'd that curiosity in
            neither can make choice of either's moiety.   (I, i, 1–7)

After this hint that Albany and Cornwall may need to be separated, they are treated (in accordance with Lear's view of them) as a pair, just as their wives too form a pair. All four – the two men and the two women – seem evil. Three of them are evil, but from early on there are signs that Albany does not quite fit into the category apparently assigned to him. Somewhat feebly at first – even evasively – but gradually more strongly and openly, he stands out against the evil of the other three. When Cornwall dies Albany is freed from the pairing: he seems to break free of evil, although for a while he continues in an uneasy alliance with Edmund, who in many respects is equivalent to Cornwall. It is possible to feel that Edmund is also equivalent to what Albany himself *was*: the Bastard replaces Albany in Goneril's affections, as he also replaces Cornwall in Regan's. The role of the just leader is increasingly assumed by Albany. Where Edmund and the evil sisters have no scruples about making war on the invading French, Albany must review matters carefully before his integrity is satisfied:

> Sir, this I heard; the King is come to his daughter,
> With others whom the rigour of our state
> Forc'd to cry out. Where I could not be honest,
> I never yet was valiant: for this business,
> It touches us, as France invades our land,
> Not bolds the King, with others, whom, I fear,
> Most just and heavy causes make oppose.   (V, i, 21–7)

Inevitably, after the victory over the French, Albany and Edmund come to the point of quarrel – the fate of Lear and Cordelia is at issue. Edmund has taken upon himself to have them imprisoned. 'Sir,' says Albany, 'by your patience,/I hold you but a subject in this

war,/Not as a brother' (V, iii, 60–2). Albany's authority is in turn
questioned, by Regan directly, and indirectly by Goneril. The outcome is settled by way of Albany's formal challenge to Edmund,
which Edgar successfully champions. At the end of the play when
Lear has died, Albany seems to appoint Edgar and Kent as joint rulers
– unless he himself may be supposed to rule with the twain as a
third friend:

> . . . Our present business
> Is general woe. [*To Kent and Edgar.*] Friends of my soul, you
> twain
> Rule in this realm, and the gor'd state sustain.
>
> (V, iii, 318–20)

But Kent, too, is dying. Either Edgar rules alone – he has the last
speech – or he rules with Albany.

As the play proceeds, therefore, Albany moves by moral grada-
tions from worst to best; or at any rate, from worst to better, if one
assumes that the very best lies beyond the militancy of Edgar, Kent,
and Albany. In Albany, one might say, man's mixed moral nature is
spread out through time: yet the direction of the change also shows
man's good side prevailing. Now, because Lear's moral understanding also advances as the play proceeds – though erratically, and notwithstanding his final reversion to childhood innocence – Albany's
advance may seem to serve as a sort of index, a simplification of the
King's much more complex state. Originally (before the play) Lear
could apparently distinguish between good and evil, he preferred
good to evil though he was associated with both Dukes. The power
to distinguish has been lost, however, and at the opening of the play
good and evil, Albany and Cornwall, seem like each other – and
indeed, in dramatic terms they *are* like each other; Lear thinks of
them both as good. When the King begins to be harried his moral
discrimination improves somewhat – improves overall, one might
say – but there is much error and confusion, so that only very slowly
does Albany establish himself as *genuinely* the better of the two Dukes:
correspondingly, Cornwall comes to show as worse. Albany's support for the King against evil suggests a new discrimination, a
restoring of the time when 'the King had more affected the Duke of
Albany than Cornwall'. And, finally, Albany makes sure that the aged
man is invested once again with the full Kingship, which could not

be conferred on younger strengths, nor the name only retained, while life lasted.

Albany   . . . for us, we will resign,
              During the life of this old Majesty,
              To him our absolute power.   (298–300)

Lear's old Majesty has only one more heartfelt cry to make.

15

Matthew, xi, 28: 'Come unto me, all ye that labour and are heavy laden, and I will give you rest' (saith the Lord). Critical thought, and thinking about criticism, they are no lightsome burden. I am like a figure in a strip-cartoon, weighed down and more weighed down in every picture by a swelling balloon of verbal gas profoundly denser than air. I am enveloped – as in the guts of slaughtered animals, which pigs will eat. I am a whited sepulchre, my pretences are legion, full within of dead men's bones and all uncleanness. I am proud to be my own white elephant. Or, like a filthy rag-and-bone intellectual, whose pedestrian faculties bear the load of rubbish down the long rational miles, I sag, I shuffle, I stumble under my sacks, wander out of my wilful way – lost. I am Yahoo: or am I frenzied, tragic, right–wrong Gulliver, ignorant of his Swift? Am I, at times, a fool?

I am a critic, and Gulliver is of course a critic too, the author presenting him as a typical specimen of twentieth-century academic man in departments of English; thus much will not be doubted, save by a few habitual dissidents whose function is merely to illustrate freedom of speech. That Gulliver eventually turns against criticism shows ... hardly a change of heart, rather a determination to press home his principles. The critic merely outdoes himself. The fourth voyage makes this point most plainly – finalises it – although the other three voyages hint at the same outcome. After the mutiny of his crew (in the fourth voyage, to which I shall confine myself) Captain Gulliver comes to know the purely rational Houyhnhnms; God-like in mind but having the incidental bodies of beasts. He believes that he partakes essentially of their condition, he stresses his rational faculty, he identifies himself with the great system of reason, as does any aspiring critic. And yet he is putting forward a claim not altogether represented by the facts: some uncertainty attaches to his

rational status, and a confident manner does not prevent his inadequacy from becoming obvious. The trouble is literature. It would be
unnecessary for Gulliver to show critical prowess if literature were
rational: on the other hand, he has to assume that literature is not
irrational. Commitment to criticism is commitment to literature.
Gulliver the critic, to impress the Houyhnhnms, must prove that he is
like them both because of literature and in spite of it; an under-
taking which smacks of the impossible. Houyhnhnm literature sur-
passes ours, presumably is more rational, is not literature as we
know it – Houyhnhnm criticism does not exist having no possible
function to fulfil. In his tell-tale *desire to be* a Houyhnhnm, the critic
refuses to allow his literariness to seem a taint upon him. Gulliver
stands up for it stoutly, he can only make a virtue of it, otherwise he
concedes defeat; thereby he cuts a different figure from his Master (all-
reasonable). However, the more literature's identity with criticism is
insisted on, the less does literature seem criticism: it is neither
wholly compatible with the reasoning system, nor (perhaps because
of this) is it anything but separate – far from being interchangeable
with criticism it remains still itself. The critic moves backwards from
his goal. He manages to exult in success to come, but he may be
driven to know that success will never come.

Naturally Gulliver in his efforts to justify criticism allies himself
with European criticism as a whole, both because his claims will
then appear to be more than merely his own, and because he must
establish that he is not of the horrible Yahoo race, whatever his looks
may suggest. But when he realises that criticism is only Yahoo sophis-
tication, he has no alternative but to shift his ground: having claimed
to be a critic he must now claim not to be one: from all that is Yahoo
he stands apart, and declares himself a unique creature. It will be
obvious to everyone in his right senses, if to anyone, that Gulliver
thus passes into a more extreme intellectual state – the critics themselves continuing to occupy the position that was Gulliver's own
before he turned against them. In a sense he has not turned against
them. Rather he has done what they, by a false method, try to do.
They pretend to thinking and the rule of reason, but unfortunately
they involve themselves in literature, which is not finally amenable to
their plan. Gulliver believes that nothing less than total rejection of
non-thinking will enable him to trot like a horse. The original
dilemma remains, though, even after he has put so much of his

humanity from him. True, he can congratulate himself on being no
longer a critic: he is superhuman or more: and yet he is after all not
indistinguishable from the gods. He is in a sense curiously humble,
only because he feels that his true self is greater than himself. So
enormous is his intellectual pride that he is not blind to the justice
of his rejection by Houyhnhnmality, despite the fact that he has
repudiated affinity with critickind.

Pride enters deeply into selfhood. Often (by no means always)
it is the intellectual, thinking aspect of the mind which claims our
sense of identity. This is Gulliver's case to an extreme degree. He
excludes the part of himself which is not 'himself', because it cannot
be fully assimilated, nor its independence engrossed. He will stand
on his own two feet, feels himself strong, needs strength; refuses
sustenance. In the furious effort of selfhood alone he must find,
somehow, the strength to get strength. He becomes the dead weight
of his own thinking, the weight of his own dead thinking: falls
beneath the unbearable burden. The moment of supreme divinity
turns out to be a grappling with despair, since all his pride was a
false assumption concerning the nature of thinking. The critics are
dishonest enough to insist that they are gods because they are men:
if they seldom despair it is because, as men, they keep the strength
to keep trying to be gods, and the strength and the trying are a kind
of hoping. Gulliver's pride is worse, and the penalty is worse which
he pays. He is dishonest enough to insist that he is a god because he is
not a man. The critics unintentionally accede to a psychic reality
which Gulliver, truth-loving Gulliver, does all he can to evade. They
lay hold on non-thinking in their effort to convert it into thinking,
where Gulliver thrusts non-thinking violently away: critical activity
implies a state of productive contrast between thinking and non-
thinking. Gulliver cannot tolerate the foolishness of critical preten-
sions, but fails to realise that these (in themselves quite unjustified)
subserve a valid end. The pride of critics, so reprehensible, is not inconsistent with wholeness of a sort.

Critics flower in the Fall, that autumn which is yet humanity's
springtime. Consciousness, a brave showing, marks the onset of our
winter life and death. It is a courageous separation from unconsciousness, in one sense rebellious, in another sense independent and
responsible. With fallen perception is associated identity of selfhood:
a moral frame of reference is recognised, and, in this respect as in

others, knowledge comes. At the flowering-time of the Fall there is
much confusion over moral knowledge. Whilst it is the case that
moral orientation has become possible and necessary, the actual
discrimination between good and bad is subject to error – we have
become moral beings, but our judgement is unreliable. At first we
believe that evil is good, or are able to persuade ourselves that it is.
Later we may improve, or we may not: but even if we do begin to
see things more clearly we may persist in attitudes which inhibit
advance, we may continue under various mistakes as to the true
nature of good and evil: in particular, pride clouds our vision, for as
long as it exists it seems good. Strangely (in some respects) the early,
confused phase of the Fall is the most successful as regards human
achievement. Its energy, verve, resourcefulness, though corrupt, seem
rather incipiently than actually so. Confusion between good and evil
makes potent creatures of us, and the final destruction of ourselves is
unforeseeable. Autumnal springtime declines towards man's prosperous summer. Long-unwithering as chrysanthemums (bonny
plants) in pride of manhood proud critics think and reason: but
Gulliver comes to hate the Garden of the Fall. His reaction is comparable in certain ways with that of Lear or Gloucester. However,
where Lear seeks to deny the Fall by reverting to innocence, and
where Gloucester accepts it patiently while life lasts, Gulliver in
aspiration advances beyond our lapsed mentality to enter his own
heaven on earth. The disaster does not consist in his recognition of
evil in the critics. He sees clearly the corruption around him but will
own to none personally: it is in this that his disaster lies. In judging
himself he ceases to set beside good, evil; this process being impossible because he believes that in him evil has no existence. In other
words he is determined to avail himself of the status conferred on
him by the Fall – that of a creature whose innocence has become
moral being – yet at the same time is hell-bent on laying claim only
to goodness. He has no notion, as regards himself, that good is not
good unless in proper relation to evil, that good without the
presence admitted of evil is evil. To enjoy the good consequences
of the Fall he denies its ill consequences, suffering however only
those: or rather, in his death-like pride, enjoying only those; perhaps, indeed, he is more like Lear and Gloucester at the play's beginning than at its end. And Hamlet? – how does Shakespeare pursue and
explore the consequences of the Fall there? What I began I must finish

I AM NOT PRINCE HAMLET

at last, returning: to the state of man in Denmark, rotten as the doomed labour of rational criticism; a mode none the less of contact with the non-thinking which is literature.

But before I leave the satirist Gulliver to his fate at the hands of the satirist Swift, it may be worth while to deal with the flaw in my argument. The effort of the critics to rationalise literature seemed like an attempt to turn evil into good; their false confidence and absurd pride spoilt the good, although literature itself presumably stayed evil. And Gulliver's subsequent rejection of literature (when he ceased to practise criticism) was seen as a disastrous denial that evil had a place in his being. Surely literature is not evil! But quite apart from the critics and Gulliver there is Pedro de Mendez to consider, the Portuguese sea-captain who rescues Gulliver, and who so charitably provides for him notwithstanding our hero's ill-conditioned rudeness. Pedro opposes evil by forgiving it; and forgiveness is the wrong word if it suggests superiority. He forgives because he is not Gulliver's superior. He knows that Yahoo evil (non-thinking literature?) is unavoidably a part of our humanity, knows that human goodness depends first on acceptance of the fact. Undoubtedly Pedro de Mendez is a good man — and what he displays is right-thinking. Is not this Swift's message?

In a sense it is. And yet the patient captain could never have written Gulliver's Travels. Even Gulliver, who supposedly can and does write it, is so to speak the inadvertent author of a masterpiece against himself — as far as he is concerned he has written another book. Gulliver's Travels is not the product of good or bad human thinking, nor of any thinking, even the most Houyhnhnm-like. And it is certainly not produced by non-thinking of a Yahoo kind. The achievement of the actual author, Swift, runs counter to the apparently prevailing ideal of thinking as good consciousness — that ideal which Pedro lives up to, and which the critics and Gulliver betray. The book is good consciousness and non-thinking: literature. Now although the performance, like the message, tends clearly to good, the opposition between them sets up dangerous and fascinating uncertainties, possible and perhaps actual reversals of value. Swift is concerned with thinking as the ordinary mode of consciousness. What form such thinking should take, he explores, and the disaster of man's thinking ambitions. In the figure of Pedro the norm is realised. It is everyman's norm; or if it is beyond the reach of everyman, still it represents, Pedro represents, a sort of perfected commonness. The Pedro-message is calm. *Gulliver's Travels* as a whole is otherwise, anything but calm. It is wrested directly out of unconsciousness; brought into complex order at high risk of chaos; inspired, in the way that literature must be. Thinking is not more conscious ultimately than non-thinking, but it is more safely conscious, for it claims the continuity of system, does not endure flux, cannot. Swift favours the divine Houyhnhnms in one way, in another he is anti-Houyhnhnm (being their god-like opposite). The author who gave us *Gulliver's Travels* did not create right-thinking Pedro (that Dean-like figure) in his own image.

16

When I tried to discuss the possible madness of Hamlet I may have already begun thinking about madness in *King Lear*; that play may have influenced the points I made at the time concerning the Prince, as well as illustrating them. Or perhaps only when madness in *Hamlet* was confronted did critical ideas begin to take shape which had a bearing also on *Lear*: later, in the context of *Lear*, the ideas on dramatic madness were more fully developed.

I wonder how deeply I saw into Hamlet's enigmatic state. I seem to have realised, though surely not as well as I ought to have done, that Hamlet is brought into contact with the possibility of madness so as to raise a kind of felt query about whether he is in the right moral position. Near the end of the play the hero himself apparently passes judgement on his earlier madness, his sinfulness. It is difficult to think that the old plan to be 'antic' holds any place in the apology he offers Laertes before the duel:

> Give me your pardon, sir. I have done you wrong,
> But pardon't, as you are a gentleman.
> This presence knows, and you must needs have heard,
> How I am punished with a sore distraction.
> What I have done
> That might your nature, honour and exception
> Roughly awake, I here proclaim was madness.
> Was't Hamlet wronged Laertes? never Hamlet.
> If Hamlet from himself be ta'en away,
> And when he's not himself does wrong Laertes,
> Then Hamlet does it not, Hamlet denies it.
> Who does it then? his madness. If't be so,
> Hamlet is of the faction that is wronged,
> His madness is poor Hamlet's enemy.   (V, ii, 224–37)

The Prince seems not to be mad when he speaks these words: nevertheless, one is uneasily reminded of the occasion in Gertrude's
closet (III, iv) when he claimed not to be mad but used his mother's
'health' as a criterion of sanity. Either he was sound then, in which
case his apology to Laertes (referring ultimately to the death of
Polonius, killed by Hamlet in the closet) is suspect because a sound
act is now called mad and wrong: or he was then unsound, in which
case can one feel that the present speech to Laertes is necessarily any
healthier? – (if the moral condition of the person addressed does
have any bearing on Hamlet's words, one should perhaps recall the
imperfections of Laertes along with those of the Queen).

I doubt whether I had got far towards seeing that the reader or
member of the audience who contemplates Hamlet's madness as a
possible fact will experience mixed feelings about it. If Hamlet is
mad and therefore in the wrong he may be understood to embody a
principle of goodness strained out of its true nature by outside evil,
or (equally) he may be understood to embody a principle of evil
within himself. Lear is subject to this double interpretation, and
despite the immense differences between the two heroes, so is
Hamlet – at any rate on the assumption that he is mad; which
assumption, however, cannot be confirmed, neither can it be denied.
The possibility of madness keeps in commotion a multiplicity of
moral meanings. Hamlet makes his way back to Denmark from exile,
having escaped in the sea-fight on his way to England – the country
of the mad, so the sexton would have it. He agrees eventually to a
duelling match, but does so in an unaccustomed frame of mind,
lacking in angry bitterness or self-reproach, at once light-hearted,
even-tempered, and stoically aware: he seems not unwilling to oblige
the King, he does not mind being named as the King's man in a wager
which he will try to win for him. This is far from being the attitude
we have come to expect of Hamlet: perhaps now he is no longer
mad. Yet here, as elsewhere in the play, his condition remains
problematical considered by itself – an uncertain phenomenon of
even more uncertain significance. It has to appear like this, potentially anything, because the Prince lives in a flux of powerfully
conflicting forces which never attain stability. Notwithstanding the
fearful moral confusion that always threatens to become chaos, however, moral coherence of a rapidly evolving sort is effected by the
structure and movement of the play as a whole. The hero's moral

state is indicated precisely enough in formal terms if in no other
terms. It thus has conferred upon it the particularity of being
something, and by the same token is prevented from being anything else,
which with almost equal likelihood might have been realised from
the dangerous flux of potentiality. The tragedy's final phase emerges
out of and completes the structural implications of its first and
middle phases.

When vengeful Laertes returns home he first holds the King
responsible for Polonius's death. Subsequently he collaborates with
the King in a plot against Hamlet. But the plotters lose control of
events: Laertes is mortally wounded in the duel along with Hamlet,
who, before he dies, suddenly accomplishes the King's death also.
From what essential standpoint does Hamlet kill Claudius – is he
irrevocably confirming partnership with his father, or is this the
moment of successful rivalry? Whichever is the case (if one is), are
the moral implications as ambiguous as ever? Where does the
Queen's death figure in the outcome? – for she, she of all people,
does not escape.

'The point envenomed too!' – cries Hamlet when Laertes, in
extremis, reveals the truth. 'Then, venom, to thy work' (V, ii, 319–20).
He stabs Claudius: but Claudius does not immediately die. Presumably he would have died, since Laertes and Hamlet are doomed
by the same sword. Nevertheless he calls for help: 'O, yet defend me,
friends, I am but hurt'. Hamlet's response is to seize the poisoned
cup and force it to the King's lips. 'Here, thou incestuous, murderous, damnéd Dane,/Drink off this potion.' The potion, designed to
kill Hamlet in case the rapier-attack failed, has already killed
Gertrude. By itself it would certainly have killed Claudius. In
fact, either the sword or the cup would have killed the King, but
he is destined to die of a double cause. Perhaps ultimately it is
a single cause: even so, Hamlet inflicts death in two different
ways.

'Then, venom, to thy work.' What is the fated 'work' which
Hamlet commands to its fulfilment? In Act IV, scene vii, when the
plot to destroy Hamlet is being formed, Claudius says –

> Or with a little shuffling, you may choose
> A sword unbated, and in a pass of practice
> Requite him for your father.   (136–8)

Laertes will thus have his revenge, will confirm himself as the son in
partnership: 'I will do't', he says. But he goes on:

> And, for the purpose, I'll anoint my sword.
> I bought an unction of a mountebank,
> So mortal, that but dip a knife in it,
> Where it draws blood, no cataplasm so rare,
> Collected from all simples that have virtue
> Under the moon, can save the thing from death
> That is but scratched withal.   (139–45)

Laertes' poison, the vengeance-poison, originates from a mounte-
bank not from Claudius: one observes that Claudius framed the first
version of the plot, hence is implicated, but that the plot did not then
contain the idea of poison at all. The poison is Laertes' embellishment. The King produces an embellishment of his own a moment
later, and it calls for the use of poison too. However, the chalice-
poison belongs to Claudius himself; Laertes is of course implicated
in this further development, although the sword remains his primary
concern.

The duel between Hamlet and Laertes brings latent conflict to
a head. The meaning of the past becomes more meaningful. The
import of partnership and rivalry undergoes intense, rapid development. What the duel gathers up and intimates is projected towards
the tragic climax.

It is presumably beyond dispute that Laertes is a son seeking
revenge for his father's death, and this leads one to think in terms of
partnership; revenge and partnership, though, have long ceased to
appear automatically good. Laertes in his quest for revenge seeks the
death of Hamlet – the Prince is the person aimed at in the joint plot
with Claudius. Could another relationship than that of father/son be
in some way relevant? At the beginning of the duel Hamlet says that
he 'will this brother's wager frankly play' (251). And earlier he
seemed to describe a kind of brotherhood when he compared his own
case with that of Laertes:

> But I am very sorry, good Horatio,
> That to Laertes I forgot myself;
> For by the image of my cause I see
> The portraiture of his.   (V, ii, 75–8)

Laertes avenges his father's death: we ought to look carefully at the underlying realities which are subsumed within the son's act of loyalty. Is the sword, whose work is to revenge fathers, doing everything it might be supposed to do when Laertes drives its poison into his enemy? Undoubtedly Hamlet killed Polonius: in retaliating upon the killer, Laertes seems to achieve the kind of partnership defined for us by the Prince's own revenge situation. Yet Old Hamlet died at the hands of a brother – here was fratricide. The death of Polonius was caused not by a brother, not even by a member of that generation, but by a 'son'. Comparison is therefore imperfect: the object of Hamlet's vengeance is his father's brother, the object of Laertes' vengeance is his father's 'son'. At the very least, partnership as achieved by Laertes differs from partnership as we once understood it. The murderer of Polonius, however, did indeed commit fratricide by a remote structural analogy: if Hamlet ran his weapon through the arras hoping to reign incestuously with his mother, that is if he acted in rivalry, then he resembled the incestuous fratricidal King whom he would have usurped. We are familiar with the complications. Whatever the nature of the partnership actually achieved by Laertes – and surely he achieves partnership of a sort, morally sound or not – this hints at a rivalry in Hamlet his enemy; fatally wounded by the first use of the poisoned sword.

The emphasis given to revenge serves to obscure the changed circumstances in which revenge occurs, for our prior assumptions operate, seem justified because they are partly justified. We have looked at qualifications underlying Laertes' partnership and the rivalry of Hamlet which is called up by it. Looking at these qualifications again, we can make out that they tend in the direction of Laertes' rivalry and Hamlet's partnership. Thus the father who is in some measure Claudian and incestuous and evil, Polonius, is the father with whom Laertes wants to be identified. And Hamlet, whose sexual relationship with Ophelia might have led to legitimate marriage: is he not (via Laertes, via Polonius) like Old Hamlet the victim of Claudius? Partnership in the case of Laertes conceals something of rivalry, just as Hamlet's rivalry hides the element of partnership. The brotherness within the past reaches out.

When Hamlet wields the sword against Laertes it is put to use for the second time. There appears to be a complete reversal: the same basic arguments, turned round, apply. At the beginning of the duel

Hamlet was overtly a rival, covertly a partner, because he was pitted against Laertes, overtly a partner, covertly a rival: one might put it like that, or one might employ brackets to suggest the hidden side of each contender: the sword having now changed hands, Hamlet is partner (rival), Laertes is rival (partner). Perhaps, after a fashion, the Prince is revenged for his father's death, although his opponent never did that murder. He commits an action which could be indicative of his essential outlook; his mood being in any case not as light as it seems – 'thou wouldst not think how ill all's here about my heart – but it is no matter' (210–11). Unknowingly, he inflicts death with the sword of vengeance. This same ignorance, however, characterising the second use of the sword, bears on the reversal process in such a way that further meaning emerges; meaning not inconsistent, not altogether unexpected, yet still in some sense new.

It would have been highly misleading, if not absurd, to attribute ignorance to Laertes, who gave the first wound. He aimed to strike down his father's assassin. The loyal son was in a state of knowledge, consumed by knowledge of vengeance, possessed. Still, he was far from aware of the rivalry inherent in his action: rivalry has no place in the assumptions to which an avenger commits himself, it is accounted the opposite of revenge. But now, as regards Hamlet when he stabs Laertes: surely this cannot be seen as avenger's work, for he has no thought of currently fulfilling the role? Probably what we register most clearly is the immediate 'brotherness' of the duel, the junior brotherness of the contestants themselves: that which formerly went unnoticed because the revenge interpretation distorted our judgement, we now realise was visible all along. The duel we would willingly reckon no more than friendly strife, if we could, competition between brothers, rivalry (the word springs naturally to mind): that is the light in which Hamlet would like to regard it: but we are too well aware of fatal reality. Fratricide – we may call it such – is being mutually committed at the level of the younger generation. Laertes killed Hamlet for love of Ophelia (as Claudius killed Old Hamlet for love of Gertrude); he had a further motive besides – Hamlet had killed Polonius. For love of Ophelia Hamlet strikes back; his love, unlike that of Laertes, is legitimate, yet on the other hand Laertes had not killed Hamlet's father. Each junior brother is guilty and each is extenuated: can murder ever be extenuated? The compelling fact of the duel is before us, its meaning cannot be fully separated from the past. Increasingly, sonship becomes morally equivalent to, and is seen as, a complex relationship between brothers. It is Hamlet's relative ignorance which makes brotherness more apparent, junior and senior: yet the general sense of reversal, resulting from the sword's use by Hamlet instead of Laertes, enables us to feel at the same time that all this is latent in the idea of revenge. The reversal process is initiated, never completed: the new meaning which is brotherness takes its place, a full revision of the old.

Hamlet's position is perhaps hardly less ambiguous than it was when he killed Polonius (the accidental quality of that action, which could be regarded as purposeful, is in fact comparable with the semi-accidental killing of Polonius's son, except that Laertes is Hamlet's 'brother'). However, despite the ambiguity, Hamlet at the end of the duel more resembles Claudius than Old Hamlet, or so it seems to me. The same judgement would apply to Laertes for different (in a sense opposite) reasons. These junior brothers (notwithstanding that they poison each other) are neither of them unlike Old Hamlet, but I am saying that on the whole they are more like Claudius. Their sonship is no longer so dominant: that is the most important thing. Is not Hamlet's sonship still the central issue?

When he cries 'Then, venom, to thy work', and stabs the King, Hamlet seems to be putting the sword to its intended use. Although the word 'revenge' is not uttered, the poison calculated to revenge a father is being driven home. Moreover, Claudius belongs to the slaughtered father's generation, not to the generation of the son, so there is no confusion over the murderer's age: Claudius is the original fratricide. Still, the fact remains that the word is not uttered. In view of the changes wrought upon vengeance as an idea, one wonders whether the word could have been used – has it not become, within the terms of the play, an obsolete term? If Hamlet thinks he is avenging himself on Claudius he must be unaware of the emergent brotherness which has so altered the real meaning of his situation. He must be unaware that he is more like Claudius (who gave occasion for revenge) than Old Hamlet (on whose behalf it is undertaken): the prosecution of revenge being thus as pointless as a vicious circle; revenge impossible because it was always an impossible conception. How much does Hamlet know when he stabs the King?

Laertes knew he wanted vengeance, and to that end he allied himself secretly with Claudius: vengeance might be evil, but the

possibility produced in him no sense of inconsistency. Laertes seemed
Claudian to the audience because of this complicity if for no other
reason (other reasons there were, however). It comes almost as a
surprise to remember that Hamlet, too, is directly aligned with
Claudius. He fights on the King's behalf – just for the wager – yet the
earlier dark intrigue was not more striking than the openness of this
alliance: 'the King drinks to Hamlet': drum, trumpet, cannon.
Hamlet entered on the duel without knowledge – that is true in a
way, although his light approach was qualified by a deep oppression,
and he felt he was defying augury: and he remained in ignorance
while the duel was being fought – until after the second use of the
sword in fact. Certainly when he comes to stab the King he knows
more. The basic question reasserts itself, how much does Hamlet
know? I reject altogether that general view of the play which sees
him as a mere opportunist, who finds he has a chance to kill
Claudius at last and takes it. For such a view denies the Prince any full
understanding of his action – on this reckoning it denotes only
naïve revenge. By way of refutation one can look ahead to Hamlet's
dying speeches, where he hints at a greater awareness than he is able
to specify. He tells Horatio –

> Had I but time, as this fell sergeant, Death,
> Is strict in his arrest, O, I could tell you –

and then he breaks off the sentence (334–5). Again a little later he
begs Horatio 'to tell my story', distressed by the realisation that a
false meaning will otherwise replace the true one of which he is
aware –

> O God, Horatio, what a wounded name,
> Things standing thus unknown, shall live behind me!
>
> (342–3)

It is possible that these statements are conventional, in which case
they can hardly be held to establish anything. But another convention – an undoubted one, and much more powerful – works wholly
against the idea of Hamlet as opportunist; thus suggesting, even if
the passages quoted above are conventions lacking in proof, that
they reflect Hamlet's knowledge nevertheless. When a firm move is
made on stage to inform a character who has been in some ignorance,
he must be supposed to lose that ignorance even should the infor-

mation be sketchily conveyed. It is clear that Laertes before he dies (and just before the King is killed) informs Hamlet. The question of Hamlet's knowledge therefore involves Laertes' knowledge: perhaps it involves the audience's knowledge too, which may not be quite the same as Laertes' – the functioning of the convention blurs the difference if there is one. Laertes is no longer wholly deluded by the chimera of vengeance. His enhanced awareness is passed to Hamlet: if the audience's awareness is still greater, Hamlet may possibly be the recipient of that also. The Prince is informed. One has to suppose, moreover, that he is not a passive learner. What is discovered to him may serve him as a key to further discovery. For why should he be less able than the audience, than Laertes, to grasp at the meaning of events past and present? The Queen falls and dies:

Hamlet	O villainy! ho! let the door be locked –
	Treachery! seek it out.
Laertes	It is here, Hamlet. Hamlet, thou art slain . . .
	The treacherous instrument is in thy hand,
	Unbated and envenomed. The foul practice
	Hath turned itself on me, lo, here I lie,
	Never to rise again – thy mother's poisoned –
	I can no more – the king, the king's to blame.

(309–18)

I cannot other than believe that Hamlet is aware of his situation, aware of much of its meaning at any rate, when he strikes the King. I believe he is aware of it through the play's form, as is the audience. Where are the quotations to prove this? They are absent: a play's form, though verbally produced, does not have to include verbalisations about its own nature. I am far from wishing to imply, however, that anyone's awareness at the time of the sword's third use is fully achieved – my position is quite the opposite. As the play progresses, so it urges its identity formally: the pattern is always potentially more than it seems: awareness is always behind itself, hence ahead too. In short there is a process of development not yet complete.

The idea of vengeance is superseded by a far more complex idea which has been evolved from it, but the original is in some degree discernible and indeed alluded to in Hamlet's exclamation, 'Venom, to thy work'. He has been apprised of the terrible realities underlying

the duel: knowledge such as it is replaces ignorance such as it was:
he takes an instant decision and he acts. The poison, with its element
of Claudian brotherness, is thrust into the body of the King. Just
before this happens a connection is formed between the sword-
poison and the cup-poison (of the King's preparing) and thus a
further emphasis is given to the sword's Claudian element, which is
discovered to be stronger than it seemed and more important. Hamlet
is probably aware of the connection, and it has to do with his
decision. 'The point envenomed *too*.' Conceivably, just conceivably,
the point is envenomed *as well as* being unbated: that might be the
force of the word 'too'. Yet the Queen as she died declared herself
poisoned, having drunk of the cup: and Laertes, in the confessional
statement to Hamlet which followed immediately afterwards, spoke
of Hamlet's poisoning and his own and the Queen's in terms which
hardly precluded all these from partaking of the same treacherous
foul practice: the same blame – King's blame. The assault on the
King by the sword, then, gathers into itself something of the cup's
significance (a significance already inherent in the sword, and perhaps not altogether latent): much more likely that the word 'too'
alludes to this assimilative process. Hamlet's action with the sword
is inflected, one might say, by the cup, and is precursor to his action
with the cup itself: does that final assault on the King take on a
qualified meaning by its following upon the work of the sword
(completion, duplication)?

> Here, thou incestuous, murderous, damnéd Dane,
> Drink off this potion.   (323–4)

The cup of poison was prepared by a father for a son: but it is
administered by no father and drunk by no son (the Queen's case I
shall come to in a moment). It is administered by a son who thus
takes on something of the father's role: and drunk by a father who
thus becomes a sort of son. This mutual confusion of functions
leaves the two men in a state of equality, for each is composed of the
same mixture, part son, part father: they are 'brothers'. It is as
though the final phase of the conflict, the moral conflict, finds
Hamlet older or Claudius younger, so that they are like Old Hamlet
and Claudius, or even, perhaps, like Hamlet and Laertes. The drawing
together of the two generations into one gains support from the
manner of Gertrude's death (or else I repeat my error). The cup-

poison is designed to operate downwards through the scale of generations (the sword-poison is aimed upwards, at the father's brother): the cup-poison is designed to kill the rival son – thus Claudius will keep the incestuous sister to himself. But it is Gertrude who falls: by a sort of logic, the poison confers upon her the status of the younger generation, the son's generation. She seems his sibling. If her real age is still known, despite the logic of the poison, then Hamlet as her sibling assumes the mantle of the older generation, because of the logic of the poison. Apparently (the same kind of idea offers itself as before) Gertrude is younger or Hamlet older: in a sense each of these propositions is true. When the Queen drinks she is carousing to Hamlet, not to Claudius who tries in vain to prevent her from drinking: 'I will, my lord, I pray you pardon me' (289). Although incest with Claudius may be said to cause her death, incest with Hamlet is a kind of substituted cause. Since she exchanges the former lover for the latter, Hamlet is (in her intention) more success-ful than Claudius (but Hamlet in reply 'dare not drink yet, madam – by and by': I reserve discussion of his reluctance till later). Sibling-incest is the most potent – Hamlet becomes her brother. And Claudius her father? The two levels of generation tend to become one: Claudius remains her brother – rivalled by Hamlet, his brother and hers. So did Claudius, for love of Gertrude, rival Old Hamlet. For in this matter of the cup-death, Claudius's killing of Old Hamlet by poison should be taken into account. That first poison was poured into the ear, and it was not necessarily the same as the poison which Hamlet forces to the King's lips. Some difference can be discerned between them, since the one was for use against a brother, the other for use against a son. Yet Claudius prepared them both, and for reasons which in both cases concerned Gertrude. The two poisons are bound to be associated, to seem alike: and the other poison, the poison on the sword, bears affinity with these as we have seen. Hamlet's killing of the King by the sword first and then by the cup enhances the implications developed through the duel: sonship and brotherness are conflated into one thing, and it is brotherness. If the sword-poison had in it something of goodness, the evil of the cup is influenced towards goodness, possibly. On the other hand the evil of the cup may retrospectively influence the meaning of the sword – towards evil. It is difficult to see any sort of poison as good: difficult not to see the victory of the Prince over the King as Claudian.

And yet there is Horatio's elegy: but doubt has often been cast on it as a final summing up of Hamlet's moral position.

> . . . Good night, sweet prince;
> And flights of angels sing thee to thy rest!   (357–8)

Horatio may merely be voicing his own pious hope (it is argued) which the audience can indeed share, but which will not necessarily be fulfilled in the hereafter. The fallibility of witnesses is of course always possible in drama. If we doubt Horatio's conjuring of Hamlet into heaven (as perhaps we should) should we not also doubt Hamlet's conjuring of Claudius into hell? A Prince not fit to go to heaven might be mistaken in supposing his slaughtered victim damned. For it cannot be denied that Claudius is a victim, whatever his faults. On the other hand Hamlet is a victim too, dying, pierced by the sword, of which the poison may be the same as that in the cup, or may be little different. From the beginning, Hamlet and the King have been inextricably involved each with the other; their deaths demand to be considered together – so correspondent yet so opposite their fates.

Fratricide, which took place before the action of the play began, initiated the call to vengeance. Vengeance thus rises from a suspect source, the avenging son's role is suspect, although the only alternative which appears open to him is worse: less distinct from that worse alternative the role becomes as its implications develop, and morally the commitment to it becomes more desperate. The Ghost called for revenge in Act I, scene v, and retired with the words 'remember me': Hamlet passionately exclaimed –

> O all you host of heaven! O earth! what else?
> And shall I couple hell?   (92–3)

At the end of the next Act, Hamlet speaks of himself as being

> Prompted to my revenge by heaven and hell.

And later in that same speech, contriving the mousetrap play, he reflects:

> . . . The spirit that I have seen
> May be a devil, and the devil hath power
> T'assume a pleasing shape, yea, and perhaps

> Out of my weakness and my melancholy,
> As he is very potent with such spirits,
> Abuses me to damn me.   (II, ii, 602–7)

The Prince seeks to be convinced that revenge is good, but much later in the play another revenging son, Laertes, does not care whether it is good or bad, though he rather understands it to be bad. He confronts Claudius, IV, v:

Laertes	Where is my father?
Claudius	Dead.
Queen	But not by him.
Claudius	Let him demand his fill.
Laertes	How came he dead? I'll not be juggled with.

> To hell allegiance, vows to the blackest devil,
> Conscience and grace to the profoundest pit!
> I dare damnation. To this point I stand,
> That both the worlds I give to negligence,
> Let come what comes, only I'll be revenged
> Most throughly for my father.   (128–36)

By the end of the play the fratricidal theme is again recognisable; from revenge, which is fratricide's seed, has grown the plant.

Hamlet's eventual killing of his 'brother' Claudius is comparable with Claudius's act of fratricide earlier: one may have to accept this as true, but what is also true is that Hamlet's fratricide (assaulting the King) suggests retaliation by Old Hamlet himself (assaulting the King) – an idea apparently close to the notion of a son's revenge but crucially different. The moral problem of revenge derives from the brotherness of good and evil. A son's outlook is derivative: he owes duty and responsibility to a condition of life, the very nature of which leaves final duty and responsibility in older hands. He inherits a situation: is part of it: must develop it on his own account, yet in a way its essence lies always at one remove. All this is unavoidable, and also proper (so far as the prior victory of evil allows anything to be proper). Nevertheless, he must somehow enter upon morality's original. The brotherness of good and evil, their struggle, must be entered upon by the son free-willed. Only then can the father's cause be taken up, and it will be done not for the father but as the father: in reality, as himself. Hamlet's triumph apparently resembles a triumph of evil. And the reason for this is that his likeness to Old Hamlet does not make him unlike Claudius. The perennial problem of good's retaliation upon evil is acutely present. Good becomes evil if it militantly destroys the evil brother (who in some sense becomes thereby good) – fratricide is fratricide. True, Hamlet (Old Hamlet) seeks to destroy evil, not to bring about its victory, yet the assumption that fratricide can be justified and distinguished from unjustified fratricide comes under great pressure. The brotherness of good and evil, notwithstanding the permanent antithesis which subsists between them, is no straightforward matter – how unstraightforward, the play's form shows, and how inadequate is the simple assumption that good should retaliate. For all this, the feeling remains that militancy is morally preferable to evil committed by and for evil alone: fratricide in a good cause is *less bad* than fratricide in an evil cause. 'And flights of angels sing thee to thy rest'? At least Hamlet, though Claudian, may be better than Claudius; despite the King's being a victim; perhaps because the Prince is one as well.

The hero is Claudian in the way that Old Hamlet is Claudian: the son-who-is-his-father does not seem fully equivalent to the evil brother, the King slain. Or at any rate, full equivalence must not be allowed to develop. Is there not something to engage our pity in Claudius's death – 'O, yet defend me, friends, I am but hurt' – to which the Prince's fury is a necessary corrective? The King is a victim, and his evil is transmuted to goodness, transient goodness, deriving from Hamlet's act of fratricide. Surely Hamlet atones for his own evil by dying: indirectly the sword has made him the victim of himself, more indirectly still it has made him the victim of Claudius. These indirect causes of his death find a direct form in Laertes' deadly challenge: just as (perhaps one makes out that there is a reversal) Hamlet's slaying of Laertes is in some sense an indirect figuring of the King's direct death to come. Yet the 'brothers' Hamlet and Laertes, as soon as Claudius has fallen, come together through mutual forgiveness:

Laertes   Exchange forgiveness with me, noble Hamlet,
            Mine and my father's death come not upon thee,
            Nor thine on me!
Hamlet   Heaven make thee free of it! I follow thee . . .

                                              (328–30)

The King may be justly served, but Hamlet's victim Laertes is comparable with the King in significant ways (and the same applies to Laertes' father Polonius, he too being Hamlet's victim): Hamlet himself, who killed them both, has an affinity with Claudius, as well as an affinity with Old Hamlet which is not altogether different. The exchange of forgiveness brings into being a possibility, remote, experimental, retrospective, of reconciliation between Claudius and Hamlet. Its realisation is held fully in check: the King was justly served: Claudius remains and must remain the source of evil. For he is incestuous, and if Hamlet's Claudian quality allows him finally to be unlike Claudius it is because he, the Prince, has put incest from him, destroys it.

Hamlet's sexual attitude towards his mother, which enters so deeply into his slaughter of the King, seems to have undergone subtle changes. He draws back from her somewhat when she is willing to accord him the place of Claudius: Gertrude's willingness is implied by her offering the poisoned cup after carousing to her son, who replies, 'I dare not drink yet, madam – by and by' (291). He seems to think of her as damned by reason of that incest from which he has detached himself: 'Is thy union here?' he demands with ferocious irony, administering the cup to a Claudius whose future damnation he cannot question, 'Follow my mother' (324–5). Perhaps he merely shrinks from the knowledge of his own incestuous inclination, as he always has done when experiencing its force. His final utterance on the subject of his mother, however, suggests complete disengagement, which is replaced not by indifference but by judgement and pity both. 'Wretched queen, adieu!' Those haunting words are his only comment on the death of a woman who has hitherto obsessed his imagination. There is no explicit moral evaluation, though I feel that moral evaluation of some sort enters into the sentiment. Is Gertrude seen as deceived and erringly human rather than wicked on principle? Does Hamlet, through pity, pardon her? – thereby pardoning, changing, his own sexual self? The farewell to his mother comes directly after the exchange of forgiveness:

Hamlet   Heaven make thee free of it! I follow thee . . .
          I am dead, Horatio. Wretched queen, adieu!
          You that look pale and tremble at this chance . . .
                                                              (330–3)

No mention at all is made of Ophelia. Yet at the level of his own generation the exchange of forgiveness with the alter-ego Laertes cannot but shake into a new ordering Hamlet's attitude to her; for upon her the quality of his dealings with Laertes have finally depended. Here it is difficult not to over-affirm. The exchange of forgiveness, and the farewell to the Queen, hint at a new kind of relationship between Hamlet and Ophelia, which is sexual as well as moral, hence comparable with the love of Old Hamlet and Gertrude. The Gertrude of incest is condemned, pitied, left, in order that Old Hamlet, namely Hamlet, may be the true husband of her, namely Ophelia. But all this is born only into the death of life. Perhaps it increases Hamlet's chance of heaven, despite the murder he committed before the change took place.

One feels that another element could be important too. Hamlet says, summoning the last of his strength –

> But I do prophesy th'election lights
> On Fortinbras, he has my dying voice.   (353–4)

Horatio's elegy to the 'sweet prince' follows in the next speech. Immediately after that, Fortinbras makes his martial entry. The hero's death is indeed strangely mingled with the triumph of the Prince from Norway. He it is who prospers, alone among the three sons in the play. Like Hamlet, like Laertes, he is touched by the urge to vengeance – a sort of vengeance at least: on the battlements of Elsinore, at the time when the Ghost was first seen, a strict watch was being kept because of hostile measures against Denmark. Horatio explained:

> . . . young Fortinbras
> Of unimprovéd mettle hot and full,
> Hath in the skirts of Norway here and there
> Sharked up a list of lawless resolutes
> For food and diet to some enterprise
> That hath a stomach in't, which is no other,
> As it doth well appear unto our state,
> But to recover of us by strong hand
> And terms compulsatory, those foresaid lands
> So by his father lost; and this, I take it,
> Is the main motive of our preparations,

> The source of this our watch, and the chief head
> Of this post-haste and romage in the land. (I, i, 95–107)

Our assessment of Hamlet's actions and death must pay due attention to Young Fortinbras – he is part of the tragic meaning as a whole.

I ought to say here that the reader's dissatisfaction may not exceed mine. I have been doing my best to think clearly and write clearly about the play's closing phase, but I acknowledge that the results are not everything they might be. The question is, what might they be? I am not trying to avoid blame when I assert that expository writing, thinking writing, is ill-adapted to describing literature when literature operates at the highest pitch of imaginative (i.e. non-thinking) complexity. I am not trying to imply that clear expository writing devoted to very complex literary effects is impossible: I am only wondering about the adequacy of that clarity. And if the clarity should also happen to be of great thinking complexity (as well as being thinkingly clear) I am still wondering about its adequacy. Critical coherence is not altogether the mark of critical success. My own failure need not be excused, and I make no disingenuous plea on my own behalf: yet one may be defective, and rightly be censured for it, whilst having reason to insist that even under better direction criticism could only be less of a failure, not a success. The critical march through this part of the play is ambushed, mines blow, bombs fall from nowhere, machine-guns open up on all sides; Shakespeare must have been a soldier in the lost years. We are exposed to the multiple effects of dynamic formal meanings, and this makes demands on criticism which cannot be met, even by overstraining sequential and analytic resources superior to those which I possess. Thinking is too unlike non-thinking.

*

The Fortinbras who takes charge at the end of the play and presumably becomes Denmark's next King, is very different from the unauthorised adventurer of the beginning. His courage and activity are the same, but as time goes on he becomes more respectable, more ideal. In IV, iv he 'craves the conveyance of a promised march' across Denmark against the Poles. Hamlet, who at that time is being dispatched into exile, sees the expedition, enquires about it of a captain, speculates, and then passes into soliloquy. His leaping thoughts are not easy to follow, but his attitude seems deeply ambiguous. On the one hand he feels the futility of the new war (as indeed does the captain, who told him – 'We go to gain a little patch of ground/That hath no profit in it but the name'; 18–19). 'Two thousand souls and twenty thousand ducats', observes the Prince, 'Will not debate the question of this straw!' (25–6). Of course he is not content to leave the matter there. He seems to suggest that the war (war-like aggression in general, perhaps) is a result of prosperity at home, and that death by war is really caused by some older (and inevitable?) condition of the life beforehand. I find the idea difficult and disturbing, and I shall return to it –

> This is th'imposthume of much wealth and peace,
> That inward breaks, and shows no cause without
> Why the man dies. . .   (27–9)

On the other hand, and notwithstanding the negative view he takes of the war, Hamlet notices positive features which seem to him if anything more important. He admires the vigorous efforts of Fortinbras, which 'spur my dull revenge'. The long soliloquy, of which the following is an extract, is all directed to the achieving of Hamlet's revenge:

> . . . Examples gross as earth exhort me.
> Witness this army of such mass and charge,
> Led by a delicate and tender prince,
> Whose spirit with divine ambition puffed
> Makes mouths at the invisible event,
> Exposing what is mortal and unsure
> To all that fortune, death and danger dare,
> Even for an egg-shell. . . . Rightly to be great
> Is not to stir without great argument,
> But greatly to find quarrel in a straw
> When honour's at the stake.   (46–56)

By IV, iv Young Fortinbras has become, therefore, a 'delicate and tender prince'. He ceases in fact to be disreputable in II, ii when Voltemand returns from his mission to Norway with news which, summarised, amounts to this. Old Fortinbras (who succeeded to the Norwegian throne after his brother's defeat by Old Hamlet) ordered

at first the suppression of his nephew's levies, having mistakenly supposed them destined for Poland: Young Fortinbras showed himself
willing to acquiesce – moreover, rebuked, he promised never to
repeat his attempt against Denmark: this submissiveness and this
promise were so gratifying to the old bed-ridden King, that he has
now commissioned Young Fortinbras to retain the levies and use
them *actually* against Poland, supplying him with funds for the purpose: Voltemand brings back with him a polite request for passage
over Danish soil. The response of Claudius to all this is: 'It likes us
well' (80).

Young Fortinbras, compliant to his uncle's commands – indeed,
obedient ultimately to Claudius himself – seems to stand in some
contrast to Hamlet. Yet one feels that this difference can be accounted
for by the differing situations of the two nephews. The hostility of
Young Fortinbras was necessarily directed at Claudius, the reigning
monarch, but he was concerned with the wrongs done him by Old
Hamlet:

Claudius   Now follows that you know, young Fortinbras,
           Holding a weak supposal of our worth,
           Or thinking by our late dear brother's death
           Our state to be disjoint and out of frame,
           Colleaguéd with this dream of his advantage,
           He hath not failed to pester us with message
           Importing the surrender of those lands
           Lost by his father, with all bands of law,
           To our most valiant brother.   (I, ii, 17–25)

One has to say of Old Hamlet that he is, or was, a 'Claudian' figure
to Young Fortinbras, despite all the difference made by lack of family
ties, and despite the mutual treaty drawn up by those first comba-
tants, Denmark and Norway. For Old Hamlet killed a 'brother' King,
who was Young Fortinbras's father. So far as revenge alone was
aimed at by the son (as opposed to revenge *and* *redress*) Claudius has
proved to be on the side of Young Fortinbras – having in fact
destroyed the object of revenge already, Old Hamlet. Thus the
switching of the attack to Poland is the outcome not just of obedience
but of a situation subtly different from Hamlet's own; obedience is
easier for Young Fortinbras, and more natural. Hamlet's Claudius,
defying vengeance, still lives.

Nevertheless the fact that Young Fortinbras is so to speak morally instated during the course of the play, and that this process brings him into a kind of alliance with Claudius (who permits the passage of Norwegian troops across Denmark) sets us pondering the question of the King's good aspect. It seemed he might have one, transiently, when we considered him as Hamlet's victim. The question may be more general, not applicable only to the end of the play. Actors often convey the impression that Claudius has a good side, whether they intend this or not. Others play the part in such a way that anything good about Claudius is seen to be merely his hypocrisy. I have never seen a production in which Claudius is denied even the semblance of goodness – I doubt whether an approach of that sort could be successful. On a political level the King is simply too king-like. He holds the fate of Denmark, and despite evidence of national unrest he wields his authority convincingly: his procedures are sometimes hardly distinguishable from those of a wise and just ruler – this is true, for example, of his handling of the Norwegian crisis. Of course, the interests of the state are now his own, and self-interest is made worse by the nature of the self that is interested, whose domestic morality is founded on murder and incest. Yet even here there is some extenuation (not enough) because he can suffer remorse. Hamlet might have taken his revenge pat. His decision not to do so (in one sense, perhaps, anything but a decision) sets the revenge ethos in its ugliest light, and this may direct some of our sympathy to the lonely suppliant who needed to pray so much.

> And what's in prayer but this two-fold force,
> To be forestalléd ere we come to fall,
> Or pardoned being down? then I'll look up. . . .
> My fault is past, but O, what form of prayer
> Can serve my turn? 'Forgive me my foul murder'?
> That cannot be since I am still possessed
> Of those effects for which I did the murder;
> My crown, mine own ambition, and my queen;
> May one be pardoned and retain th'offence?
>
> (III, iii, 48–56)

Claudius is not without some genuine kindness, and this shows in the way he treats Ophelia when she is mad. Strangely, his feelings for Gertrude, at least as he expresses them himself, are less vicious than one might suppose from the tale Hamlet tells of them. Are these feelings for her, which he reveals to Laertes apparently with reluctance, wildly removed from what we might recognise in another man's case as love? – Laertes is under the impression that the King behaved too leniently towards Hamlet after the murder of Polonius:

Laertes   . . . but tell me,
             Why you proceeded not against these feats. . . .
Claudius   O, for two special reasons,
             Which may to you perhaps seem much unsinewed,
             But yet to me they're strong. The queen his mother
             Lives almost by his looks, and for myself,
             My virtue or my plague, be it either which,
             She is so conjunctive to my life and soul,
             That as the star moves not but in his sphere
             I could not but by her.   (IV, vii, 5–16)

In point of fact Claudius had arranged for the death of Hamlet in England, and he is now with some skill manipulating Laertes' anger. Still, his words seem more like Hyperion's than a satyr's – here one recalls that passage in the earliest soliloquy, spoken by Hamlet in praise of his father:

             So excellent a king, that was to this
             Hyperion to a satyr, so loving to my mother,
             That he might not beteem the winds of heaven
             Visit her face too roughly.   (I, ii, 139–42)

It is possible that Claudius has some real goodness in him, alongside, or beneath, or above (however one wants to put it) the undoubted evil. Yet one may certainly talk about his *appearance* of goodness, whether this represents reality or not.

The audience will recognise a dreadful irony in the King's acting like a substitute Old Hamlet towards the Prince. Royal benevolence is displayed publicly:

                     . . . think of us
             As of a father, for let the world take note
             You are the most immediate to our throne,
             And with no less nobility of love
             Than that which dearest father bears his son,
             Do I impart toward you.   (I, ii, 107–12)

Is Claudius conscious of being hypocritical? He may be: if he is not, perhaps he is all the worse for that. Hamlet himself feels the irony keenly. Indirectly, but with as much openness as he dares, he rejects the relationship which Claudius seems to offer: when Claudius requests him (virtually commands him) not to go back to Wittenberg, the Prince takes care to agree only with his mother, who has made the same request.

Hamlet	I shall in all my best obey you, madam.
Claudius	Why, 'tis a loving and a fair reply,
	Be as ourself in Denmark. (I, ii, 120–2)

Hamlet never ceases to reject Claudius: nevertheless he is *also* drawn into something like acceptance. In Act V he consents with very little objection to play the King's wager for him, although he might have been expected to feel and show resentment – I drew attention to this on another occasion.

| Hamlet | Sir, I will walk here in the hall, if it please his majesty. It is the breathing time of day with me. Let the foils be brought, the gentleman willing, and the king hold his purpose, I will win for him an I can, if not I will gain nothing but my shame and the odd hits.   (V, ii, 174–8) |

Hamlet is not of course wholly the King's man: if some degree of highly qualified acceptance has developed, this evidently abates nothing of his rejection, which exists concurrently. In any case, is Hamlet accepting Claudius as Claudius? Is he, perhaps, accepting him as though he were Old Hamlet, in the manner indicated earlier by Claudius himself? If the latter – which indeed is hardly likely – then the continued rejection of Claudius, to which I have referred, may have in it some element of rejection for Old Hamlet likewise. It is difficult to discriminate between acceptance and rejection, all the more so because it is difficult to decide who is being accepted or rejected. Sometimes Hamlet's apparent loyalty to Claudius late in the play is the effect of total irony. He sends the King a letter, for example, announcing his arrival back in Denmark: it has the appearance of service but – as Claudius would guess and the audience is well aware – none of the substance.

High and mighty, you shall know I am set naked on your kingdom. Tomorrow shall I beg leave to see your kingly eyes, when I

shall, first asking your pardon thereunto, recount the occasion of
my sudden and more strange return.   HAMLET   (IV, vii, 43–7)

On the other hand sometimes he wavers, is less than committed to
irony – he may not believe in it much when he agrees a second time
to take part in the duel:

> I am constant to my purposes, they follow the king's
> pleasure.   (V, ii, 199–200)

The voyage to England – that strange episode which is like an active
hiatus between the play's middle and last phases – dramatises the
forces at work (or perhaps it does). Not without reason, describing
the voyage, does the Prince tell Horatio –

> Sir, in my heart there was a kind of fighting
> That would not let me sleep.   (V, ii, 4–5)

When Hamlet is on the high seas, one could argue, he is the captive
son-in-partnership, doomed to death by rivalry. Yet if his heart is
given to partnership why does he resist the pirates, why does he act
with the crew of the vessel which holds him prisoner? I would be
prepared to count the pirates on the side of partnership, disreputable
as it has now become in many ways. Hamlet does not willingly suffer
release from the spirit of rivalry to which he seemed opposed –
instead he opposes the pirates, gives battle aboard their own craft.
They break off the engagement, taking only Hamlet with them
(IV, vi, 15–20). He has been freed from the old imprisonment but
now experiences unwilling imprisonment of another sort: his heart
is so to speak Claudian, but he is held captive by the spirit of partnership – the situation that prevailed at the start of the voyage is reversed.

   Hamlet may come to be more associated with Claudius than he
seemed: this might (might not) imply that the partnership which he
goes on supporting reveals a degree of ugliness. What is certain, however, is that the King's public attitude to Hamlet is unvarying. It is
designed to look kindly, devoted, indulgent (so far as his son's
'madness' permits). This is apparent near the end of the play as much
as at the beginning. Had Old Hamlet, not Claudius, presided over
a duelling-match which was genuine instead of managed, would he
have uttered sentiments differing substantially from those actually
uttered by Claudius? –

> The king shall drink to Hamlet's better breath,
> And in the cup an union shall he throw,
> Richer than that which four successive kings
> In Denmark's crown have worn: give me the cups,
> And let the kettle to the trumpet speak,
> The trumpet to the cannoneer without,
> The cannons to the heavens, the heaven to earth,
> 'Now the king drinks to Hamlet.'
>
> (V, ii, 269–76)

The apparent goodness of Claudius, which is largely but not in every respect illusory: also the alliance between him and Hamlet, so deceptive, yet with traces of loyalty and obedience on Hamlet's part: in short the mockery of a reigning Old Hamlet, shadowy and unreal: these signs seem by their spuriousness to condemn Claudius, whose credit with the audience never thoroughly survives testing. But in the end it is Old Hamlet's credit which suffers more – Claudius has nothing much to lose, Old Hamlet everything. Some semblance of Old Hamlet's identity is superimposed on the evil of Claudius. What does this ghastly effect come gradually to suggest, but that the identity of Claudius perhaps underlay the living goodness of Old Hamlet? Possibly he wronged Young Fortinbras: in regard to that son he seems more culpable than Claudius. Was Hamlet's father almost as evil as the slayer of Hamlet's father? The problem of Hamlet's revenge, the whole problem of revenge at large, began in the battle (should one say duel?) between Old Hamlet and Old Fortinbras –

Hamlet	. . . How long hast thou been grave-maker?
1 Clown	Of all the days i'th'year I came to't that day that our last king Hamlet overcame Fortinbras.
Hamlet	How long is that since?
1 Clown	Cannot you tell that? every fool can tell that. It was that very day that young Hamlet was born. (V, i, 137–43)

*

The point is sometimes made that the words 'This is I,/Hamlet the Dane' (uttered when he leaps into the grave to grapple with Laertes, V, i, 251–2) refer to Hamlet's kingly status; the expression is deemed proper only for royal use. Hamlet of course is not King then or later

– even in the brief period at the end of the play between Claudius's death and his own. True, Claudius had once told the world that his adopted son was 'the most immediate to our throne' (I, ii, 109). But there is no evidence that Hamlet dies a King, quite the contrary: he himself with his last breath refers to the coming election; Horatio in the elegy calls him Prince; Fortinbras declares he was likely to have proved most royal 'had he been put on'. In fact no clear title to the throne (as I noted in an earlier chapter) is allowed him, yet not-withstanding this, the English audiences for whom the play was written will cherish a hazy conviction that Hamlet was always Denmark's rightful ruler. They are right to do so, at least they are not wrong; besides, the treachery of Claudius in secretly assassinating Old Hamlet makes this belief all the more natural. To identify king-dom with King is a familiar convention and no empty one: the power of a monarch is territorial – in a sense is territory. But perhaps just as important as the association of the country with a *male* figure is the general association of the earth with femaleness. It will be understood that my kind of mental equipment hardly allows me to undertake the demonstration of this large and age-old connection. Scholars of several kinds, approaching the topic through myth and religion, through art, and through social institutions, have produced a mass of evidence: and either because I have read bits and pieces of their work and been convinced, or else because it seems a natural thing to do, I personally have no difficulty in bringing the two concepts, earth and femaleness, together. Our own culture no longer makes the association so readily as have some past cultures, including the Elizabethan, but even today the tendency to bring it about can be felt.

It is nowhere stated in *Hamlet*, I think, that Gertrude is equivalent to Denmark, nor that any woman is equivalent to any piece of ground. The nearest pronouncement that comes to mind is the Ghost's behest, 'Let not the royal bed of Denmark be/A couch for luxury and damnéd incest' (I, v, 82–3); and here it is only too clear that maleness is involved as well as femaleness. However, some kind of equivalence (or less, association, comparability) between land and womanhood may enter the play's structure. Certain basic features of the plot make this possibility seem less than absurd. Young Fortin-bras, Hamlet, and Laertes are presented as variant forms in terms of sonship and the revenge motif: they are not of course random variants, but meaningfully related. Each of the sons sets out to right the wrong done to his father, who lost his life; and who lost land (in the first case), land and wife (in the second case), daughter (in the third). Land and womanhood could be contrasted or they could be similar: it is rather as though their togetherness were stretched apart. Are they, if not substitutes for one another, transformations – partial transformations? What has land to do with incest – that which turns away from outwardness?

I mentioned at an earlier point that I tend to see this play – and I think I have a preference for seeing all plays in the same way – as a dramatic projection of the hero's inner life. Some support for this approach, which is no doubt primarily the result of my type of temperament, I find in the convention of the Morality play, from which (and from other, quite different sources) Elizabethan drama evolved. Therefore I want *Hamlet* to evince the moral and/or psychological life of the human individual: it has then an immense significance. Yet it seems to me – others may accept this more readily, but I must accept it too – that in a major respect the play manifests outwardness which is more than the presentation of inwardness: I am thinking of the shift from one generation to the next. An individual in his single psychic experience will have within him at any given moment patterns of good and evil which may be founded upon, or fundamentally engaged with, the sexual outlook predominating at that period of his life: at different periods of his life he will hold different views about how he stands towards his parents and his children, and his basic moral patterns will change correspondingly; whether the morality is related to the sexuality as cause or effect may be difficult to ascertain. All this complex personal evolution – all this inwardness – can be brought out in a play by manipulating parent and child figures in moral situations. A central character will be necessary, for whom the other personae are relevant projections, comprising in *toto* his mental life: such projections can be more than single aspects of the hero, for they may sometimes amount to reorientated versions of his whole self, alternative embodiments; this is so at any rate in a great play like *Hamlet*. Yet despite extensive presentation of inwardness there may be and perhaps has to be exhibited also the continuity of life beyond the individual. Behaviour initiated by fathers can have long consequences which children must work out and conclude. *Hamlet* certainly deals in temporal processes of this sort. The individual hero occupies his allotted place within the sequence, he is so to speak *less* than it. Outwardness exists independently: if it remains finally attached to the hero's individuality, perhaps this has something to do with the realising, phase by phase (tragedy notwithstanding), of his proper human potential. In being fully himself he will be what his forebears became, and what he can be his children must become.

It is impossible to be altogether contented with this argument, even though a substantial concession to outwardness is made. The two systems, inward and outward, are somehow shown to interact without quite touching. Yet surely the relationship must be more unaccommodating, at least on occasion. The individual is his environment, this is partly true: but it must also be true that individual and environment are not always the same, that their identities encroach on each other, that mutual interference is as much the rule as correspondence. The hero is in a measure opposed to his environment. Characters and circumstances surrounding Hamlet thus have a double function, since they figure at times the inner hero, and at times the outwardness which is alien to his being. We have to think in terms of degrees of impingement by externality, and degrees of willingness by internality to impinge upon it. More than the question of generations is involved, though that remains of great importance. The world not only of people but of inanimate matter is involved, land, which is so obscurely the ground of good and evil, which is so womanly, as women are of the earth especially − it has been believed; men are material, too, good and evil, but differently. Matter, bodies, other minds, are all outward to the hero, and in varying degrees they impinge on his inner life, and he will impinge on them.

Perhaps we can recognise in the play an extreme human tendency. A man may turn in on himself, try to enclose and confine his surroundings within the tightest of circles, desire to exclude the world. His is an unhealthy concern with interior reality only − psychic sexuality and a morbid morality may obsess him; though he cannot wholly dispense with external concomitants, which indeed being so few are intensely important, and situated in those parts of his surroundings that have always been near attributes of himself. Another tendency can be discerned, however, representing the opposite human extreme: it too revolves sexual and moral issues. It is an attempt to correct inwardness by breaking the isolation and

incorporating exterior reality, otherness. The individual who turns
outwards endures full exposure to things beyond and different from
himself: with these he grapples in an act of self-renewal. He is
doomed to fail; for he goes about the denial of inwardness, or perhaps (is this the same thing?) outwardness when he has assimilated it
is again inwardness. No doubt we are predisposed in favour of one
tendency or the other according to temperament, yet both are ultimately necessary to each of us. The relationship between them is
general in significance, universal, despite and because of personal
preferences. Upon the reconciling of inner and outer truth depends
development (psychological, moral) in anyone. Reconciled these
must be. Fixed compromise – some stable balance of forces – is not
however to be looked for, it is not desirable: it is humanly impossible.

I have always assumed that Old Hamlet and Claudius are the
chief male figures in the older generation, for the dilemma of the
hero lies between them; more accurately (each being regarded by
Hamlet as his mother's husband) the dilemma is between their marriages. This view cannot be wrong. The relationship between Old
Hamlet and his 'brother' Old Fortinbras is subordinate. Yet if the
play's inward tendency is represented by, and culminates in,
Claudius – this one feels strongly to be the case – Old Hamlet his
opposite must represent outwardness: and on this point one feels less
confident. Rather, one is confident only if Old Hamlet's most significant outward movement is taken into account, which is to say the
combat with Norway. I seem to have to pursue the matter further,
and I think this may involve shifting the emphasis away from Old
Hamlet/Claudius, the single pair.

Old Fortinbras no doubt appears subordinate partly because he is
not among the dramatis personae, having died long before the main
action begins. He died, one infers, on the day of Hamlet's birth:
the gravedigger's comment, coming so late in the play, has the air of
Shakespearean improvisation, but it does remind us that the combat
was introduced into the play with all the force of an originating
event. It is clear to me now that some of the ideas put forward in
Chapter 4 need substantial development. Act I, scene i contains the
long narrative speech by Horatio, which is an exposition of the
essential background. He speaks of Old Fortinbras's (and Old
Hamlet's) emulate pride; of the battle itself which was inevitable;

of the prize fought for; he connects Young Fortinbras's rising with
the events of the past; and the hectic preparations for war which are
going on in Denmark he connects with the rising. Moreover, this
narration of background takes place between the first and second
appearances of the Ghost, and is certainly relevant to those visitations:

> Such was the very armour he had on,
> When he the ambitious Norway combated,
> So frowned he once, when in an angry parle
> He smote the sledded Polacks on the ice.   (I, i, 60–3)

Horatio was harrowed with fear and wonder.

> This bodes some strange eruption to our state.   (69)

The Ghost made itself visible to the watch: watch was being kept
because of the imminence of war. After Marcellus's request for information, which Horatio supplies in the long speech, Barnado accepts
what has been said. Accepting also a relationship between the natural
and supernatural events, he even supposes that Old Hamlet was *and
still is* of central importance – this is the Old Hamlet who (as
Horatio has explained) fashioned history by encountering and slaying Old Fortinbras. The present situation is made to depend in its
entirety upon that conflict, that victory.

Barnado   I think it be no other but e'en so;
> Well may it sort that this portentous figure
> Comes arméd through our watch so like the king
> That was and is the question of these wars.

>   (I, i, 108–11)

Another speech by Horatio, which is heavy with omen: and then –

> But soft, behold, lo where it comes again!   (126)

The Ghost appears to Hamlet in scene v. It speaks at last – of
Claudius: not of present preparations for war, not of the combat
long ago with Old Fortinbras: but of Claudius, Old Hamlet's brother,
who murdered the King and married the Queen – fratricidal,
incestuous Claudius: and the son is bidden to vengeance. Hamlet's
grief for his father in the intervening scenes, and his attitude to
Claudius and Gertrude, have so well prepared us to expect these

utterances that we are not likely to call the play's opening into question, not likely to fault it – although we are at liberty to wonder whether Claudius and Old Fortinbras, events recent and events past, have anything in common. Are they in fact opposites? The haunting strikes us as a single, necessary process. If not opposites, then, are they the same – the Claudius of the present and the Old Fortinbras of the past? In a way these questions are proper, but only up to a point, for the assumptions on which they rest are simplistic. The absurd answer to both questions would be yes; or alternatively, no.

Everyone is familiar with those advertisements, often pictorial, which rely on the idea of BEFORE and AFTER. Perhaps one can imagine a cartoon, a sort of anti-advertisement, in which BEFORE is shown to be better, and the AFTER-state is worse. Would this be like (mere cavilling aside) the situation before and after Old Hamlet took his sleep in the orchard? It would seem to be like it, in that two epochs are apparent – the first good, the second evil. But it would be unlike it in that the second appears to usurp the first, without the first seeming to turn into the second. The right kind of causality, the right kind of connection, is absent. Or rather it is present, as I might have some chance of showing if I could opt out of the ad-man's rat-race backwards. I resume sullen critic; dignity's the thing wherewith if with anything I'll catch the conscience of a King.

The combat with Old Fortinbras is presented as an initiating event. It is the only event of Old Hamlet's reign to receive strong emphasis and detailed treatment, although there are hints of wars; the Ghost has 'that fair and warlike form/In which the majesty of buried Denmark/Did sometimes march', I, i, 47–9); he frowns as he did when he struck at the Poles, I, i, 62–3 (but later, Hamlet asking 'What, looked he frowningly?', Horatio replies, I, ii, 232, 'a countenance more in sorrow than in anger'). Shakespeare not infrequently creates contradictory impressions. Despite the emphasis given to the single-handed combat, despite the supporting indications of royal activity in war, we somehow come to believe that the reign was generally prosperous and peaceful. The sense we have of Hamlet's golden childhood may be held largely responsible for this other impression: we remember Denmark quiet, contented, fruitful – everything it has ceased to be since the accession of Claudius. Because the main combat in Old Hamlet's reign took place long ago, perhaps we are allowed to think of all the battles as long ago: two phases, warlike followed by peaceful. It does not matter how we arrange the history – we hardly undertake chronology anyway. Both impressions existing, the important underlying idea develops that war abroad makes for peace at home. The good epoch as a whole, i.e. the reign of Old Hamlet, is characteristic of, and is produced by, the outward orientation of the King. Outwardness always predominates. Aggression is turned against foreign evil: it is designed to establish good power: but the further aim of such power is the contemplation of its own being. Outwardness, though preserved, begins to give way to inwardness. Foreign evil is not finally conquered but only assimilated: the imposthume of evil is within the peaceful prosperity that emerges from war. The reign draws to a close, contemplating its own successful nature, declines towards the evil which is there unseen: which is seen at last and embraced as the true objective of inward-turning – eruption breaks in Denmark, Claudius replaces Old Hamlet, marriage becomes incestuous. The good epoch has died into the bad, for the bad has murdered the good. Yet bad and good together comprise a new whole. The duality of the good epoch is seen to be one half of a greater duality whose other half the bad epoch constitutes. Perhaps the bad epoch is itself a subordinate duality, like the good, grounded in the violence of fratricide and enjoying the uneasy peace thus won. Such direct comparison, however, serves only to enforce the more general reversal. The weakening of outwardness in Old Hamlet's reign is matched by the weakening of inwardness in the reign of Claudius; for Claudius dies in his turn. The bad epoch is the separated opposite of the good, also its sequel.

Separation and sequel belong to time – in human life a reality no less than in drama. The death of Old Fortinbras becomes, via the death of Old Hamlet, by temporal process the death of Claudius. I am not underestimating the significance of time when I say that good and evil also exist together simultaneously – they are inseparable, unsequential, co-present in their relationship. Time alone allows realisation – time which is the lag of spontaneity: it is crucial, for example, in the achieving of moral victory, as Old Hamlet's prosperity shows. And yet, with the long time-lag of the peace eliminated, we can see that Claudius is the form of Old Hamlet triumphant over his 'brother' Old Fortinbras. By killing Old Fortinbras, Old Hamlet turns himself into Claudius. He might indeed have failed, as Old Fortinbras failed in the same attempt. But for time (without which a duality is only both its aspects, instead of one) but for time and the accident of defeat, proud, emulately outward Old Fortinbras would be the Claudius of fratricidal inwardness who is Old Hamlet dared to the combat, emulately outward, proud, the victor of the peace. One does one's best, but Shakespeare, no critic, does much better.

Old Hamlet is associated with Old Fortinbras, and is thus revealed in his outward aspect. Old Hamlet is also associated with Claudius, and shown in his other aspect, inward-turned. Beyond the time-factor, all three Kings are one another. Thus analysed (and time rather admitted than excluded) Old Hamlet is paired in two different ways, as he veers between extremes. Now, Hamlet the son is concerned, one feels, with only the second of these pairs, namely Old Hamlet/Claudius: and, as I have already noted, this assumption can hardly be wrong; his principal aim must be to put right the situation bequeathed him by the murder. He does not see the combat as something to be acted on, nor see how far it is really part of the murder. Does he see it as part of the murder at all? Does the audience? There is little warrant for answering these questions affirmatively. On the other hand they cannot be answered negatively with any confidence, for the opening of the play abounds in suggestive detail. Combat and murder are gathered into a context, yet still it is possible for Hamlet to concern himself, primarily, with Old Hamlet and Claudius — possible, natural, perhaps even inevitable. Believing as he does that his father represents goodness, he believes further that his father should be loyally followed. Hamlet is claimed by partnership. Yet he is not altogether in his father's position — he cannot be in it, and he ought not to try to occupy it. A son necessarily belongs to the generation below his father: Hamlet must be prepared to turn outwards from, or outwards against, Old Hamlet; he must not turn inwards to his own origin. Partnership is a retreat, or rather it is a non-advance, a betrayal of the son's real condition as a new man: to this extent Hamlet's loyalty to Old Hamlet does not represent good, and his belief that it does so is mistaken. On the other hand loyal partnership is at one remove from incest with the mother, since she is approached through the father, whose love for his wife is legitimate. Partnership, if it turns inwards, at least does not turn inwards with the full evil of rivalry — the maleness of the son's origin is somehow less extremely inward than the femaleness. Hamlet must oppose his father, but this will bring his attitude close to rivalry, for Claudius

too (whom the son would replace in the mother's affection) opposes
Old Hamlet. Alongside incestuous rivalry there develops another
rivalry which is not incestuous. This latter is competitive in an outward way, being aggressively emulate. Only through the new generation powerful in its own right (i.e. through the son's development
into manhood) can it arise: it implies competition between equals:
between brothers. It makes possible legitimate, outward-turned
marriage. The father who was once his partner, Hamlet has to rival
so as to be like him: in the process he cannot but rival Claudius, his
father's enemy and his own.

Can he rival Claudius without becoming unlike Old Hamlet? I
find myself again reviewing the ideas I had when I dealt with the
final struggle between Hamlet and Claudius, and wondering whether,
after all, I would do better to abandon that part of the account
entirely – simply scrap it. Why should the reader be troubled with an
unmatured theory? I suppose I retain it because I have come to feel
that no theory of Hamlet can be matured to the point of finality. Only
an evolving awareness (thinking awareness) seems possible, whose
latest version is shaped out of its own past before shaping its own
future. Not that any theorist thinks it necessary to rely on the future,
however he may choose to rely on the past; and indeed time does
run out even for the proudest race (a consummation devoutly to be
wished). Speaking now as a critical tyrannosaurus, I cannot disown
the intentions and ideas of that primitive running-lizard my ancestor
– he loved truth, take him for all in all he would be a man. Hamlet
and Claudius come to a death-struggle, one may say, in which both
are killed. Whilst this is in some sense surely true, one has to bear in
mind that Hamlet is actually killed by Laertes: Claudius is perhaps
felt to be the ultimate source of Hamlet's death, but Laertes is the
agent. It is in the first phase of the duel that the hero receives his fatal
wound and thus falls victim to his brother. So far as the duel is
analogous with the original combat between brother Kings, Hamlet
appears to be like Old Fortinbras, the victim of Old Hamlet; that is
to say, Hamlet does not appear to be like his father. Rather, Laertes is
like him; and the fact that Laertes is a loyal son lends support to the
comparison, since the revenge motif derives from Old Hamlet's
Ghost. Moreover, if the combat and the murder are regarded as
associated events, Old Hamlet triumphant has potentially the face of
Claudius, so that Laertes' Claudian connections (the intrigue, the

poisoning) are not incompatible with his playing Old Hamlet in the duel with the Prince. It can be argued – rightly, I think, although the form of words is somewhat absurd – that Hamlet as a victim makes Claudius potent via triumphant Laertes (via, through, in) : Laertes, like Old Hamlet, becomes by his triumph an incestuous murderer. And yet Old Hamlet triumphant does of course postpone the onset of Claudius, because of the time-lag. In a way he is destroying Claudius temporarily by fighting and destroying Old Fortinbras. The mortally wounded Hamlet of the duel, therefore, who is like Old Fortinbras in defeat, not only empowers Claudius, but also in a sense destroys him – which is seen to happen a few moments later in the play when he *does* destroy him.

On the other hand – and this too I would accept, though it seems contradictory – Hamlet's killing of Claudius may be regarded as the consequence not of Old Fortinbras's defeat but more simply of his victory ; the combat might well have gone the other way, and now, in being refought, it does so. Laertes is killed by the Prince ; that is to say Old Hamlet (Laertes), visible as Claudius, is (are) assaulted by Hamlet the Old Fortinbras figure. Yet why – since Old Hamlet is supposed to be defeated – is he visible as Claudius at all ? He is Claudius because, as Hamlet's outward enemy, he embodies Hamlet's own inward Claudianness ; similarly, in the actual combat of long ago, Old Hamlet fought his inner Claudius when he fought outwardly against Old Fortinbras. Hamlet's assault on the King, besides its being equivalent to the *defeat* of Old Fortinbras and the triumphant postponement of Claudius by Old Hamlet, is also representative of Old Fortinbras's *victory*, his triumphant postponement (in defeating his outward enemy Old Hamlet) of Claudianness within himself. What I would suggest amounts to this : whether Hamlet as Old Fortinbras is seen to be victim or victor (either view being possible for he is both) he is hardly separable from Old Hamlet triumphant or defeated (the adjectives in that order) for no matter which turn the combat takes Claudius is destroyed ; the causes of his destruction are two, opposed, the same, one.

The Prince victimised by Laertes (ultimately by Claudius) allows the repetition of Old Hamlet's triumph ; the Prince victimised like Old Fortinbras. Victorious, the Prince is comparable with the Old Fortinbras who, had he won, would have been as Old Hamlet actually was. Either way the Prince must change his form. For the combat is over, and what is to follow? Young Fortinbras begins his reign. He is the new form of Hamlet; of Old Fortinbras, therefore, but also of Old Hamlet, and Claudius. It is necessary that the son should enter upon his adult aspect through opposition to his father: in this way and in no other can Hamlet achieve the outwardness which was his father's best quality. Had the Prince remained in partnership, had he, instead, adopted the rival's stance which aimed more directly at incest with the mother, he would still have been committed to the inward orientation, still have been turned in upon his origins. Outwardness implies rivalry of a legitimate sort: a rivalry which is not incestuous, a legitimacy which has nothing to do with partnership. In order to establish himself, then, as a younger version of his father, Hamlet assumes the role of his father's outward enemy: he must lose the battle against Old Hamlet, otherwise Old Hamlet would never be able to reign in prosperity: he must also win this battle, otherwise Hamlet's own right to a prosperous reign would be forfeit. The son of the King of Denmark inherits Denmark as the son of the King of Norway. And Young Fortinbras, he who is an aspect of sonship separate and independent until he attains to Denmark — at which time he commences a new form, being also that of the new Hamlet: Young Fortinbras too, in his former aspect, needed to oppose his father, becoming his father's outward enemy. He (Young Fortinbras) had to become Old Hamlet and not Old Fortinbras precisely because of that forfeit paid by the loser: the victimhood which Hamlet has just suffered, Old Fortinbras suffered once. And yet the defeated King in everything but defeat was the same as the victor; his attitude was emulate and outward; his victory in prospect was realised by his 'brother', and again much later by his own son.

Young Fortinbras at the play's end is in no simple sense a unified form of all brothers, including the Claudian brother who is held in abeyance: a unified form of the senior brothers; of the junior brothers; of senior and junior brothers together. Young Fortinbras at the end can scarcely be called a composite, still less a compromise figure, for despite his being all the brothers he is nevertheless one of them only, he is (or rather he is like) Old Hamlet. Prior to the emergence of the unified version, Fortinbras the son was pursuing his own separate and independent existence, as I have mentioned. What was the relationship, the implied relationship, between Hamlet and

Young Fortinbras during the penultimate aspect? – implied, because they were not in actual contact, Hamlet being in the hall of tragedy at Elsinore Castle, Young Fortinbras marching towards it at the end of his campaign. I yield to the conviction that in some sense they were locked in mortal combat. Hamlet (Old Fortinbras) struggled with Young Fortinbras (Old Hamlet). Young Fortinbras won. Perhaps this helps to explain 'the soldiers' music and the rite of war' (397), a tribute which he orders for Hamlet dead; 'such a sight as this/ Becomes the field, but here shows much amiss' (399–400). Hamlet's move outwards had its true reflection, found its true reality, on the battlefield. Yet the struggle properly occupied only the penultimate aspect of the play (in the hypothetical way I have indicated). The result of the struggle constitutes the final aspect. The triumphant figure who comes to power is no less the loser's form than the winner's. The rite of war is for a great father displaced by a great son, it is for a twin brother displaced by a twin brother; am I saying it is for evil displaced by good?

    I would not wish to ignore what might be termed the physical continuity of Young Fortinbras. In his final identity he is, as I have attempted to explain, a unifying figure of dramatic complexity, yet he has a personal history. His was the ready route to maturity, not agonisingly and uncertainly experienced; this statement perhaps has to be amplified. Is it not the case that the inwardness of the male (no less than his outward tendency) concerns femaleness? His worst evil is incestuous. For some reason which I do not pretend to understand, however, the male experience of femaleness is not associated wholly with women, although (the use of the word 'femaleness' implies this) women are a principal focus: another possible focus (not the only one) concerns land; I return to that forgotten topic. It seems likely enough that women are the most potent form of femaleness experienced by man, but whether this is so or not it is certainly true in the play. We know nothing of Young Fortinbras's attitude to women, though he must have had a mother and could have had sisters: for all we know to the contrary he may be courting or he may be married. My point is that his inward tendency, which necessarily involves his attitude to femaleness, is known to us only through his attitude to land. It is as though he has half-solved the problem of inwardness already, for no struggle with incest is shown. His attempt – his rather disreputable attempt – to recover the lost land (whether on behalf of his father or for himself is not altogether clear) raises the partnership/rivalry issue, but raises it somewhat faintly, indirectly, one might say safely; the urgency of incest is not felt. Perhaps because his inward orientation has already begun to turn outwards, Young Fortinbras is soon willing to convert his attack on Denmark to an attack on Poland: he engages in foreign conquest. His is the personality which as it were stands behind the final unifying figure. The route to power has been straightforward and untroubled. Young Fortinbras is not, of course, the hero of the play. But the play which centres round Hamlet explores the underlying development and meaning of manhood, the transition between generations; explores Young Fortinbras's and all 'natural' manhood – explores Hamlet's own. A cycle of life is made apparent, which is relevant to individuals within the succession of the ages. The completion of this cycle can perhaps easily be mistaken for a final resolution, instead of being seen as a temporary resting-place. The unspecified but vaguely felt formation of a double kingdom has much to do with this – the Prince of Norway claiming the crown of Denmark. Resolution does indeed occur. It is extremely important and in every way an extraordinary achievement. The double kingdom is necessary because forgiveness has been exchanged between Hamlet and Laertes (in a sense Young Fortinbras is involved in this as well): evil has been ousted. It is also necessary because the authority and validity of a good reign must seem to occupy the future. But the reassurance is not aimed at fairy-tale finality. For the nature of a good reign has been exposed to doubt – within wealth and peace is the imposthume. What is required is that the driving back of evil inwards, by an outward movement against it, should not appear to make a grand lie of morality. Goodness, though achieved only temporarily, is not invalidated by its unavoidable relationship with evil. The relationship is proper, goodness depends upon it. Prosperity is a reality, and through the unifying person of Young Fortinbras we are reassured, but it is not of course a permanent reality.

There are victims in Hamlet but no willing victims. No character makes a sacrifice of himself (or herself). There is no one who resembles, or in any way performs the function of a redeemer. Shakespeare's concern, one might say, is with the ordinary rather than the extraordinary. I don't mean that he is concerned with anything which is superficial or trivial, for he presents 'natural' life in all its underlying complexity. Ordinary life is heroic; dominated by an assumption which precludes meekness as unthinkable, out-of-this-world, weak. We naturally struggle for independence, we value our desire to implement goodness. We are proud. In this condition we live and die surrounded by moral facts to which we respond not altogether imperfectly. We do our best as we see it, and, by instinct or judgement, our best may turn out worthily, may force back evil; goodness is furthered in the world by true militancy, and on these terms love seems possible. That success is temporary does not invalidate success: human nature being what it is, permanent success is beyond our grasp whether we approach life in this or in any other way. Our ordinary approach, heroic and militant as are its assumptions, is not more deluded in this respect than the extraordinary approach which is based on meekness and sacrifice, although in certain respects the latter is superior. Is it superior – can we finally take for granted the inferiority of normal human achievement, worldly goodness, greatness? That rhetorical question shows the tenor of our existence. The play, at any rate, sets beside the militant maturity of the older generation the innocence of the younger. Yet childhood Falls, the inner evil is known, the son's situation in this next phase is that of Sophoclean or Freudian Oedipus. The Fall of the son is associated with something like a re-activated Fall for the father, whose goodness is overpowered by the evil within. During the next phase, the third, whilst the father's power declines further into evil, the son begins to grapple with inward evil by turning outwards. The son's militant maturity and the father's death are comprised together in the last phase.

These phases need to be focussed more clearly. As regards Hamlet's age at the time of the Fall, there are difficulties. This phase (the second) is associated with the murder; and since the King is 'but two months dead, nay not so much, not two' (I, ii, 138), the Prince was adult at the time of the murder – to all intents and purposes as adult as we see him to be in the play (his precise years are variously computed). Can his childhood innocence have lasted so long? One feels inclined to locate the Fall at a much earlier period of life, but the evidence of the play seems to rule this out. It is possible that Shakespeare equated the beginning of moral awareness with what he saw as the beginning of sexual awareness. The latter could be held to occur later in childhood, but hardly later than puberty. Hamlet, however, is more than pubescent. I am inclined to believe

that his life is shown in compression at the specific period of early
adulthood: in the few weeks covered by the play the young man's
whole development is shown, up to and including the point of his
maturity. The very recent date of the murder need not, and I think
does not, mean that Hamlet's years of innocence (or any son's) are
strangely prolonged. Another, related reason for the recent date of the
murder concerns Old Hamlet. It is desirable that his good reign
should be known to run its full course: the King's second Fall is
latent in his militant success against Old Fortinbras, is inherent in it,
yet the time-lag is the only period of human greatness. The father's
second Fall is thus deferred in accordance with the real importance
of calendar time, whilst the corresponding Fall of the son is deferred
to accord with the requirements of dramatic time. Old Hamlet's
reign, and Hamlet's years while his father lived, make up between
them the first phase of the cycle within the terms of the play. The
third phase (after the second phase of the murder) is represented by
the decline inwards of Old Hamlet as Claudius, whose reign amounts
to an extension of his brother's, and it is during this period that
Hamlet gradually turns outwards and confronts his own inner evil.
The treatment of time presents continued difficulty, for as I have
already suggested Hamlet's development is compressed: partly
because of this Old Hamlet's decline is foreshortened, and partly it is
foreshortened because, as I have also shown, the prosperity that pre-
cedes it must be stressed. Hamlet finally establishes his maturity,
militant and heroic, with the death of Claudius. Perhaps in real life
the phases of father and son are seldom mutually concurrent, yet a
fundamental pattern connects the older with the younger generation.
This pattern, of interdependence, of reciprocity, the playwright
reveals.

   Hamlet must die because he is a son: the hero cannot be rede-
fined as a father and still remain Hamlet. Sonship aspires to and
achieves maturity in the tragic death of sonship. Young Fortinbras
lives changed, coming to power. Nothing is said about his future but
we can predict it. Already he has defeated Poland, as once Old Hamlet
'smote the sledded Polacks on the ice': and at that time, or afterwards, he in some sense 'the ambitious Norway combated' (Hamlet
as Old Fortinbras). Already, perhaps, he has wooed and married
Ophelia/Gertrude; if not, he will presently do so. At the end of a
long and good reign he will die of the evil in him, brother to the

good, and live on in the form of that brother, still married to his own
widow; the imposthume of peace will have broken − what was
always the truth, because it was potentially true, will come true.
He will have left behind him from his good years a son, whose
symbolic if not whose actual birthday occurred at the very beginning
of the reign (V, ii) when Young Fortinbras claimed his vantage. This
Youngest Fortinbras will know and fight the ascendant interior evil
of his uncle: 'Wretched queen, adieu', he will say to his dead mother
at the last, himself dying, having killed the King. But another Prince is
waiting in the wings: the son of Hamlet, one might say: a hypothetical reality and literal implication, a retrospective offspring (as it
were) of the Hamlet who was emulate victim, and who was transforming into emulate victor. At the time when Young Fortinbras was
secretly assassinated this Prince was raising levies against the kingdom
of his father's enemy. However, he diverted his attack to unhappy
Poland, and is now newly come from victory there. It is his turn to
take the Danish crown. He orders military honours for Youngest
Fortinbras, who, had he been put on, was likely to have proved most
royal − 'Go, bid the soldiers shoot'. Nothing is said about the new
King's future, but Old Moore is always ready (he is his son). Meanwhile they are still mad in England without knowing it, or else,
knowing it, they cling to their condition like a grief, as did Shakespeare grieve on the death of Hamnet?

17

In university departments of English, and not only there, the assumption is made that criticism is essential to the nation's literary culture. Experts have always been looked up to, but today every one else is looked down on: the literary experts are critics. It is true that most individuals (of those who are not critics) have doubts about the very point which they feel obliged to concede. Criticism can hardly be other than essential, they feel, and yet it is not actually essential to them. One may say that to a greater or lesser (especially lesser) extent, critical routines enter into literary experience, and that such routines are considered important; for literary experience is held to be of consequence only as it is critical. Where critical practice is rudimentary it may indeed seem to occupy no significant position: yet I feel that the desire to stress criticism, the assumption that it is essential for the expert if not for the tyro himself, the *status* accorded to thinking, all these must make their impact on the literary experience concerned, and thus the influence of criticism is less slight than it appears. The more sophisticated the criticism, however, obviously the more influential it becomes. Critical education has its greatest effect in what might be termed the central cultural areas of literature. It is clear that the literary scene which we know today (and I include here our awareness of historical as well as contemporary works) could not exist without criticism. But this is not of course to say that literature depends on criticism: I see no reason to suppose that, if criticism had never been, we should necessarily lack a literary culture. In fact I see reasons to suppose the contrary, for there have been past literary cultures where criticism has played little part. The matter is doubtless one of emphasis. But surely it is true that no literary culture of the past has been as permeated by criticism as ours is today.

All the more harmful, therefore, is the fact that so few people are really able to benefit from a critical education in literature. Education

in literature implies critical education, for what other way of presenting literature have we got at our disposal? Variations in intelligence
or talent among those taught must dictate the intensity of the critical
approach employed by a teacher: but the aim is always to teach
criticism so far as possible. According to their abilities, children and
young adults learn to criticise. Those are fortunate whose powers
equip them to succeed. They are strongly disposed to literature and
can respond to the non-thinking demands which it makes, but they
also, and just as strongly, know the opposite demands of thinking:
literary criticism enables them to relate two major aspects of their
experience. They achieve for themselves a unity of contrast (more
intricate, indeed, than might be supposed) which is valid in terms
of personality, less valid in terms of the claims that are made on its
behalf. People who are constituted differently, whether gifted or not,
will get little from a critical education except tedium and frustration.
By the exercise of thinking faculties they will feel themselves severed
from literature, and, if they enjoy it despite this, they will try to
remain in contact by keeping up their criticism as best they can: they
will believe themselves at fault, not the criticism which they dislike.
Even Honours students of English in the universities are not, many of
them, fundamentally cut out for criticism, although with some
success, and at some psychic cost, they grow critics. The thinking side
of their minds is developed: perhaps a good thing in itself: but it is
forced to make close contact with literary non-thinking, and this
process is neither absolutely necessary nor, except for a few people,
is it desirable. If non-thinking awareness can give rise to maximal
meaning, and it can, why should that meaning have to be modified
into something else maximal which involves thinking?

    I must accept that a critical approach does sometimes, and up to
a point, help people who are not really critical (as defined above).
For such people criticism in small doses is like a useful drug which
cures or stimulates. The drug becomes a poison in larger doses, and
it must never be mistaken for staple diet. I am willing to be an anti-
critic if only because excessive criticism is an evil. Criticism is becoming ever more excessive − but the pendulum will swing. We
need to develop some method of teaching literature which is not
based on thinking. Protesting critics will regard me as Antichrist: or
rather (since they are not likely to overrate me) I am the Whore of
Babylon's Sporus, who, as the prompter breathed, the puppet

squeaked. Yet I am not advocating the replacement of intellectual rigour by vapid enthusiasm. Non-thinking can be just as rigorous as thinking: literature shows this: if there is any doubt we have only to consider that the whole endeavour of criticism is to further the proof. Since literature is proven to be rigorous by criticism, literature is rigorous without criticism. Shakespeare's plays, for example, were as great before criticism as after. Could people ever, can people now, come to appreciate the plays fully in the absence of critical intervention? As I should be most unwilling to argue that the high place the plays have always held in our literary culture is owing to the influence of critics (owing to that fundamentally) I must believe in the possibility of appreciation which is quite independent of criticism; obviously, however, without criticism there would not be *critical* appreciation, and unfortunately most readers will receive this latter phrase as though it were 'would not be appreciation'. The pendulum will swing; or perhaps it is the wheel which will come full circle. I do not know what the method of presenting literature will be, but I assume that in the transmission of literature, as in the transmission of culture generally, the older generation has a duty to help the younger. I was going to write 'teach' instead of 'help'. But that begs the question, for by 'teach' we seem to mean only 'help thinkingly', whereas the point at issue is how to help non-thinkingly the younger generation's non-thinking. The necessary method may take a long time to develop – the critical method itself did not develop overnight.

Purists will say that universities are nothing if not places of intellectual rigour. Dilute the thinking, they will say (introducing a metaphor of their own to describe the change), and you begin to destroy the university. I am not sure whether the purists are old-fashioned in their view or new-fangled. It seems to me that universities are concerned with preserving and promulgating civilisation: of course they are not alone in being responsible for this, but they play their part. Must their part be one of thinking, of thinking alone? The purists confuse the means with the end – and it is easy for them to do so because, as men much given to thinking, they have difficulty in recognising the validity of non-thinking. In the evolution of the human race thinking was of late emergence. Yet thinking is not therefore superior, nor can it exist alone: it is a different mode of awareness, which exists alongside the older conscious mode. The

older and the newer modes are equally contemporary for us now –
not to recognise this is grotesquely to misunderstand our nature.
We have certainly done wrong to over-value thinking, and the forces
which will right this situation are as large as half our being. The
image of the pendulum or the wheel could be much too simple.
There is even the possibility that non-thinking and thinking are no
less intricately related than good and evil. In one way or another the
change will come to the universities – they can make their civilising
contribution by non-thinking as well as by thinking means, if
appropriate procedures are developed. Knowledge will be acknowledged to the full, not confined to thinking knowledge. English
studies have in some sense always been dedicated to precisely this
aim, but of necessity the aim has been proclaimed otherwise, and
what has been proclaimed has come to be believed. For English was
admitted to the curriculum only because it promised intellectual
rigour. Perhaps it was admitted on false terms. Intellectual rigour,
criticism too much emphasised, is bad for literature, and bad ultimately for the universities. Either English ought to be rejected as un-
suitable for study, in which case literary culture may not wither in the
nation, or it should be retained and allowed to modify the concept of
the university.

The relationship between non-thinking and thinking has always
presented difficulties, for whole societies as well as for individuals,
but perhaps the problem has never been more widespread than it is
in the civilised world today, or more urgent. Not that the problem is
seen to be urgent, or even a problem – that is the nature of its
urgency. We have a modern maxim (or if we haven't, here it is):
Think well and all is well. Such crude one-sidedness is our way of
relating non-thinking and thinking, our hardly-acknowledgement of
the basic dichotomy. The persistence of non-thinking among us is
awkward, especially as some of its manifestations we cannot but
value, art being a case in point. We feel that art is as it were right, yet
we cannot square this with the fact that it is the opposite of thinking.
People involved in the literary culture are exposed together with
everyone else to the problem of the larger dichotomy in its acute
latter-day form: but (all is not well) the underlying difficulties are
made worse for them and more confusing, because literature which
partakes of non-thinking is pitched so close to criticism which
partakes of thinking.

I have been talking about a dichotomy, non-thinking/thinking. Another dichotomy has obtruded upon it, good/evil. Now, it is as plain to me as it is to anybody that these two dichotomies are not one and the same. We cannot call non-thinking good, and thinking evil: it would be absurd to define goodness as non-thinking, and evil as thinking. Yet it is equally clear that the dichotomies overlap, inter-penetrate, cannot be fully separated. For good and evil must be ex-perienced through either non-thinking or thinking, one mode or the other: also, non-thinking and thinking whenever they occur must promote either good or evil. Are the dichotomies (overlapping, inter-penetrating, inseparable) related in any permanent manner? At any given moment, in a given context, they are related transiently – and always their relationship matters. As regards the literary context: there, non-thinking engages to a considerable degree with *good*, although these two elements, each from a different dichotomy, can never be identical. Thinking, on the other hand, engages to a certain extent with evil.

One needs to say, and to insist despite its being obvious, that *Hamlet* does not treat of non-thinking/thinking. I am neither looking for nor finding symbols of that dichotomy in the play; readers who smilingly accuse me of symbol-hunting may care to bear the point in mind. Yet the play is at first perceived via non-thinking. There was a time – critical apprehension being then impossible – when the larger dichotomy was evoked only because the operation of one of its halves ultimately and automatically implied relationship with the other half. I do not believe that the relationship was historically less present, or less important, than it is today. The emergence of criti-cism as a fact of literary life has led to a situation which is changed rather than wholly new. Our experience of the play directly involves both sides of the dichotomy. The old ascendancy of non-thinking is now questioned, or rejected outright in favour of thinking. The relationship is undergoing, has undergone, convulsion.

Hamlet is an artefact. The text, considered as an object, is not like any phenomenon of unhuman nature. More important, the text as an object is not *Hamlet*. One may believe that stones or trees exist unperceived: there can be no proof, perhaps, but no disproof either, and on the whole it is easy to assume that they do not *need* to be perceived – their perceptual existence is so to speak only for the con-venience of ourselves. The text on the other hand does need to be perceived – that is its raison d'être: it needs to be read, or (more properly) to be evolved into theatrical production and apprehended by members of an audience. When Hamlet is registered by and in the perceiver, not until then, it is the play. The text, the stage production, are at the centre of the perceiver's attention, but the centre implies the presence of its circle, otherwise it is nothing at all. In short, we are an essential of the play, for in being itself it is us, we are it. The play beheld is a focussing, an organisation, of our nature. To experience Hamlet is to orientate our identity for a moment in a certain way. It is our own potential which is realised through Shakespeare's art: the originating causes of the tragedy are within us, and they come to expression when we apprehend the form of his drama. We respond to the stimulus of this form because, impossibly, we could have created it. If Hamlet had never been written, never been beheld, we should still be thoroughly affected in our lives by its origins. People who have never come across the play actually are in such a state of influence: for them, the powerful self-focus of that particular centre is yet to come. It may be urged, here is subjectivity run riot! Any play, of course, in a sense is many plays, all different, and this can seem alarming – so much so that an illusory objectivity is preferred before subjectivity. We are surely not altogether wrong in believing that the play is better realised in some people than in others whose literary powers are less developed: an idea which invites the postulation of a best Hamlet, hence an only Hamlet. Subjectivity, however, is consistent with due stability. 'Better' may be admitted, even though the heavenly logic of 'best and only' has to be dispensed with. The play beheld is a conscious formulation, deriving from our more or less uniform human unconsciousness, and relating also to our particular culture. Common conditioning of common stock: within limits (notwithstanding the variation of individuals) this must lead to common response when a stimulus is in common (granted that drama varies as regards performance).

Hamlet organises the perceiver's moral dichotomy into a cycle. Perhaps this cycle implies or induces a corresponding cycle governing the other dichotomy, i.e. non-thinking/thinking: alternatively, all basic dichotomies may organise their own two halves in essentially the same way, the moral dichotomy therefore affording a highly important instance of the general rule. I doubt, at any rate, whether non-thinking/thinking, necessarily activated as I take them to be by the process of apprehension, are meaninglessly associated with the pattern of good and evil – randomly associated or varyingly related: a degree of significant connection is all the more likely when non-thinking and thinking are at odds within the individual perceiver. The conflict between them is acute for me personally; of this the reader will be too well aware. My experience of the play, in which such conflict bears a part, may be less peculiar than it seems – it may not be untypical of the modern response. For Hamlet's modern existence (it no longer has an Elizabethan one) is bound to be influenced by the realities of non-thinking and thinking pressing upon us, and this is so whether or not prevailing assumptions correctly view the facts; I have said that the great faith we have in thinking generally, the denial of conflict, does not rule conflict out – is likely to enhance it, lending present urgency to something that has always mattered. But now, what of that third dichotomy, outwardness/inwardness? – in regard to which, the difficulties I have encountered were probably no less obvious. Here my reaction may indeed be more personal. With some hesitation, though, I conclude otherwise. No doubt I represent a rather extreme case temperamentally, and have been betrayed into absurdities for that reason. It seems I began the book with an outward flourish and much trumpeting: my recommended course of action, if action it could be called, was for a wholly inward withdrawal: eventually it was this same inwardness which obliged me to recognise, through Hamlet, the outwardness I had apparently forgotten. That the third dichotomy is so germane to Hamlet, a play of wide general appeal, surely shows a concern with outwardness and inwardness to be more than idiosyncratic, whatever the vagaries of my response may have been. The dichotomy which is outwardness/inwardness is associated with good/evil: and with good/evil is associated non-thinking/thinking. Are we to discern a circular logic: A equals B, B equals C (where ABC respectively are each of the three dichotomies): are we then to projetc the conclusion, A equals C? That is, outwardness/inwardness equals non-thinking/thinking? Can we, however, actually feel a connection between outwardness and non-thinking on the one hand, between inwardness and thinking on the other? Outwardness may just as readily, perhaps, be associated with thinking – in which case the parallelism between the dichotomies could be more like opposition:

and may not inwardness be associated with non-thinking, the opposition being thus completed?

The present-day literary scene can hardly be disentangled from the educational set-up, for every literary person has been more or less exposed to the teaching of English. One may wish to insist that literature is inwardly experienced or not at all: to this extent it may appear to be *essentially* inward. Yet it has its outward aspects too, it is a public phenomenon, and the outwardness seems finally to be no less essential. Moreover the literary medium, language itself, is poised between inwardness and outwardness (the dramatic medium too, so far as this differs from language): for its meaning is an inward realisation, yet it belongs to the physical world (sounds, print) and this physicality is fulfilled only through promulgation and public effect. The conflict between non-thinking and thinking, which enters into the realisation of *Hamlet* and is viewed under the play's influence, cannot be regarded only as an inward concern, for the modes of apprehension are properly associated with outwardness also. I have suggested that in terms of literary inwardness, non-thinking appears 'good' because it is the primary mode of realisation, and thinking appears 'bad'. My reaction has been to espouse the cause of the murdered sovereign, although at the same time I am drawn into rivalry with usurping criticism. In the end an obsessive inwardness must be recognised, rejected painfully: it prevents that which seems to oppose evil from being good: nothing less than a movement outwards can reverse the morbidity of self-absorption. Outwardness such as that which truly characterises the play itself I can only achieve by emulating and overcoming the *Hamlet*-criticism which is now its public and apparently authentic face – this latter-day aspect is an outwardness corrupting into extreme inwardness. To succeed thus in thinking would presumably be to succeed in the non-thinking of literature (for if outwardness against criticism *remains* criticism it has failed): literature that illustrates *Hamlet* uncritically and unfalsely, postponing by its victory the necessary onset of criticism in the more distant future. I speak tentatively, however, not confident that the experience of the play implies so much for the modern literary scene.

Hamlet was a man of destiny, but I am not Prince Hamlet. Am I rather Claudius – an inferior Claudius, of course? For my own attempt at least has failed, sub-critical. Beyond question I no longer

I AM NOT PRINCE HAMLET

belong to Hamlet's generation: at my age I could only be, if not an
inferior Claudius, an inferior Old Hamlet. Perhaps, accordingly, I had
better dedicate this work to my son William, born 1970; a rag-book
for my successor. How embarrassed he will be when he grows up
(pray God he lives). Remember me in my academic gown.

> But howsomever thou pursues this act,
> whatever it may be
> Taint not thy mind, nor let thy soul contrive
> Against thy mother aught.
> Am an attendant lord.